GODS THAT FAIL

Modern Idolatry & Christian Mission

VINOTH RAMACHANDRA

InterVarsity Press
Downers Grove, Illinois

Published in the United States of America by InterVarsity Press, Downers Grove, Illinois, with permission from Paternoster Press, Carlisle, Cumbria, United Kingdom.

InterVarsity Press® is the book-publishing division of InterVarsity® Christian Fellowship, a student movement active on campus at hundreds of universities, colleges and schools of nursing in the United States of America, and a member movement of the International Fellowship of Evangelical Students. For information about local and regional activities, write Public Relations Dept., InterVarsity Christian Fellowship, 6400 Schroeder Rd., P.O. Box 7895, Madison, WI 53707-7895.

Typeset by WestKey Ltd., Falmouth, United Kingdom

Cover photograph: SuperStock, Inc., Jacksonville, FL.

ISBN 0-8308-1896-0

Printed in the United States of America ∞

Library of Congress Cataloging-in-Publication Data

Ramachandra, Vinoth.
   Gods that fail : modern idolatry and Christian mission / Vinoth Ramachandra.
     p.   cm.
   Includes bibliographical references.
   ISBN 0-8308-1896-0
    1. Apologetics.   2. Idolatry—Controversial literature.
   3. Philosophy, Modern. 4. Rationalism—Controversial works.
   5. Civilization, Modern—20th century. 6. Missions—Theory.
   I. Title.
   BT1200.R345   1997
   261—dc21   97-12922
                                            CIP

19	18	17	16	15	14	13	12	11	10	9	8	7	6	5	4	3	2	1
13	12	11	10	09	08	07	06	05	04	03	02	01	00	99	98	97		

Acknowledgement

This book has been long in the womb. It began life four years ago, but was then left to languish while I turned my attention to a very different book about mission, one dealing with the theological challenge from within the Christian Church itself. Some of the material in the present book first saw the light of day as addresses to students, Christian and non-Christian, in various Asian countries. I am grateful to my friends Nishan De Mel, Dilani Peter, Prabo Mihindukulasooriya and Shehan Williams who perused early drafts of some chapters and commented on their readability.

So, I dedicated this to the students, graduates and staff of the IFES movements of Asia, who have shared and enriched my journey of faith. As they enter the brave new world of the next millenium, may they seek and hold fast to the old-fashioned virtues of truth, simplicity and righteousness.

'I almost think that we are all ghosts, all of us, Pastor Manders. It isn't just what we've inherited from our father and mother that walks in us. It's all sorts of dead ideas, and all sorts of old and obsolete beliefs. They are not alive in us; but they are lodged in us and we can never free ourselves from them . . . There must be ghosts the whole country over, as thick as the sands of the sea. And then we are, one and all, so pitifully afraid of the light.'
—Mrs Alving in Henrik Ibsen's play *Ghosts*

'Those who believe they believe in God, but without passion in their hearts, without anguish of mind, without uncertainty, without doubt, and even at times without despair, believe only in the idea of God, but not in God Himself.'
—Miguel de Unamuno (1864–1937), *The Tragic Sense of Life in Men and Nations*

'Once you said "God" when you gazed upon distant seas; but now I have taught you to say "Superman".'
—Friedrich Nietzsche (1844–1900), *Thus Spoke Zarathustra*

1

Introduction: Modernity & Idols

'Constant revolutionizing of production, uninterrupted disturbances of all social conditions, everlasting uncertainty and agitation distinguish the bourgeois epoch from all earlier ones. All fixed, fast-frozen relations, with their train of ancient and venerable prejudices and opinions, are swept away, all new-formed ones become antiquated before they can ossify. All that is solid melts into air, all that is holy is profaned . . .'
—K. Marx & F. Engels, *The Communist Manifesto* (1848)[1]

These famous words, written a century and a half ago, are still an apt description of social changes taking place all over the world. Modernity has come to encircle the globe, its effects felt in the most remote rural villages and not only in university campuses, urban shopping malls and government bureaucracies. It is not simply one civilization among others, but the first truly global civilization to emerge in human history. For Marx, 'modern' conditions were those created by technological progress and the ever-expanding commerce of nations. Capitalist production was the nerve-centre of the monster of modernity. Ancient communities were uprooted and people thrust into competition with each other in the new jungle of a capitalist social order. But, for Marx, the horrors of modernity also contained a potent promise. The collapse of 'all fixed, fast-frozen relations' liberated modern human beings from the 'ancient and venerable prejudices and opinions' of traditional peasant life. It created a historic opportunity for humankind, represented initially by the new industrial working class, to seize control over its existence through collective revolution and thus put an end to all irrational and arbitrary authority. The monster of modernity could not only be tamed (since it was, after all, a human creation) but would become a necessary means to human liberation.

Another well-known image of what it feels like to live under modern conditions was given by Max Weber (1864–1920), one of the founders of modern sociology. For Weber capitalism was part of a broader phenomenon of increasing rationalization, appearing for the first time in the West in the late-sixteenth and seventeenth centuries. Like Marx, Weber believed that capitalism was an historically specific economic form, not a universal human drive. Unlike the pursuit of gain or ruthless expropriation common to most human cultures, the modern epoch of capitalism was a system of rational rule-governed behaviour, organized around a central motivation: the continuous accumulation of profit *as an end in itself.* Modernity was like an 'iron cage' that drew an ever-tightening noose of impersonal, abstract, instrumental rationality around its victims, leading to the suppression of spontaneity, diversity, and mystery, and the widespread 'disenchantment' of the world.[2] This is an image that has come to dominate much of the fictional and sociological literature of the twentieth century. It has bred a widespread mood of pessimism and near-fatalism.

(Weber's characterization of bureaucratic rationality as the 'iron cage' of modernity, and of its almost absolute rigidity, has not gone unchallenged. From Durkheim onwards, empirical studies have shown that often large-scale organizations make room for autonomy and spontaneity that are less achievable in the closed world of smaller social groups).

An alternative image to both Marx and Weber is offered in the recent writings of the eminent British sociologist Anthony Giddens. He likens life in the modern world to being aboard a 'careering juggernaut . . . rather than being in a carefully controlled and well-driven motor car'.[3] The English word 'juggernaut' comes from the Hindi *Jagannath*, one of the titles for the god Krishna. A huge chariot was used to take an idol of the deity out of its temple in Orissa once a year, and as it trundled through the streets devotees would throw themselves under its wheels and be crushed to death. The modern juggernaut is an engine of enormous power which 'collectively, as human beings, we can drive to some extent but which also threatens to rush out of our control and which could rend itself asunder'.[4] The ride is by no means unpleasant. Riding on the juggernaut of modernity is often exhilarating and rewarding, but there are times when it veers away violently in directions one cannot foresee or control. It crushes both its devotees and all those who stand in its way.

Giddens refuses to *identify* capitalism with modernity, seeing the former as simply one of a cluster (an 'institutional nexus') of movements that constitute the complex affair we call modern life. The most significant others are industrialism (the transformation of nature into 'created environments' through science and technology) and the growth of the nation-state (with its control of information, supervision of the population, and monopoly of the means of violence). If it is the case then, as some allege, that we (or, at least North America and Western Europe) have moved into a new epoch of 'post-modernity', this can only imply that the trajectory of social development has taken us beyond these modern institutions into a new and distinct type of social order.

Giddens is sceptical that we have moved 'beyond modernity' into a 'postmodern social universe', but does recognize 'a few glimpses of the emergence of ways of life and forms of social organization which diverge from those fostered by modern institutions'.[5] Instead of using the term postmodernity, which is thus misleading, he prefers to speak of the 'radicalization' of the consequences of modernity at the end of the twentieth century, so that we are living in a period of 'late' or 'high' modernity. As for the related term 'postmodernism', also in vogue today, it is 'best kept to refer to styles or movements within literature, painting, the plastic arts, and architecture. It concerns aspects of *aesthetic reflection* upon the nature of modernity'.[6]

1.1 The End of Modernity?

Western sociologists disagree as to how to describe the transformations of modernity that have gathered pace in recent years. For those who accept some version of the modern–postmodern distinction, once again it seems that 'all that is solid melts into air'. If we follow Giddens' juggernaut metaphor, 'postmodernization' is best understood as a continuation of the processes of modernization but with increasing intensity and scope; but the result of that intensification has been to erode the stability of modernity and to throw it into some confusion. No longer subject to control and prediction, its cultural and institutional effects may even be reversed.

No doubt aspects of the 'premodern', 'modern' and 'postmodern' will co-exist well into the twenty-first century, in

societies rich and poor, but in varying and bewildering con-
figurations. Announcements of the 'death of modernity' are
premature and, to paraphrase Mark Twain, somewhat exaggerated.

In addition to postmodernists, the intellectual landscape in
recent years has been peopled by post-structuralists, post-
Marxists, post-industrialists, post-Fordists, and other apostles
of a new dispensation. Christian theologians, especially in the
United States, have not been tardy in leaping aboard the
freewheeling bandwagon, declaring the advent of a new
'post-liberal' and 'post-evangelical' theological agenda. The
irony has often been pointed out that those who see a *fundamental* global transition as having occurred in recent decades,
with 'postmodernity' superseding modernity, have invoked
the very thing that they have declared to be impossible under
'postmodern conditions': namely, giving to history an intrinsic
coherence, and being able to locate ourselves within its relentless movement. For one of the characteristic emphases of the
postmodernist intellectual temper (dominant more in the
humanities than the sciences) is that all universal theories,
truth-claims and teleological readings of history- 'totalizing
metanarratives', in the jargon of the day- are obsolescent.
Writers who speak of a new 'postmodernist' epoch are still
employing a master narrative to celebrate the demise of all
master narratives. They still operate within the same intellectual framework, since sceptical subversion of traditional narratives has been as much a part of the world of modernity as
is the creation of overarching storylines.

It has often been remarked that modern men and women
have little sense of history. We are all prone to consider our
own generation as somehow special, unmatched in the depth
of its crises no less than in its achievements. So it comes as
some surprise to be reminded that many of the themes that
have dominated the second half of the twentieth century were
first conceived in the European 'cultural crisis' of the 1890s.
Amidst the declining glory of Hapsburg Vienna, for instance,
there emerged the study of the subconscious and its role in the
irrationalities of everyday life, the notion of nationhood as the
basis for political identity, and a preoccupation with language
and its effect on the 'construction' of reality . . . The decade
also saw the the rise of sociology as an organized scientific
discipline with its inquiries into mass urban culture, rationali-

zation and bureaucracy, suicide and *anomie*. Significant as recent global socio-economic changes are, especially in the past two decades, they should not be exaggerated. For, as even that guru of the new 'knowledge society', Daniel Bell, admitted in a footnote in his famous book, *The Coming of Post-Industrial Society*, 'In terms of *daily life* of individuals, more change was experienced between 1850 and 1940- when railroad, steamships, telegraph, electricity, telephone, automobile, radio and airplanes were introduced- than in the period since when the future is supposed to be accelerating. In fact, other than television, there has not been one major innovation which affected the daily life of persons to the extent of the items enumerated.'[7]

Those who subscribe to the more radical postmodernist creed also hold that long-held distinctions between reality and appearance, truth and falsehood, valid and invalid reasoning, ethical principle and social convention, are relics of a now-discredited Platonic-Christian-Enlightenment (Kantian, Marxist, or whatever) heritage in the West. The argument sometimes starts off on the liberal premise that truth-claims have often gone along with a notion of privileged access by an elite who have used their intellectual authority and political power to impose their version of the truth on others. It ends with variations on the Nietzschean theme that 'truth' is nothing more than the product of a specific human discourse, with postmodern life the belated recognition and celebration of multiple and conflicting discourses.

Hence the American pragmatist Richard Rorty's cheery recommendation to his fellow philosophers that they join theologians in giving up their deluded notions of dealing with matters of ultimate truth, and rejoin the cultural 'conversation of mankind' on equal terms with sociologists, literary critics, novelists and others who never entertained such high-minded ambitions. We should substitute 'solidarity' for 'objectivity', a sense of shared consensus-based values and beliefs for the attempt to 'get things right' from a critical standpoint. Talk of 'truth' now becomes simply a rhetorical device, a label of convenience attached to those ideas which currently enjoy widespread approval. It can be re-defined for all practical purposes as 'good in the way of belief'.[8]

Such recommendations have a less than benign aspect when we consider how easily public opinion can be manipulated and consensus-values engineered to serve some very illiberal forms of political behaviour. Those versions of the pragmatist-post-modernist creed which are suspicious of 'outworn' ideas such as truth, critique and ethical accountability, are simply unable to discriminate between a *true* consensus based on beliefs arrived at by open argument and debate, and a *false* consensus that rests solely on collective prejudice, mass-media distortion and the *force majeure* of propaganda. Like those fashionable slogans proclaiming the 'end of history' and the 'end of ideology' they end up serving to legitimatise the cynical interests of American *realpolitik*.

Thus Francis Fukuyama, a Rand corporation protégé, became an overnight celebrity on the US lecture circuit-in those heady years between the collapse of the Berlin Wall and the beginning of the Gulf War—by pronouncing, with splendid assurance, the 'end of history'.[9] Since the whole world—or the world that really mattered- had now em-braced free-market capitalism and liberal democracy, ideo-logical conflict was now a thing of the past and history had effectively come to an end. Of course there would be those awkward 'trouble-spots' around the world which refused to accept the New World Order, and critical intellectuals everywhere who still indulged in Canute-like gestures to fend off the tidal waves of change, but these could be consigned to the scrapheap of history. In a later article on the Gulf War, Fukuyama wrote: 'A large part of the world will be populated by Iraqs and Ruritanias, and will continue to be subject to bloody struggles and revolutions. But, with the exception of the Gulf, few regions will have an im-pact—for good or ill—on the growing part of the world that is democratic and capitalist. And it is in this part of the world that we will ultimately have to make our home.'[10]

Here is the classic pattern of ideological scape-goating: the projection of blame on to a racial or cultural Other (the 'Iraqs and Ruritanias' in the new geopolitical order), which enables 'us' (that civilized part of the world which 'we will ultimately have to make our home') to live with an easy conscience, convinced of our moral superiority despite all the evidence of western connivance and complicity in the 'bloody struggles and revolutions' in the non-western world. Barbarism always resides elsewhere. Fukuyama's 'end of history' sloganeering disguises the massive hypocrisy, political betrayals, economic blackmail and proxy violence that have so often attended western talk of defending democracy and exporting 'free world' values. Media coverage of the Gulf War, like the coverage of American domestic political campaigns, provided a depressing spectacle of public-opinion management far more ruthless than any existing in pre-modern societies. The first casualty in the build-up to, and prosecution of, the war was *truth*: the re-writing of regional history, the 'whitewashing' of Kuwaiti and Saudi Arabian despotism, bogus casualty-figures issued for public consumption, massive urban destruction concealed by talk of 'precision bombing' and 'surgical strikes', and so on . . . But how can such a critique emerge from intellectuals who can no longer distinguish between truth and what the majority have come to believe, and how can such a critique be sustained in a world mesmerized by cable TV?

For those of us unfortunate folk who happen to live among the 'Iraqs and Ruritanias' of the late twentieth-century world, the perspective is rather different. The political naivete of writers such as Rorty and Fukuyama raises searching questions about the 'postmodernist' paradigm. Is all such talk of 'truth' and 'reality' as being fictive and imaginative constructions, having no extra-linguistic reference (often advanced, para-doxically, as a genuine and liberating insight), simply a reflec-tion of the pervasive influence of the electronic media today? In other words, has the cultural ascendency of advertising agencies, public relations experts, opinion-poll samplers, and 'virtual reality' engineers, lent plausibility to such notions, a plausibility that is lacking in earlier phases of modernity and in those countries that have still to fall completely under the spell of the electronic high-priests? I am inclined to think so.

Writing fifty years ago of a famous CBS radio war bond sales-drive, the American sociologist Robert Merton observed shrewdly that these propagandists were 'technicians of senti-ment' and warned that 'a society subjected ceaselessly to a flow of "effective" half-truths and the exploitation of mass anxieties may all the sooner lose that mutuality of confidence and reciprocal trust so essential to a stable social structure'.[11] It is open to serious question whether any participant democracy can function for long on the basis of consensus-values derived via the mass media. Today's 'technicians of sentiment' have achieved a level of sophistication so great that, for the bored youngsters of the affluent world, MTV and Disneyland have become the paramount reality. Madonna, of course, is the great icon of postmodernism: a kaleidoscope of shifting images (the *femme fatale*, the vulnerable Monroe, the androgyne, the gangster moll, the arch-capitalist, et al.), a celebration of fragmentation and the loss of depth that, as we shall see, are the hall-marks of the late modern world.

Having rejected both a biblical theology of creation and humanist talk of a 'universal human nature', writers such as Rorty are hard pressed to find a moral framework within which we can locate a sense of place and of human 'solidarity'. Rorty can only fall back on a pragmatist appeal to nationalist sentiment as a basis for policy. Thus he remarks on 'the attitude of contemporary American liberals to the unending hopelessness and misery of the lives of the young blacks in American cities. Do we say that these people must be helped because they are our fellow human beings? We may, but it is much more persuasive, morally as well as politically, to describe them as our fellow *Americans*—to insist that it is outrageous that an American can live without hope.'[12] Whether such appeals are persuasive to the inhabitants of Fukuyama's 'Iraqs and Ruritanias'— who are now being wooed into the benefits of liberal democracy and respect for 'human rights'—is open to serious doubt. It is paradoxical that just as talk of 'truth' has historically been used to consolidate power by dividing people into 'us' and 'them' (a point stressed repeatedly by postmodernist critics of modernity), here even the language of 'solidarity' serves only to cement narrow sectarian interests . . .

1.2 Modernity as Paradox

The renowned Czech philosopher, novelist and statesman Vaclav Havel has identified the most distinctive feature of modern life as a 'loss of co-ordinates'. He writes, 'I believe that with the loss of God, man has lost a kind of absolute and universal system of co-ordinates, to which he could always relate everything, chiefly himself. His world and his personality gradually began to break up into separate, incoherent fragments corresponding to different, relative, co-ordinates . . .'[13]

Havel was reflecting on the inherent weaknesses of modern western societies, the very model his newly independent country was being persuaded to follow. He saw the consumerist culture of the West to be as oppressive to the human spirit as the repression Eastern Europe had suffered for most of the present century. The recent history of Eastern Europe, he believes, holds up to the West a convex mirror, giving a grotesquely magnified image of the West's own inherent tendencies. Modernity had let loose forces that bred conformity, a herd culture, either in the overt form of totalitarian regimes or the covert homogenizing pressures of consumerism. The banal freedoms of choice, represented by the ubiquitous Coca-Cola ads, shopping malls and McDonald's fast-food chains (which have become the universal symbols of modernity), conceal a loss of human freedoms at deeper, more profound levels. For every achievement of modernity, there is also a demonic underside. Liberal capitalism and Marxism were actually twin aspects of the same phenomenon, generated by the loss of coordinates in the modern world. They followed the 'irrational momentum of anonymous, impersonal, and inhuman power-the power of ideologies, systems, bureaucracy, artificial languages and political slogans'.[14]

Havel's mathematical imagery is instructive. Co-ordinates express the way things are related to each other. They provide a point of reference, a scale by which entities may be measured and seen in their true proportions, a map which helps us find our bearings and our way around reality. The belief in God had been the traditional unifying focus for such a system of co-ordinates in western culture. So, in one important perspective, the modern condition is characterized by a *displacement* of God from that focal position. It is not the case that God has been explicitly expunged from modern consciousness (though this was vigorously attempted, for instance, by the French version of the eighteenth-century Enlightenment[15] and also by the latter's Marxist successors in the twentieth); but rather that God has been pushed to the fringes of consciousness, and his function taken over by surrogate deities (e.g. Nature, Posterity, The State, The Market, and so on).

The historical origins of modern secular culture are still a matter of scholarly debate, and I do not propose to venture into this complex terrain. What has become increasingly clear, however, is that the popular self-image of modernity, namely as representing a radical break with a Christian worldview and the emancipation of human reason from the oppressive grip of ecclesiastical interests, lacks historical plausibility. There seems to have been more intellectual freedom in the late medieval period in Europe than in the heyday of the French Enlightenment, more participatory citizenship in the medieval 'free cities' of Europe and the 'holy commonwealths' of Puritan New England than in many of today's so-called 'advanced democracies'. The roots of modernity itself were nourished by Christian theology as much as by the pre-Christian philosophies of Greece and Rome. Max Weber's famous thesis that Puritan rationality and piety furnished the character-formation necessary for the rise of a capitalist economy is now recognized to have been greatly exaggerated, but it has served to draw our attention to the unique intellectual climate in which modernity emerged.[16] This is seen especially in the rise of experimental natural science which remains the most prominent and influential aspect of modern society. Not only were Christian values embodied in scientific practice, but the enterprise of science itself was founded on a specific understanding of God, human beings and the world which sprang from Reformation theology.[17]

Furthermore, the political philosopher Charles Taylor has recently highlighted what he calls the 'affirmation of ordinary life' which was given new and unprecedented significance at the beginning of the modern era. This, Taylor believes, has also become 'one of the most powerful ideas of modern civilization'.[18] By the 'affirmation of ordinary life' he refers to the biblical notion, re-discovered in the Reformation, that the everyday life of human production and reproduction, of work and the family, is the main locus of the good life and carries an inherent dignity and worth. Taylor points out: 'According to traditional, Aristotelian ethics, this has merely infrastructural influence. "Life" was important as the necessary background and support to "the good life" of contemplation and one's action as a citizen. With the Reformation, we find a modern, Christian-inspired sense that ordinary life was on the contrary the very centre of the good life. The crucial issue was how it was led, whether worshipfully and in the fear of God or not. But the life of the God-fearing was lived out in marriage and their calling. The previous "higher" forms of life were dethroned, as it were. And along with this went frequently an attack, covert or overt, on the elites which had made these forms their province.'[19] What Taylor asserts here with regard to Aristotelian ethics is also valid for the monastic religious traditions of Asian societies.

However, there is another aspect to modernity that eventually submerged whatever Christian paths may have led to it. The indirect and unforeseen political consequences of the Reformation, reaching a climax in the bitter Wars of Religion in the late sixteenth and early seventeenth century, provided the momentum which propelled the European states towards a social and political order that was based on 'natural religion' rather than on any particular confessional creed. In his massive work *The Authority of the Bible and the Rise of the Modern World*,[20] Henning Graf Reventlow has explored the widespread influence of ancient Greek, and especially Stoic, sources on the thinkers of the early modern period, and the way in which the Bible, while still an undisputed authority in political and ethical argument, came increasingly to be read within the framework of an alien rationalist temper. The God of the Bible became the abstract, a historical deity of philosophical theism.

The God who is displaced from the co-ordinating centre of human thought and life doesn't simply disappear. God may cease to be the transcendent Other, standing over and above the human world, but he resurfaces in the guise of the human Self. René Descartes (1596–1650) is typically taken as the founder of the modern concept of knowledge: knowledge which takes mathematical certainty as its ideal, independent of the authority of the past, grounded in the individual human subject. A straight line could be drawn in the history of ideas from this approach to Feuerbach's (1804–1872) position, deeply influential in the Marxist tradition, that all the attributes of a transcendent God refer, in reality, to the collective human consciousness. Theology has now been translated into anthropology.

The straight line extends naturally and inexorably to what is today often referred to as the 'End of Enlightenment' or, 'high modernity' in Giddens' less dramatic terminology: a temper of mind that is dismissive of central Enlightenment notions such as objectivity, truth, critique, right reason and 'progress'. Even the reality of a unified human subject is now denied. In the early phases of modernity, the threatening experience of 'all that is solid melts into air' was countered by locating order and meaning in the autonomous human self (thinking, willing and judging); but now, that semi-divine self has splintered and dissolved into numerous 'subject positions' each thrown up by some context-specific human discourse. The human self is simply the point of interaction of myriad social and cultural forces. To use a famous metaphor of the French writer Michel Foucault, it is inscribed in sand on the ocean's edge, soon to be erased by the incoming tide.

Here it seems that postmodernism is simply modernism come home to roost. A movement that sought to guard the objectivity of truth from theological 'interference' has ended up doubting the very concept of truth. A movement that gloried in reason and exalted it above divine revelation has come to spurn the rational in every area of life. A movement that began with the divinization of the self has culminated in the loss of that very self.

These are but some of the many paradoxes of modernity. An age that began with a vigorous defence of human individuality spawned, in the regions of the world most influenced by modernity, either totalitarian states more all-embracing than any in antiquity or an equally oppressive consumerist conformity. The belief in human progress through the conquest of nature unleashed forces that now threaten the human species itself with extinction. The installation of Man as the Creator of all meaning and value, in an attempt to throw off the dead weight of the past and 'begin all over again', has as its outcome the denial of any meaning to the world and any significance to humankind. Modern life-styles promise freedom but lead to slavishly followed 'fads' and to new and powerful addictions. Modern relationships place a high premium on intimacy and authenticity, but are prone to fears of manipulation and one-upmanship. The marginalization of religion has itself bred numerous new religious movements, so that some of the most secularized states of the world are experiencing a flourishing of 'religious' interest. On modern college campuses in the West, works on astrology, mysticism and shamanism are evidently more popular than the works of Hume or Locke.

The peoples of the modern West (and the middle classes of non-western cultures) are better fed, better housed, better equipped with health care than those in any previous age in human history. But, paradoxically, they also seem to be the most fearful, the most divided, the most lonely, the most superstitious, and the most bored generation in human history. All the labour-saving devices of modern technology have only enhanced human stress, and modern life is characterized by a restless movement from place to place, from one 'experience' to another, in a frenetic whirl of purposeless activity.

1.3 Modernity and Fragmentation

The loss of co-ordinates which troubled Havel has led inevitably to the fragmentation of knowledge and life, so prominent a feature of modern society. The British linguistic philosopher, Mary Midgley, bemoans the way in which knowledge has come to be identified with the gathering and storage of *information*. 'It is now claimed,' she writes, 'and claimed by some as a sign of progress, that human knowledge is doubling itself exponentially every seven years, a process held to have begun in the late 1960s. The grounds given for this are that the number of scientific papers published in the world is increasing at this rate. Does anybody suppose that the reading-time available has increased so as to allow all this stuff to be read and digested? All academic departments are now bombarded with floods of incoming articles, only a tiny proportion of which could they possibly read, even if they did nothing else . . . The main effect of this flood of paper (apart from exhausting the world's forests) must therefore be to pile up articles which, once they are published, nobody reads at all.'[21] No bibliographies are up to date. The mass of books and critical essays, of scholarly articles and dissertations produced each day in Europe and the United States, has the blind weight of an avalanche.

Such 'information-processing', split up among so many disciplines and sub-disciplines, no longer constitutes knowledge in the traditional sense. Hitherto, knowledge has been seen to involve *understanding*, the ability to relate myriad pieces of information into meaningful wholes. For all the great philosophers of the past, whether Christian or non-Christian, knowledge was an aspect of wisdom: it was part of an understanding of life as a whole, out of which a sense of what really mattered, what was really worth pursuing in life, would emerge. Merely holding information as an inert piece of property and passing it on like a slab of meat to one's students would have invited contempt in any other age. At an academic level, Midgley believes that things could be dramatically improved if the quality of reasoning shown in books and journals were given far more weight than the mere number of papers published– 'a number which, considered as a measure of merit, is of little more value than the number of the writer's hairs'.[22] She also points out that what is needed is not simply that different specialities need to be related to each other, but they all need to be related to everyday thinking and feeling, and made responsible to it. Just as music recorded on tape and stored forever unheard in archives is music wasted, what counts as knowledge today is similarly futile. But music is also wasted when heard by those who cannot see the point of it. So too with knowledge.

This does not mean that all scholars should attempt to be polymaths, let alone try to master all the details of their own limited fields. That feat would have been impossible in any age. What is needed, says Midgley, is that 'all should have in their minds a general background map of the whole range of knowledge as a context for their own specialty, and should integrate this wider vision with their practical and emotional attitude to life. They should be able to place their own small area on the map of the world, and to move outside it freely when they need to'.[23]

But this 'general background map' is precisely what modernity has ceased to have ever since its loss of cognitive and moral co-ordinates. Immanuel Kant (1724–1804), perhaps the most influential philosopher of the Enlightenment, brought about a synthesis of reason and sensory experience such that the realms of truth, goodness and beauty were radically and permanently fragmented. The human individual splintered into the abstract, non-communicating faculties of reason, will and emotion. Scientific reason was taken to deliver objective truth, the will (which, though rational, inhabited a different level of reality) centred on morality. Emotion became the channel for aesthetic perception. Thus a world of 'facts' was separated from that of 'values', knowledge parted company from faith, and aesthetics became a matter of purely subjective judgement. The Kantian legacy, which divorces science, ethics and art from each other, is still visible on every university campus.

Weber reinforced the splits with his doctrine of 'differentiated spheres' in modern society. According to him, law, religion, administration, science, art, ethics, economics, etc, each inhabited an 'autonomous sphere' in which its own unique system of norms and rationality prevailed. There was no possibility of communication between spheres. So, for instance, it was not permissible to bring aesthetic criteria into science, or ethical judgements into discussions about economics. The purest form of rationality was practised in science, and this 'instrumental reason' encroached on other spheres as modernity advanced. But each sphere occupied an autonomous, though limited, space in society. Weber believed he was describing what happened to societies under the impact of capitalism and scientific technology, but his descriptions were influenced by his own Kantian framework of thinking. Thus immediately following his depressing assessment of modernity as an 'iron cage', he remarks: 'No one knows who will live in this cage in the future or whether at the end of this tremendous development entirely new prophets will arise, or there will be a great rebirth of old ideas and ideals, or, if neither, mechanized petrifaction . . . For of the last stage of this cultural development, it might well be truly said: "Specialists without spirit, sensualists without heart . . ." *But this brings us to the world of judgements of value and of faith, with which this purely historical discusion need not be burdened . . .'*[24]

A large sociological output has emerged in recent decades on the erosion of public life under modern conditions, its transformation into a realm where the mass of people perceive themselves as passive and helpless, and the elevation of the domain of personal relations into a refuge from a harsh social world and the arena for self-realization. Mass commodity consumption has accelerated this process. One could say that while the literature of modernism (for instance, the poetry of TS Eliot) experiences fragmentation as loss, the cult heroes of postmodernism (for instance, the novelist Milan Kundera) celebrate it.

1.4. Modernity and Meaning

In a fascinating discussion on the loss of meaning in modernity, the eminent literary critic George Steiner argues persuasively that 'any coherent account of the capacity of human speech to communicate meaning and feeling is, in the final analysis, underwritten by the assumption of God's presence'.[25] Steiner believes that a historical inventory of all that has been compelling in literature, art and music demonstrates them to have had a religious inspiration and reference:

> Referral and self-referral to a transcendent dimension, to that which is felt to reside . . . outside immanent and purely secular reach, does underwrite created forms from Homer and the *Oresteia* to *The Brothers Karamazov* and Kafka . . . Music and the metaphysical, in the root sense of that term, music and religious feeling, have been virtually inseparable.[26]

What Steiner is expressing here is his intuition that in a culture where God's presence is no longer held to be a tenable supposition and where God's absence is not felt as an overwhelming loss, certain dimensions of thought and creativity are no longer available. Indifference to the metaphysical and theological leads to a radical break with aesthetic creation and reception. All poetics is now in the age of the 'after-Word' where the 'contract between the Word and the world', the basis of all meaning and creativity, has been severed. Steiner writes, 'It is my belief that this contract is broken for the first time, in any thorough and consequent sense, in European, Central European and Russian culture and speculative consciousness during the decades from the 1870s to the 1930s. *It is this break of the covenant between word and world which constitutes one of the very few genuine revolutions of spirit in Western history and which defines modernity itself.*'[27]

The vacuum created by the loss of artistic creation and responsive experience is filled in the late modern world by what Steiner pungently calls the 'mandarin madness of secondary discourse'.[28] The secondary has become our narcotic.

> Literate humanity is solicited daily by millions of words, printed, broadcast, screened, about books which it will never open, music it will not hear, works of art it will never set eyes on. A perpetual hum of aesthetic commentary, of on-the-minute judgements, of pre-packaged pontifications, crowds the air. Presumably, the greater part of art-talk or literary reportage, of music reviews or ballet criticism, is skimmed rather than read, heard but not listened to . . . Like sleepwalkers, we are guarded by the numbing drone of the journalistic, of the theoretical, from the often harsh, imperious radiance of sheer presence.[29]

Journalism insinuates itself into every nook and cranny of our consciousness. All over the modern world, we are bombarded by a barrage of 'information', in the press and on the TV screen, images of fleeing refugees in Rwanda and Bosnia jostling with images of the rich and the famous, and vying for our attention with the latest sexual gossip involving the American president or the British monarchy. Football and politics, soap operas and religion, beauty contests and ecological calamity, they are all more or less of equal import and—with the exception of the soaps—last only for the day. Such a flood of instant information has a stupefying effect, often retarding education by robbing us of the ability to *feel* what we see. The information flow that reaches us down the Global Super-Highway does not carry with it any value-framework that helps us to discriminate between the significant and the trivial; that value-framework has to be generated from outside, and, in a pluralist society lacking a moral consensus, it is the owners of the press and other media who determine what counts as News.

The media are much more than a commercial enterprise. Modern journalism articulates what Steiner accurately calls an 'epistemology and ethics of spurious temporality'. The ambiguities of life are avoided in favour of what is straightforward, arguments replaced by slogans, narrative must give way to novelty. The most awesome beauty and the most unspeakable horror, along with the crass and banal, are all shredded at the end of the day. 'Correspondingly, the content, the possible significance of the material which journalism communicates, is "remaindered" the day after. . . . We are made whole again, and expectant, in time for the morning edition.'[30]

It is not only erudite scholars like Steiner who deplore the loss of depth and discrimination in modern media. The veteran *Washington Post* journalist Carl Bernstein (of Watergate fame) is even more scathing in his criticism of what he calls 'this new culture of journalistic titillation'. Through its obsession with trivia ('the lurid and the loopy'), modern journalism panders to its readers and viewers and avoids its responsibility to challenge people. It thus helps to create 'what deserves to be called the idiot culture. Not an idiot subculture, which every society has bubbling beneath the surface and which can provide harmless fun; but the culture itself. For the first time, the weird and the stupid and the coarse are becoming our cultural norm, even our cultural deal . . .'[31]

In her examination of the mental habits and work-styles of advertising art directors and copywriters (usually referred to as 'creatives' in the US), Janice Hirota observes that such folk are 'commercial experts with symbols' who must be able 'to dispense with traditional notions of "truth" and employ instead a notion of "story", a habit of mind that obtains whether one is fashioning advertisements for a detergent, a presidential candidate, a corporate image, or a public service safety campaign'.[32] She concludes her observations with the following sober appraisal:

> The endless storytelling, promotion, dramatization, and symbol manipulation that permeates advertising's structure, also disseminate to mass audiences the ethos of advertising work itself. As it happens, this ethos celebrates the manufacture of image, the adroit framing of perspectives and issues, and the style of presentation-that is, how one tells a story- far more than it celebrates the content of a tale, the substance of an issue or, indeed, the reality of experience.[33]

That this mentality has made deep inroads into the modern church should be obvious to anyone familiar with the contemporary evangelical scene. Under the influence of television and advertising, Christian gatherings in affluent societies have experienced major shifts from Word to Image, from passion for truth and righteousness to cultivating intimacy and 'good feelings', from exposition to entertainment, from integrity to novelty, from action to spectacle. The reduction of knowledge to information, and the growth of a specialized, esoteric 'knowledge class', which Midgeley and others lament, are evident in church-affiliated theological seminaries no less than in university faculties of theology. Many seminary graduates are now skilled in management techniques, or counselling skills and even 'church-planting' methodologies, but lack any integrating *theological* vision. Even mission has come to be a specialized discipline of professional study—'missiology'—an item of consumer choice and subject to all the fashionable computer gimmickry and statistical quantification beloved by the new mandarins. That *all* study and life should, for the Christian, be motivated by, and orientated around, a sense of mission, seems too radical a thought for the modern seminary.

1.5 A Mutual Challenge

The famous novelist G.K. Chesterton once remarked that when a man turns his back on God, he doesn't just believe in nothing, he believes in anything. The same is true for whole societies. The so-called secular world of modern men and women, no less than the traditionally religious world, is heavily awash with gods. The present book is built around the conviction that the displacement of the God of the biblical revelation, which is the most distinctive feature of modernity, has paved the way for the rise of new gods which, like their ancient counterparts, eventually devour their devotees.

This book is addressed primarily to students and other thoughtful Christians who intend to serve God in the midst of 'secular' occupations in the modern world. It does not, for the most part, assume any acquaintance with academic theology or philosophy. Nor does it aim at originality, and I am aware that even those insights which I may think are original probably derive from sources which I tapped a long time ago and have since forgotten. I myself write as one who has been shaped largely by the culture of modernity, but I am grateful for the privilege and responsibility of exposure to other cultures. I am grateful too for the great benefits that modernity brings to our nations, especially in breaking the stranglehold of traditional religious and political elites and social (including gender) hierarchies. No one, whether Christian or non–Christian, who cares about human emancipation can rejoice in the 'end of modernity' chorus emanating from certain quarters of the Western world. But we also stand in great need of discernment lest we identify the 'spirit of the age' as the Holy Spirit, the Spirit of truth who mediates the reality of the risen Lord in the midst of historical change and uncertainty.

It has become a cliché to contrast the secular materialism of the West with the religious spirituality of the East. Such generalizations are unhelpful and misleading. In fact, materialism as a philosophy flourished in India long before the rise of modernity, and some Buddhist thinkers have sought to interpret Buddhism as essentially a secular way of living. Materialism as a cult of acquisition and ostentatious consumption is as prominent in the cities of Asia as it is in Europe. The engine of modernity, at least in its technological and economic dimensions, seems to have shifted to East Asia; and it is often forgotten that even India, noted for its mass poverty and its antiquity, is the tenth largest industrial power and has the second largest middle-class population in the world. Young professionals, whether in Bangkok or London, whether in medicine or accountancy, testify to being 'driven' by the pressures to conform to the values of a profit-obsessed work environment and to finding the life and teaching of their local churches increasingly irrelevant to their concerns.

It is the sheer diversity of Asia that makes generalizations about an 'Asian mind' or 'Asian theology' so specious. What-ever can be said to be true of Asia, the opposite can also be shown to be true. The same applies to the recent emphasis on 'Asian values', popularized by the Chinese regime in Beijing and anglicized South-east Asian politicians like Singapore's Lee Kwan Yu and Malaysia's Mahathir Mohammed. Such talk serves to legitimate paternalistic or authoritarian forms of government in Asia, and to justify the suppression of civil liberties such as freedom of political expression and political action.

It is also intriguing to observe some points of convergence between modernity and the dominant religious-intellectual systems of Asian cultures. They tend to share an understanding of human liberation as self-mastery; a preoccupation with *technique*, in the pursuit of material progress (in the first case) and spiritual or psychic power (in the other); a common belief that historical events can never convey ultimate truths, that truth must be directly accessible to the individual human being (in the one case through the faculty of reason, in the other through mystical insight); and (especially in late modernity) a common distrust of language, rejection of the subject-object distinction, and the assumption that the world of temporality, plurality and change is essentially meaningless . . .

The dialogue with modernity, therefore, no less than that with traditional religious faiths, throws into sharp relief the distinctiveness of the biblical gospel. But, as in all authentic encounter, it also forces us to re-examine our own Christian traditions. Any critique of modernity can carry credibility only if it begins with self-criticism. For modern secularism, while historically appropriating many Christian beliefs and concerns, has also been the most powerful protest against the deficiencies of much Christian theology and moral practice.

The American Jesuit Michael Buckley believes that the

origin of atheism in the intellectual culture of the West lies 'in the self-alienation of religion itself'.[34] His contention is that much of the responsibility for the modern displacement of God must be attributed to the way 'God' became increasingly abstract and impersonal in the western theological tradition. The great medieval synthesis of faith and philosophy (what is called 'natural theology') involved a 'downplaying' of the work of Christ and the Holy Spirit, so that Christians in seventeenth-century Europe tended to defend Christianity without appealing to anything distinctively Christian: 'The absence of any consideration of Christology is so pervasive throughout serious discussion that it becomes taken for granted, yet it is so stunningly curious that it raises a funda-mental issue of the modes of thought: How did the issue of Christianity vs atheism become purely philosophical? To para-phrase Tertullian: How was it that the only arms to defend the temple were to be found in the Stoa?'[35]

By turning away from the person and work of Jesus Christ and the experience of the Christian community and turning instead to philosophical apologetics in order to demonstrate its inherent 'reasonableness', Christian theology at the beginning of the modern era had already surrendered its own competence. Attempts to develop so-called 'physico-theologies' (deducing God's existence and nature from the worldview of Newtonian science) backfired on biblical theology. As philosophy developed into natural philosophy and then into mechanics, the latter 'established its own nature by denying that its evidence possessed any theological significance and by negating any theological interest'.[36] Over the centuries that followed, physics, medicine, mathematics and other disciplines could assert their own auton-omy from physico-theologies only by denying their own theo-logical character. If they moved into atheism, Buckley argues, they did so because theology had made them the primary area of its evidence and of its argument. Thus the theologians who had deposited their entire inheritance with them gradually found themselves bankrupt . . .

Thus there is much that contemporary Christians can learn from the modern critique of Christian faith. My travels in Asia and many parts of the western world have convinced me that eighteenth-century European and Platonist/Hindu concep-tions of God are alive and well in the most conservative of Christian circles! It is not surprising, for example, that many

Christians today have reduced the doctrine of creation to an account of the temporal origins of things ('how things began') rather than about their relatedness to God. It is impossible to understand the cross and resurrection of Christ with such an inadequate theology of creation.

Modern secularism, then, can best be understood as a systematic Christian *heresy*, taking heresy to mean a one-sided development of an important Christian truth. It is thus parasitic on Christian life and doctrine (just as postmodernism is parasitic on the achievements and conceptual framework of modernity). So, for example, most forms of political liberalism derive from the traditional Protestant belief in the inherent dignity of the individual and the consequent right of individual conscience. But by absolutizing the individual it turns into a philosophy of individualism: namely, the dogma that I can be myself without my neighbour. Thus the 'other' can be perceived only as a threat to my freedom, and human society becomes the clash of competing wills as each asserts his or her 'rights' against the other. Thus a genuine human plurality is denied. Late (or 'high') modernity is no different in this regard. As the fashionable language of 'political correctness' well illustrates, authentic 'otherness' is suppressed in the name of equality. By reducing everything to the same value, and not admitting distinctions of truth and falsehood, right and wrong, beauty and ugliness, the much vaunted individualism of late modernity is actually oppressively homogenizing.

The challenge to us modern Christians is to return to our biblical roots, but to articulate that biblical faith in conversation with the thought-patterns that shape today's world. The current renaissance of Trinitarian theology is a most welcome development, for modern secularism is, in part, a justified rejection of inadequate conceptions of theism. Monism and fragmentation seem to be two sides of the same coin. However, if the triune God is the source of all being, meaning and truth, it should be possible to develop a theology that integrates the different realms of human thought, action and culture; and in a way that recognizes their distinctives while also tracing the concrete shapes that sin assumes in all areas of thought and life. That undertaking, alas, is beyond both the scope of this book and my own theological competence.

My primary concern has been to let the Bible speak. I have drawn largely from the Old Testament scriptures, mainly because of their relative neglect in our contemporary churches. The context from which I write is that of a South Asian society swept up, for better and for worse, into the global march of science, technology and transnational capitalism. In keeping with the introductory and essentially 'bridge-building' character of the book, I have chosen to dispense with footnotes (apart from, of course, references to sources) and the endless qualifications that must necessarily attend a more academic presentation.

The book's sub-title is deliberately ambiguous. Does Christian mission involve a confrontation with 'the idols of our time'?[37] Or does Christian mission, at least in some prominent aspects, unconsciously disseminate forms of idolatry around the globe? Or are large sections of the Christian Church so riddled with idolatry that their missionary vision has been paralyzed? The burden of this book can be summed up by saying that all three questions require the emphatic answer: 'Yes' . . .

In a missionary engagement with the world, we tell the biblical story in the face of all the other stories that the world offers for its ultimate *raison d'etre*. If the gospel is *true*, it must be relevant to every aspect of human activity. However, in that act of engagement a process of mutual conversion occurs. Even as the fundamental lie of the world is unmasked by the gospel message, so too is the church challenged to a deeper apprehension of, and obedience to, the fullness of 'the truth that is in Jesus' (Eph. 4:21). Hence the double thread that runs through the present book, two moods that alternate and interweave: the one apologetic and didactic, the other self-critical and exhortatory . . .

Although I shall touch on a wide range of issues, the discussions are not intended to be rigorous and exhaustive but illustrations of a theme in the text. The reader must not expect a compendium of modern idols, least of all regard this as a manual/handbook for Christian apologetics. My aim is more modest: to provide my fellow-pilgrims, who are attracted, repelled or confused by modernity, with a few historical and biblical compasses that may help them in their journey beyond modernity to the counter-culture of the kingdom of God. I am acutely aware that a book of this nature may well fall between two stools, irritating the more academic reader who may feel I am trampling on his or her specialist grass as well as presuming too much with regard to the capacities of the general reader. But I think the risk is worth taking.

Chapter Two centres on the biblical critique of religion. The way into this is via two famous, and still influential, secular humanist critiques of Christianity. *Chapter Three* seeks to retrieve the biblical doctrine of creation from the neglect and misuse it has suffered at the hands of both traditional Christian apologetics and the popular writings of eminent modern scientists.

No talk of a Creator can evade the vexed problem of unjust suffering. *Chapter Four* turns to the ancient book of Job which was probably the earliest written dialogue on the question that many still ask today: how can we speak of God in a suffering world? Shockingly, the conventional theological answers of Job's friends are revealed to be idolatrous.

Chapter Five explores the process of idol-formation and its impact on human lives in the modern (and modernizing) world. Various illustrations are given from different walks of life, and these also provide the backdrop for our reading of two stories, familiar but ever fresh, from the early chapters of Genesis.

Chapters Six and Seven are of a more philosophical nature. The first deals with the various ideologies that cluster around the domain of science, the most influential of modern idols. Some of the sources from which the growing critique of science have sprung are described in a brief survey. Suggestions are given as to what form a Christian response could take.

Chapter Seven may be omitted on a first reading. It is an extension of the preceding chapter, exploring further the manifestations of idolatry in human reasoning and the epistemological crisis that many critics believe lies at the heart of modernity. The work of Michael Polanyi is described briefly and commended as an alternative approach to knowing in the formation of a Christian worldview and missionary engagement.

Finally, *Chapter Eight* turns to the Cross and the defeat of idolatry. But no discussion of the Cross can evade the charge that the church has betrayed the Cross in its missionary history. The charge is considered seriously, and some of the implications for contemporary global Christian mission drawn out.

That we are dealing with matters of life and death, and not

indulging in arid intellectualism, can be illustrated by the growing debate all over the world on the 'sanctity' of human life. The fiercely anti-Christian polemic of Peter Singer and Helga Kuhse's book *Should the Baby Live?*[38] shows the yawning gulf between Christian and secular humanist assumptions in moral debate. Singer and Kuhse attack Christian morality as the dominant and restrictive ideology of the West, an ideology from which we need to be liberated if we are to address responsibly moral issues such as severely handicapped infants. In particular, we need to detach ourselves from the belief that human life has a special sanctity, a belief that is no longer tenable in a modern, pluralist state. The distinction between human life and other forms of life is morally irrelevant, and a hangover from a Christian past. How do modern Christians respond to the accusation that 'the traditional principle of the sanctity of human life is the outcome of some seventeen centuries of Christian domination of Western thought and cannot rationally be defended'?[39]

Remember that Singer and Kuhse's argument deals not with abortion but infanticide- the killing of newborn infants who might otherwise live. That this is the natural implication of a world-view that rejects the God of the biblical revelation should not come as a surprise. That the loss of divine co-ordinates has far-reaching practical consequences was seen a century ago by that eccentric, anti-Christian visionary, Friedrich Nietzsche (1844–1900). Dismissing the moralism of English novelists such as George Eliot, he writes: 'They have got rid of the Christian God, and now feel obliged to cling all the more firmly to Christian morality . . . When one gives up Christian belief one thereby deprives oneself of the right to Christian morality . . . its origin is transcendental . . . [Christian morality] possesses truth only if God is truth—it stands or falls with the belief in God . . .'[40]

The choices are stark. Whatever the modernities we inhabit, whether of the past-Christian West or the anti-Christian East, that to which we tune our hearts in worship is what, in turn, shapes the form of our humanity.

Notes

[1] K. Marx & F. Engels, *The Communist Manifesto* (1848) (Introd. AJP Taylor, Harmondsworth: Penguin, 1967) p. 83

26   *Gods That Fail*

2 M. Weber, *The Protestant Ethic and the Spirit of Capitalism* (1904–5) (New York: Scribner, 1958) esp. pp. 180ff

3 A. Giddens, *The Consequences of Modernity* (Cambridge: Polity Press, 1991) p. 53

4 Ibid. p.139

5 Ibid. p.52. See also pp. 163ff

6 Ibid. p.45 (italics in text)

7 D. Bell, *The Coming of Post-Industrial Society* (London: Heinemann, 1974) p. 318 n. 30

8 R. Rorty, *Contingency, Irony, and Solidarity* (Cambridge: Cambridge University Press, 1989)

9 F. Fukuyama, *The End of History and the Last Man* (London: Hamish Hamilton, 1992)

10 F. Fukuyama, 'Changed days for Ruritania's Dictator', *The Guardian* (London), 8 April 1991.

11 RK Merton, 'Mass Persuasion: A Technical Problem and a Moral Dilemma' in R. Jackall (ed), *Propaganda* (London: Macmillan, 1995) p. 273; originally published in R.K. Merton, *Mass Persuasion: The Social Psychology of a War Bond Drive* (New York and London: Harper & Brothers, 1946)

12 Rorty, op. cit., p. 113

13 V. Havel, *Open Letters. Selected Prose, 1965–1990.* ed. Paul Wilson (London: Faber and Faber, 1991) pp. 94–5

14 Ibid. p. 267

15 The term 'the Enlightenment' is usually used with reference to the project on which the eighteenth-century *philosophes* of France and Scotland, and their followers in northern Europe and the United States, embarked. At its heart lay the belief that the expansion of scientific knowledge along the lines opened up by Galileo and Newton would give humankind (mankind, at any rate!) rational control over both the natural and social worlds. Other seventeenth-century figures whose thought had an abiding influence on the course of the Enlightenment were John Locke, René Descartes and (especially in Germany) Gottfried Leibniz.

16 See, for example, L. Ray, 'The Protestant Ethic Debate' in R.J. Anderson, J.A. Hughes & W.W. Sharrock (eds.), *Classic Debates in Sociology* (London: Allen & Unwin, 1987)

17 See Chapters 3 and 6 of the present book.

18 C. Taylor, *Sources of the Self: the Making of the Modern Identity* (Cambridge: Cambridge University Press, 1989) p.14

19 Ibid. pp.13–14

20 H.G. Reventlow, *The Authority of the Bible and the Rise of the Modern World* (Eng. trans. J. Bowden, London: SCM, 1984)

21 M. Midgley, *Wisdom, Information & Wonder* (London & New York: Routledge, 1991) pp. 6–7

22 Ibid. p. 9

23 Ibid. p.8

24 Weber, op. cit., p. 182 (my emphasis)

25 G. Steiner, *Real Presences: Is There Anything in What We Say?* (London: Faber and Faber, 1989) p. 3

26 Ibid. p.216

27 Ibid. p. 93 (Italics in text)

28 Ibid. p. 26

29 Ibid. pp. 24,49

30 Ibid. p. 24

31 C. Bernstein, *Guardian Weekly*, 14 June 1992

32 J.M. Hirota, 'Making Product Heroes: Work in Advertising Agencies', in R. Jackall (ed), *Propaganda*, op. cit. p. 344

33 Ibid. pp.346–7

34 M. Buckley, *At the Origins of Modern Atheism* (New Haven: Yale University Press, 1987) p. 363

35 Ibid. p. 33

36 Ibid. p. 358

37 See B. Goudzwaard, *Idols of Our Time* (Downers Grove, Illinois: InterVarsity Press, 1984)

38 H. Kuhse and P. Singer, *Should the Baby Live?: The Problem of Handicapped Infants* (Oxford: Oxford University Press, 1985)

39 Ibid. p. 125

40 F. Nietzsche, *Twilight of the Idols and The Anti-Christ* (Harmondsworth: Penguin, 1968) pp. 69–70

2

Religion and Idols

'. . . union with Christ consists in the most intimate communication with him, in having him before our eyes and in our hearts,
and being so filled with the highest love for him, at the same time
we turn our hearts to our brothers whom he has closely bound
to us, and for whom also he sacrificed himself . . .'[1]

These words are part of a school-leaving essay by a 17-year old
schoolboy in 1835. His name was Karl Marx. Yes, the same Karl
Marx whose books and pamphlets changed the whole face of
this century and in whose name countless Christians and people
of other faiths have been slaughtered. Marx came from a long
line of Jewish rabbis on both sides of his family. His father,
Heinrich Marx, was a liberal Jew who received Christian baptism
for reasons of social convenience. Karl himself was baptized as a
child and brought up in a Christian environment which profoundly influenced his future development. But how did this
earnest, religious-minded youth, come not only to reject his
religious faith during his university days but eventually to become perhaps the most famous atheist in history?

The reasons are complex. But two which stand out are:
firstly, his friendship with a group of 'radical' theologians who,
under the influence of the rationalism that had recently entered
biblical studies in Germany, declared that the gospel narratives
were legendary accounts which could no longer serve as a
source for the history of Jesus of Nazareth but only for the
history of the early church. While these theologians continued
to call themselves Christians and believed they could retain the
truths of Christianity while destroying its historical basis, Marx
saw beyond them to the logical consequences of their theories:
for if the gospels did not yield a reliable picture of Jesus Christ,
then why should we bother with him at all?

But the second reason, more relevant for our present purposes,
has to do with how Marx saw the way religion in general, and
Christianity in particular, functioned in the German society of

his day. Religion was used by the ruling classes to sanction the status quo. It justified the inequities and sufferings of the present social order by explaining them as the outworking of an eternal, transcendental order. Just as doctrines of caste, *karma* and rebirth have often tended to induce in many Asian cultures a passive acceptance of one's material and social condition and an indifference towards all attempts at transforming this world, so in nineteenth-century Europe the state churches took it for granted that the 'divine will' was reflected in the present ordering of things, with the consequence that to reject the present order was tantamount to rebellion against God. Compensation for one's afflictions lay not in material changes within this world, but in another world beyond death. This popular attitude is summed up in the well-known hymn that is still taught today in some Christian Sunday-schools:

The rich man in his castle, the poor man at his gate
God made them high and lowly, and ordered their estate
(from 'All Things Bright and Beautiful').

2.1 The Hegelian Legacy

A far more sophisticated and influential version of these sentiments was expressed by the mighty G.W.F. Hegel (1770–1831), considered the greatest German philosopher of the nineteenth century and whose influence has extended well into the twentieth. It is to Hegel that the eminent historian of ideas J.N. Findlay ascribes the title 'The father of modernism'.[2] 'God' to Hegel was not a personal being but an evolving process of thought (variously conceived as Absolute Spirit, Reason or Universal Idea), unfolding itself in a dialectical way through the dominant forms of historical epochs and developing towards greater and greater self-consciousness in Art, Religion, Science and, finally, Philosophy.

Despite a ponderous style and the obscurity of his arguments, Hegel was enormously appealing. His attractiveness lay in the unique way in which he attempted to solve a problem that had worried great philosophers such as Descartes, Hume and Kant: how was the rational, thinking human self related to the external, natural world? The mainstream western philosophical tradition, including much of theology, had been dualist in its conception of persons and the world. The realms of 'spirit' and 'nature' coexisted uneasily on parallel tracks. Their mutual relationship had become even more of a problem following the success of Newtonian science. Nature, conceived as a big orderly machine, had no place within it for the autonomous, moral, thinking selves who conceive those natural and moral laws. Reason and moral choice were regarded as the bearers of human identity, but there is clearly no place for them within Nature. Reason and sensation, facts and values, spirit and matter, the individual and culture—all these had been consigned to a state of perpetual segregation by philosophies as diverse as those of Descartes, Hume and Kant.

Hegel overcame this dilemma at one stroke. He declared that the rational and the natural did meet: they meet in history. Their relationship changes over historic time, history being the story of an ever-increasing permeation of the social order by the impersonal and immanently unfolding Reason (or Spirit or Idea): 'That world history is governed by an ultimate design, that it is a rational process- whose rationality is not that of a particular subject, but a divine and absolute reason—that is a proposition whose truth we must assume; its proof lies in the study of world history itself, which is the image and enactment of reason.'[3]

Here Hegel's Reason, the deity which guides the course of world history, blends neatly with the idea of Progress which was beginning to seduce the European mind at the turn of the eighteenth and nineteenth centuries. Progress was the notion that history was the tale of continuous and sustained human improvement of which modern Europe was the crowning pinnacle. Historical change was cumulative and beneficial, ushering humankind into a more rational world order. The ever-growing convergence of Reason with social reality was guaranteed by the gradual penetration of human thought and conduct by this immanent, impersonal Reason. This Hegelian doctrine was summed up by the aphorism that initially only one was free, then some were free, and eventually, in the modern state, all are free. 'The Real is the Rational' became the famous Hegelian slogan. This did not imply that individual human agency was irrelevant. Rather, all human action, including the conflicts and tribulations of history, are endowed with a meaning derived from their appointed place within the dynamic scheme of things. Even the irrational and often base actions of human beings unwittingly serve a higher plan. They are 'tricked' into doing so by what Hegel came to call the Cunning of Reason.

In Hegelian thought, the dichotomy between culture and reason is also bridged. Culture permeates all human feeling, thinking and acting. It crystallizes into social and political formations which generate and succeed each other in an orderly array, thus endowing human life with meaning. It could now be seen as the agency of Spirit that channels all human effort towards the fulfilment of the higher cause, namely the marriage of Reason and Reality. Hegel saw this marriage already taking place in the Prussian state of which he was a citizen, and imagined himself to be the registrar at the marriage ceremony. The task of philosophy, as he understood it, was to discern the rationality which is increasingly embodied in the actual. He saw in the rise of the new Prussian State, '... The Divine idea as it exists on earth ... We must therefore worship the State as the manifestation of the Divine on earth ... The State is the march of God through the world'.[4]

The Spirit of the Age was the new deity, replacing the old personal deities; or, more accurately, the latter could be seen as different incarnations of the Spirit in previous ages. These imperfect deities, and indeed every human thought-system, culture and epoch, had been assigned a place and a role in the dynamic unfolding of Spirit/Reason within history. Hegel reinterpreted all the traditional theological language (e.g. of Trinity, revelation, incarnation, redemption) into the impersonal categories of his new world-view. The personal God of the Hebrews became a code term, one among others in the sweep of history, for the lofty Absolute Spirit of modern European philosophy. Biblical language about God was imperfect, parabolic and metaphorical, awaiting translation (by Hegel) into the pure concepts of abstract philosophical truth. Hegel's Spirit enlarged the global scope of revelation from its crude focus in the history of Israel and the mediterranean world, bringing deity and salvation to their appointed culmination in northern Europe. This enabled Hegelian theologians to continue using the traditional language of piety and Christian orthodoxy but in ways that would have made little sense to their forebears.

Hegel's ideas had a massive impact on nineteenth-century European theology, and the influence of his approach on theological method even in the closing decades of the twentieth has been considerable. It is also intriguing to observe how, historically, his ideas shaped and left their imprint on the two most powerful of modern secular religions, both of which have been in violent confrontation with each other throughout most of the present century: Nationalism (culminating in Fascism) and Marxism. Nineteenth century nationalism had its ideological roots in the romanticization of culture and the immanent Spirit of the Age. Its terrible, but quite logical, consequences were seen in the Nazi glorification of 'blood and soil' and the justification of terrible evil in terms of historical destiny.

2.2 Secularist Critiques

Marx was initially attracted by Hegel's novel reconciliation of 'what is' with 'what ought to be', but he quickly revolted against this synthesis in the light of his experience of the Prussian state. He claimed to have turned Hegel upside-down, or more accurately, right-way up: 'In direct contrast to German philosophy which descends from heaven to earth, here we ascend from earth to heaven . . . We set out from real, active men, and on the basis of their real life-process we demonstrate the development of the ideological reflexes . . . Morality, religion, metaphysics, all the rest of ideology . . . no longer retain the semblance of independence.'[5] History was not the dialectical development of human thought towards the Absolute Spirit, but the dialectical development of the material techniques of production and their social organization towards a classless human society.

Marx saw religion as creating a make-believe world which concealed the real interests of the rulers from the ruled. This corruption of reason by class interests, whether consciously or unconsciously, was what Marx called *ideology*. Religion functioned as ideology, giving legitimacy to unjust political and social structures. All who worked uncritically within such a system were victims of a *false consciousness* which could be transformed only by political action in solidarity with the industrial working class.

It is in this context that he made his most famous reference to religion as 'the opium of the masses'. The full quotation is very moving, less harsh than some of his other comments: 'Religion is the sigh of the oppressed creature, the heart of a heartless world, the soul of soulless conditions. It is the opium of the people.'[6] In a day when medical science could offer few cures, opium was widely used as a pain-killer. So to Marx, religion was a way of coping with the constant pain of dehumanizing conditions. The urbanization and industrialization of nineteenth-century Europe brought much social misery in their wake. Workers sold themselves as commodities in a capitalist society and so became alienated from their work, from their fellow workers and also from themselves. Religion was useless to liberate them from the causes of their suffering. It helped only to lessen the pain of existence. Religion itself was not the cause of suffering but, by making tolerable what was intolerable, it sapped the will to struggle for a different order of things.

To this criticism Marx added the reductionist view of religion developed by his contemporary and friend, Ludwig Feuerbach (1804–1872), also once a disciple of Hegel but now a foremost critic of the Master. For Feuerbach, all 'God-talk' is to be understood as the expression of collective human desires and ideals (such as justice, wisdom, love, etc). These ideals are personifications of human feelings and aspirations. They are then unconsciously externalized (or 'objectified') and ascribed to a non-human object that is imagined to stand over and above the human species. In this manner the religious imagination, working on religious feelings, inverts reality. Man's religion is nothing but a reflection of himself (understood collectively, though, not individually). Whereas in Hegel the subject of the dialectic of self-unfolding is the Absolute Spirit/Reason, in Feuerbach it becomes the human species. Human self-consciousness projects its contents onto the cosmos. Thus he wrote:

> Consciousness of God is human self-consciousness; knowledge of God is human self-knowledge . . . God is the manifested inward nature, the expressed self of a man- religion the solemn unveiling of a man's hidden treasures, the revelation of his intimate thoughts, the open confession of his love-secrets . . . The historical progress of religion consists therefore in this: that what an earlier religion took to be objective, is later recognized to be subjective; what formerly was taken to be God, and worshipped as such, is now recognized to be something human. What was earlier religion is later taken to be idolatry: humans are seen to have adored their own nature.[7]

Thus for Feuerbach, the worship of a transcendent God necessarily implies the suppression of human freedom. As he put it, famously: 'To enrich God, man must become poor; that God may be all, man must be nothing.'[8]

So Marx, under the influence of Feuerbach, came to believe that the criticism of religion is the foundation for all social criticism, since religious people are most likely to acquiesce in every form of social inversion and thereby obscure social reality. Not only does religion play into the hands of those who control the way society functions to their own interests, but it lulls the believer into a passive social conformity by diverting attention from the real causes of misery and oppression. Thus, religion was an enemy of freedom. It had to be defeated for the sake of humanity.

We shall never understand Marx if we fail to perceive the Judaeo-Christian background from which he speaks. His passion to expose every form of social evil, and to liberate men from the chains of oppression is the passion of an Old Testament prophet. His vision is ethical, his values often unconsciously biblical. The characteristic language of 'alienation', 'human redemption', 'the New Man' etc is directly taken over from Christian theology. Even the protest against a God who is silent in the face of suffering and appears to sanction injustice is an echo of the protest literature of the Bible. Marx believed his analysis of capitalist society to be strictly scientific, but science in his hands was not simply a theoretical tool for understanding the world but a powerful weapon with which to change the world. Although the 'scientific' aspects of his work have been invalidated by the events which followed his death (for instance, his predictions about the course of western capitalism did not come true), his followers, by and large, still clung to the supposedly scientific nature of what came to be called Marxism, and neglected these more fascinating aspects of Marx's moral and spiritual roots.

Another towering figure of Jewish origin who became an equally impassioned champion of militant atheism was the Viennese doctor Sigmund Freud (1856–1939), the founder of the psychoanalytic movement. Freud believed that 'the basis of man's need for religion is infantile helplessness'. Religion is thus associated with an infantile stage in the individual's development, and Freud tried also to show how it arose in the development of the human species. In a book called *Totem and Taboo* (published in 1913) Freud put forward some bizarre speculations on the origin of religion and morality in human pre-history. It was traced to repressed guilt engendered by a primeval act of patricide: the males in the family-group killing the chief, out of sexual jealousy at his control of all the women, and devouring his body. He then revived a discredited biological theory called Lamarckism to argue that the lingering affection for the chief was transmuted into feelings of guilt which were inherited by successive generations, thus forming the universal religious psyche. The dead father-chief became stronger than the living one! Society was now based on complicity in the common crime; religion was based on the sense of guilt and the remorse attaching to it; while morality was based partly on the needs of this society and partly on the penance demanded by the sense of guilt.

These anthropological fantasies followed his earlier theories about the origins of emotional disorders in individuals who came to him for treatment. Freud believed he had uncovered layer upon layer of unconscious motivations that arose out of repressed guilt due to childhood sexual fantasies (what he termed the Oedipus complex, after the figure in Sophocles' ancient drama who unwittingly fulfilled his destiny by slaying his father and marrying his mother). Religion expressed an immature way of dealing with this inner conflict: by projecting a cosmic 'father-figure' who appeases our fears, we escape from the pain of facing such conflicts and taking responsibility for our lives. Religious behaviour is thus a denial of reality. We create gods out of the whirlpool of our inner desires and anxieties. At its heart lies a process of wish-fulfilment.

If Marx saw God functioning for religious believers as a giant vallium tablet (the modern equivalent of his opium), to Freud he oscillated between a giant Teddy Bear and a despotic headmaster! Both men saw themselves as ushering in a new age of liberation through science, although Freud became increasingly pessimistic about the future of the human species as he lived on into the Great War and the Nazi era. Both of them saw religion as an obstacle to their programme of human liberation because it concealed the root causes of humankind's distress. Their militant atheism was aimed at bringing an end to religious illusion, to restoring human autonomy.

What is remarkable is that, in either case, the prophetic tradition of the Bible seems to have been the unconscious motivation for their attempts at transforming human consciousness. The belief in a higher destiny for humankind, the concept of human alienation, the notion (in Marx) of purpose in history and the eventual triumph of justice . . . these are all the lingering relics of a culture that was at one time deeply influenced by a biblical world-view, however much it may have denied that world-view in practice. As Erich Fromm, one of the great pioneers of existentialist psychology, observed of Freud, 'Under the disguise of a scientific school Freud realized his old dream, to be the Moses who showed the human race the promised land, the conquest of the Id [the unconscious whirl-pool of the psyche] by the Ego and the way to this conquest.'[9]

2.3   A Biblical Critique

Today many would regard Freud and Marx as largely historical curiosities. Their theories have been superseded by others, their solutions tried and found wanting, their most ardent followers left disillusioned. Very few today, compared to, say, thirty years ago, would call themselves Marxists or Freudians. Why then should we, in the closing years of the twentieth century when religious movements, far from dying out, are burgeoning all over the world (not least in the supposedly secular West) bother to listen to their critique of religion?

I suggest two reasons. The first is that their views on Christian belief are shared by a number of folk who may never have even heard of Marx or Freud (or any other influential atheist of the last century). Whenever someone refers to faith as an 'emotional crutch' for those who cannot stand on their own feet, she is invoking the ghost of Freud. Whenever anyone mocks Christian belief as 'bourgeois ideology' or 'pie in the sky when you die', he is paying homage to Marx. Both have left a vocabulary (for example: ideology, class struggle, alienation, repression, libido) which has become part and parcel of the popular stock of modern culture.

The second, and more important, reason is this: they force all who call themselves Christians to re-examine their beliefs and practices in the light of the biblical revelation. The great prophets of Israel were, no less than Jesus himself, disturbing and uncomfortable people to have around. Much of their work involved an 'uprooting and tearing down' of cherished notions about God as much as a 'building and planting' (Jer. 1:10). Could God be speaking to us today through these 'secular prophets'—just as he spoke to his hard-hearted people

Israel through their pagan enemies? Could these atheists actually have been closer to grasping the nature of God's kingdom, as revealed in the Bible, than many religious devotees whether 'Christian', 'Muslim', 'Hindu', 'Buddhist' or whatever?

Let us reflect for a moment on the radical worship of Yahweh, the covenant name of God disclosed to the ancient Hebrews. At the heart of this self-disclosure was a sharp warning against every tendency to idolatry: 'I am Yahweh your God . . . you shall have no other gods besides me. You shall not make for yourself an idol in the form of anything in the universe' (Ex. 20:2ff). Israel's distinctiveness as a people was to lie in the way they bore witness to this unique revelation (of God's character, activity and purpose) among the nations. It is important to remember that Israel was not a pre-existing nation which Yahweh chose to relate to in a special way, but rather a motley collection of landless, displaced peoples called into being by the word of Yahweh and forged into a nation by that self-same word. Israel was to be the means whereby Yahweh challenged the evil and idolatry of the world and so re-established his kingdom (rule) over the nations. This witness took the form of keeping the terms of the covenant, for it was in the way the people related to one another that they announced the uniqueness of their relationship with Yahweh. His worship was intimately tied to the practice of truth, mercy and justice among themselves and with their neighbours.

The gods of the Canaanites, as indeed all the gods of the Semitic and Indo-European peoples, were gods of nature and fertility. They guaranteed stability in the midst of chaos and social upheaval. Their worship, in carefully prescribed ritual, was designed to appease their capricious anger and to secure material benefits for the worshippers. These gods were essentially amoral; the only demands they made on men related to ritual obligations. While the gods upheld an unchanging cosmos, Yahweh, however, was the bringer of change: liberating his people from captivity, leading them through the wilderness where they learned the meaning of his holiness, preparing them to be a people who, within the twists and turns of human history, would embody a hope for all humankind. The past lay with a couple in a garden, alienated from each other, the creation and their Creator; the future with a 'new heavens and a new earth in which righteousness dwells' (e.g. Is. 65:17ff; Ezek. 47; Rev. 21; 2 Pet. 3:13).

The great temptation Israel faced, and frequently succumbed to, was to think of Yahweh in terms of a nature deity and to worship him in the manner of these surrounding religious cults. Hence the great burden of the prophets' message was that idolatry and social injustice went hand-in-hand. When religion became a sanction for social oppression or a way of evading the costly demands of the covenant by escaping into a private world of security and false peace, then Yahweh stood opposed to religion. When the gifts of Yahweh (e.g. the land, the sanctuary, the sabbath) became substitutes for Yahweh himself, so that people deluded themselves into thinking that Yahweh was always with them no matter how they treated the weak and the vulnerable, or what they did in their business practices and courts of law, then Yahweh's judgement on the nation consisted in the withdrawal of those gifts. His people were sent into exile, the sanctuary destroyed, the sabbath desecrated by foreign armies (e.g. Lev. 18: 26–28; Jer. 7:9–15; Lam. 2:5ff).

Yahweh's concern for the poor is the other side of his opposition to idolatry. The tragic fact of poverty in Yahweh's abundant earth is sometimes attributed to individual sin (e.g. Prov. 19:15; 24:30–34), but more often it is mentioned in connection with the failure of those who are not poor to live by the obligations of the covenant. When Israel settled in the land of Canaan, the land was divided among families; and regulations concerning the Sabbath year and the Year of Jubilee (Lev. 25) were intended to ensure that land (which is the capital of an agrarian society) did not accumulate in the hands of a few to the disadvantage of the many. In the Mosaic law God made special provisions for specific groups of poor people (e.g. Ex. 23:2–9; Lev 19:9–10; Deut. 15:1–18; 24:19–22). The unity of the people was a basic assumption in these provisions: they were to relate to one another in a way that reflected Yahweh's historical dealings with them (e.g. Lev. 25:42–43; Ex 23:9). So poverty was not the concern of individuals alone; the social structures enshrined in the law were intended to protect the vulnerable sections of the community and to reveal to the surrounding nations that Yahweh was a God of compassion and justice. Promises of prosperity following obedience (e.g. Deut. 15:4–5) were given to the whole community, not to individuals.

The people of Israel failed to live with the psychological tensions of social, political and religious uniqueness. When they demanded of the judge-prophet Samuel that Yahweh give them a king 'like the other nations', Samuel warned them of the consequences: militarism and violence, economic inequality and social oppression (1 Sam. 8:10f). Once the monarchy was established and the covenant law largely forgotten, social stratification became inevitable. The absolute rock-bottom was reached during the reign of Ahab when, encouraged by his Phoenician wife Jezebel, he sought to overthrow the worship of Yahweh and replace him with Baal, the centuries-old nature deity of the surrounding cultures. The seizure of Naboth's vineyard by Ahab and Jezebel (1 Kgs. 21) demonstrates how quickly the earlier laws that kept property within a family were replaced by foreign concepts of state ownership. The prophets of Yahweh spoke strongly against the injustices involved in these changes (e.g. Is. 5:8;10:1 Jer. 34:13–17; Am 2:6–8; 3:15;5:11–12). The humble poor of the land, who had no one but Yahweh to depend on for their deliverance, came to be identified with the 'people of Yahweh' in a unique sense (e.g. Ps. 9:9,10; 14:4–6; 37:14–15; Is. 3:15). They are economically destitute, socially oppressed, but have put their trust in Yahweh and not in the gods of the surrounding nations.

The absolute prohibition on 'images' which we find from the beginnings of Israelite history, and the contingent status of kingship in Israel, are unique in the ancient world. It is not accidental that the two went together, nor that they became the prime objects of prophetic critique. All systems of Near Eastern religion centred on localized, mediating images which were supervised by a royal and priestly elite. They controlled the traffic between humans and the divine realm. In arguing both that Israel was a 'priestly' community and that the divine could not be represented by any form of human imagining (and thus be manipulated by the socially powerful for their own ends), the biblical writers suggest a critique of religion as idolatry.

It is interesting to recall that the early Christians were called 'atheists' by the Romans. They did not join in the emperor cult. They had none of the paraphernalia of religious worship: no shrines or sacred buildings, no centres of pilgrimage, no special priestly class, no 'holy days' and 'auspicious times'. They did not offer the Roman empire a new religion to add to the hundreds that were already around. Nor did they teach a new philosophy or code of ethics, though their message about a crucified criminal who had been raised with a new human body to the highest position in the universe had enormous philosophical and ethical implications. They had the choice of blending quietly into the multi-religious environment of the empire: by simply acknowledging Jesus as one amongst a number of saviour figures in the Roman pantheon. In this way they would have been tolerated as a harmless religious sect and left in peace by the authorities.

We all know the choice the early Christians did make. In a sense they had no choice, given the nature of what they believed. How could you believe that among those crucified by the Roman state was one who was the Son of God himself—and not have your view of politics and power turned upside down? How could you believe that the guardians of the most developed religious and moral tradition in the world had rejected the Son of God in order to preserve their religious identity—and not rethink your understanding of religion and religions? To choose to worship Jesus on Sundays and Caesar the rest of the week was to betray the very Good News itself. For if the crucified Jesus was the risen Lord, then Caesar and Caesar's world must also bow to Jesus. Hence they paid with their lives for what they believed.

2.4 False Gospels

Compare this with much of what passes for Christianity today. The Good News is packaged and marketed (using, uncritically, all the techniques of modern advertising) as a religious product: offering 'peace of mind', 'how to get to heaven', 'health and prosperity', 'inner healing', 'the answer to all your problems' etc. What is promoted as 'faith in God' often turns out, on closer inspection, to be a means for obtaining emotional security or material blessing in this life and an insurance policy for the next. This kind of preaching leaves the status quo untouched. It does not raise fundamental and disturbing questions about the assumptions on which people build their lives. It does not threaten the false gods in whose name the creation of God has been taken over; indeed it actually reinforces their hold on their worshippers. This kind of 'gospel' is essentially escapist, the direct descendent of the pseudo-gospels of the false prophets of the Old Testament. It is simply a religious image of the secular consumerist culture in which modern men and women live. It lays itself wide open to the full blast of the savage criticism of Marx and Freud.

I often wonder what there is in this kind of preaching which cannot be offered by one of the myriad Hindu gurus or Indian religious sects that are a growing feature of the modern, no less than traditional, cultural landscape. Why is the Sai Baba cult, for example, especially popular among politicians and wealthy business executives on the Indian sub-continent? Why do those who have ostensibly rejected the ethics of their traditional faiths, nevertheless persist with meditation classes and make frequent visits to their personal astrologers? It seems to me that the attraction lies in the offer of a religion without repentance. One can have healing for one's ailments, prosperity for one's children, peace of mind and even access to supernatural powers, without anyone raising awkward questions about one's political thuggery, racist policies or dubious commercial transactions. There is no moral demand to make public confession and restitution towards all those whom one may have wronged.

The same is true of all the New Age religious movements of North America and Europe. Their patronage by the upper echelons of the social establishment (the so-called 'Yuppie' breed) is not accidental, for they offer an attractive synthesis of Western consumerism and Eastern mystery. At root lies a common obsession with power: whether social or mystical. Commercialized forms of Indian religions, often reduced to meditation techniques and novel dietary habits, have long been popular in the West among the well-to-do. Even in the last century, the European upper-middle classes were the great patrons of theosophy, spiritualist seances, Christian Science and other spurious forms of religious practice. Therapeutic religion, pandering to the narcissism of the modern self, seems to be the opium of the ruling classes.

This kind of religion, whether in Christian or other forms, is *idolatry* by biblical definition. For at the heart of idolatry is the attempt to manipulate 'God' or the unseen 'spiritual world' in order to obtain security and well-being for oneself and one's 'group' (whether family, business corporation, ethnic community or nation-state). Biblical faith, in contrast, is the radical abandonment of our whole being in grateful trust and love to the God disclosed in the life, death and resurrection of Jesus

Christ: so that we become his willing agents in a costly confrontation with every form of evil and unjust suffering in the world. This faith involves us in embracing the pain and confusion of others, and in being willing to live with uncertainty ourselves while moving towards a future that is *already at work among us.*

In fact 'hope' is used more often than 'faith' in New Testament descriptions of the Christian life, and to the writer of the Epistle to the Hebrews, at least, faith and hope are inextricably linked: 'faith is the assurance of things hoped for . . .' (Heb 11:1). Christian hope is far removed from wishful thinking. Anchored in the physical resurrection of Jesus, it takes this world, and especially the historical existence of men and women, with utmost seriousness: recognizing its ambiguities and contradictions, but believing in its certain redemption. In the words of Dietrich Bonhoeffer, languishing in a prison cell and awaiting execution for his opposition to Hitler, 'The difference between the Christian hope and a mythological hope is that the Christian hope sends a man back to his life on earth in a wholly new way . . . Myths of salvation arise from human experience of the boundary condition. Christ takes hold of a man in the centre of his life.'[10] This is the very opposite of Freudian 'wish-fulfilment', for this hope of redemption lies in the way of the Cross; and the way of the Cross fulfils no one's natural wishes! This is a theme to which we shall return during the course of this book.

The gulf between modern Christianity and the spirituality of the Bible is seen also in our selective use of the Psalms, which were the song-book of the people of Israel and the New Testament church. The psalms not only reflect every human experience (e.g. confusion, anger, fear, anxiety, depression, uninhibited joy) but they force us to stop pretending that everything is fine with the world. The psalms of lament (e.g. Psalms 10,13,35,86) are passionate complaints at God for the contradictions between his promise and the reality the people experience. These psalms are rarely used in Christian worship today. Yet these psalms are acts of courageous faith: courageous, because they insist that we must face the world as it is and give up every childish pretence; but also of faith, because they stem from the conviction that there is nothing out of bounds where conversation with God is concerned. To withhold any part of human experience, including the darkness of unanswered prayer and the negative aspects of life, from that conversation is to deny the sovereignty of God in all of life. So, paradoxically, it is those who suppress their doubts under a litany of jolly choruses who may well be guilty of unbelief: for they refuse to believe that God can handle their rage.

Thus, the psalms of protest are a powerful rebuke to what passes for faith and worship in most Christian circles today. What is ironic is that modern life perhaps exposes us to more confusion and pain than anything in the psalmist's own world; and yet we ignore the very prayers which give speech to that sense of disorientation. It is little wonder that much contemporary Christian teaching about faith is no different from the 'positive thinking' of modern management gurus, but dressed up in pseudo-biblical language. Biblical faith, however, is its very opposite.

The same is true of contemporary preaching about 'peace', a word that conveys one of the richest of biblical concepts. The Hebrew word *shalom* (the traditional Hebrew greeting to this day) has the idea of 'well-being' or 'wholeness' and is very closely associated with the themes of reconciliation and salvation. It has many dimensions, of which the most fundamental is peace with God. For the Lord to give his people peace is synonymous with turning his face towards them in the mercy of acceptance (Num. 6:26). The promised Messiah in the Old Testament is the Prince of Peace (Is. 9:6) because he will restore the eternal covenant of peace between God and his people (e.g. Ezek. 37:26). In the New Testament 'peace with God' is the first blessing that flows out of God's redeeming and justifying grace (Rom. 5:1).

But this peace has a horizontal dimension too: peace with our fellow men and women, especially those from whom we are estranged by sin. The Good News is about God's way of 'making peace' by breaking down the walls of hostility and division between social groups (e.g. Eph. 2:14ff). The prophets made it clear that this peace was costly, it could only be the result of right relationships: 'The fruit of righteousness will be peace; the effect of righteousness will be quietness and confidence for ever' (Is. 32:17). Then there is a personal peace, a deep serenity that comes not by avoiding trouble but by trusting God in the midst of trouble (e.g. Jn. 14:27, 2 Thess.

3:16). I cannot emphasize too strongly that shalom is a holistic concept. It must never be reduced, on the one hand, to merely socio-economic justice, nor, on the other hand, to a narcissistic 'feeling good' or a pseudo-spirituality that stands aloof from social injustice and physical suffering.

We have already commented on the idolatrous role of religion, both in traditional and modern societies, in its popular invocation as a justifier of the status quo. The privileged, who may also happen to be 'religious', often feel that their social and economic privileges are somehow a solemn, basic, God-given right. In many legal systems down to the present day, the sanctity of private property has been upheld (by both legislators and magistrates) with greater righteous indignation than the sanctity of human life. As the economist John Kenneth Galbraith comments, tongue-in-cheek, 'The sensitivity of the poor to injustice is a trivial thing compared with that of the rich'. He continues, 'So it was in the Ancien Regime. When reform from the top becomes impossible, revolution from the bottom becomes inevitable.'[11] But, someone may object, what about the apostle Paul's injunction to Christians to be content with their material state (1 Tim 6:6ff)? Isn't this too a classic instance of religious opium being dished out to the masses?

Not if one pays attention to the whole passage in which Paul's words appear. For, firstly, Paul is not addressing those whom modern economists would describe as the 'absolute poor': namely those people, numbering over half a billion today, whose basic needs of nutrition, clothing, health care and housing have not yet been met. He assumes (in v.8) that these primary human requirements have been satisfied; for only then is contentment possible. Where these needs have not been satisfied, it is usually because of a failure to share material resources, which in turn is a result of the arrogance of the rich and their refusal to fulfil their obligations to the poor (see v.17,18). Secondly, Paul's warnings are not directed at the legitimate aspirations on the part of the poor to be freed from exploitation and material want. Rather they are directed at human greed, the 'love of money' (v.10), the spirit of acquisitiveness which is rampant among 'the rich in this present world' and which leads to idolatry and a false sense of security (v.17; cf Col. 3:5). It is so easy for the demand for economic justice (which God approves of) to slide into a destructive rivalry motivated by obsessive greed (which God disapproves of). This is as true for churches and nations as it is as for individuals. Paul's warnings are based on the assumption that a world of gross material inequality is a world that is dominated by false gods, by empty sources of security (v. 7,17). If the rich heeded his teaching, they would no longer be rich, and the poor would no longer be poor.

Throughout most of history the great thinkers and preachers of the Christian church have affirmed the economic rights of the poor. Not only did they remind the relatively well-to-do of their charitable *duty* to the poor, but they also insisted on the right of access on the part of the poor to adequate means of sustenance. 'Not from your own do you bestow upon the poor man, but you make return from what is his', said Bishop Ambrose (339–397 C.E.) to the nobles of Milan.[12] John Chrysostom (c.347–407) argued boldly that:

> This also is theft, not to share one's possessions. Perhaps this statement seems surprising to you, but do not be surprised . . . Just as an official in the imperial treasury, if he neglects to distribute where he is ordered, but spends instead for his own indolence, pays the penalty and is put to death, so also the rich man is a kind of steward of the money which is owed for distribution to the poor. He is directed to distribute it to his fellow servants who are in want. So if he spends more on himself than his needs require, he will pay the harshest penalty hereafter. For his own goods are not his own, but belong to his own fellow servants . . . I beg you remember this without fail, that not to share our own wealth with the poor is theft from the poor and deprivation of their means of life; we do not possess our own wealth but theirs.[13]

Similarly the great Cappadocian Father, Basil of Ceasarea (c.329-c.379) rebuked rich Christians in language that is more often heard on factory picket-lines than in cathedrals: 'That bread which you keep belongs to the hungry; that coat which you preserve in your wardrobe, to the naked; those shoes which are rotting in your possession, to the shoeless; that gold which you have hidden in the ground, to the needy. Wherefore, as often as you were able to help others, and refused, so often did you do them wrong.'[14]

The suggestion one often encounters, that the concept of rights is a product of the humanism of the Enlightenment, is historically misleading. Although the word 'rights' may not have appeared with much frequency in the great patristic and medieval church leaders, the thought that the poor in society have legitimate claims on the rich (because of the latter's duty under God towards them), and that to withhold what was in one's power to grant in situations of material deprivation was to do moral injury to the poor, permeates their writings. It is morally permissible for an extremely impoverished person to take what he or she needs for sustenance from a person who has plenty. If I have food in my house which you need for your survival, but which is not indispensable for mine, then it rightfully belongs to you. You have a morally legitimate claim on it. If I offered it to you, it would not be an act of charity on my part as much as granting you your rights under God.

In his famous *Summa* the great medieval scholar Thomas Aquinas argued provocatively that all private property arrangements, which proceed from positive law (the laws of the state), must be subservient to the principle of common human stewardship which is guaranteed by the natural moral law:

> In cases of need all things are common property, so that there would seem to be no sin in taking another's property, for need has made it common . . . Now according to the natural order established by Divine providence, inferior things are ordained for the purpose of succouring man's needs by their means. Wherefore the division and appropriation of things which are based on human law do not preclude the fact that man's needs have to be remedied by means of these very things. Hence whatever certain people have in superabundance is due, by natural law, to the purpose of succouring the poor.[15]

Reasoning from the principle of stewardship whereby material things are seen as held in trust for the common welfare, Aquinas continued: 'Nevertheless, if the need be so manifest and urgent, that it is evident that the present need must be remedied by whatever means be at hand (for instance when a person is in some imminent danger, and there is no other possible remedy), then it is lawful for a man to succour his own need by means of another's property, by taking it either openly or secretly: nor is this properly speaking theft or robbery.'

Aquinas doesn't specify how best to succour the poor nor how to secure their economic rights without infringing on other rights; but the point I wish to underscore here is his clear conviction that all human beings have a natural right to genuine and fair access to means of sustenance. That such statements should appear so remarkable to many modern Christians is indicative of how far the church has moved from its biblical traditions (which Aquinas, Chrysostom and others saw as simply being interpreted and handed on by them to their communities). Many churches, both in the West and in Asia, tend to be comfortable havens in the midst of appalling poverty. Christians have often tacitly condoned laws and judicial sentencing which punish the poor more severely than the rich. Most sermons on stewardship are simply appeals to rich members to contribute their 'tithe' towards financing church projects in the neighbourhood and abroad. They rarely, if ever, raise disturbing questions about the way people acquire their wealth or what they do with the wealth that is left over from tithing. Least of all do modern Christians give time to explore how their professional work and their church 'programmes' may actually be reinforcing structures of exploitation in their world and thereby contradicting the very message they are eager to proclaim.

2.5 Turning the Tables

Militant atheism of the kind espoused by Marx and Freud has been on the wane in recent times. The atheism of our present age is really a shallow preoccupation with individual consumption and indifference to the deeper issues of life and death. It hides behind a casual talk of 'tolerance' that is usually a respectable term for apathy. Marx and Freud, at least, believed in absolute truths and moral judgements. They were committed to stating categorically that certain beliefs were wrong and should not be followed. This older atheism, as I have indicated, was very much a hang-over from an earlier theistic outlook on life. The modern atheist is more likely to be a relativist in his attitude to life ('all beliefs and values are culturally conditioned and so equally valid'). I myself have much greater admiration for the older, militant atheism because it is a more honourable position to hold, and it also encourages genuine debate.

Christians who engage in that debate will find that it compels them to re-discover elements at the heart of the gospel which have been obscured. The criticisms of Marx and Freud are on target where many forms of Christianity today are concerned. Ever since the Christian church ceased to be a subversive movement within the Roman world and became aligned with political, social and economic power, Christian discipleship itself has been transformed into another sub-species of the genus *religion*. We have been creating a God (and a Jesus) in our own image who gives us what other religions give their devotees. In this kind of climate it is impossible to see the uniqueness of Jesus Christ and the truly revolutionary nature of the liberation he announced and accomplished. The South African theologian Charles Villa-Vicencio laments that 'the mention of the Christian God within the South African constitution [under apartheid] has probably done more to alienate black people from the church than any secular or atheist state philosophy could ever have accomplished'.[16]

In the light of that gospel it is easy to see how Marx and Freud themselves are victims of the same self-delusion, idolatry and wish-fulfilment that they attribute to religion. Marx simply transferred religious 'pie in the sky' from a heavenly realm to the end of history (the 'classless society'). For Marx salvation, the exploitation-free social order in which all human potentialities would blossom and bloom, was guaranteed to dawn in the fulness of time. The self-correcting, providential ordering of the productive process would see to it. In this, his outlook, for all its pessimistic assessment of bourgeois society and its values, was essentially Hegelian in its optimism. While scoffing at the eternal moral order which religion had taught, he proclaimed, with more naivete than the simplest religious devotee, the inexorable march of societies to the music of 'scientifically established' laws of historical change. His belief that class struggle was the engine of social dynamism had its origin more in personal wish-fulfilment than in historical argument. As a true bourgeois intellectual, he transformed the industrial working-class into an *idol*, seeing in them a Messianic community that replaced the pretensions of the Christian church. So, with hindsight, we can see how Marx's historical materialism displayed all the features of 'false consciousness' which he attributed to traditional religion Little wonder that it became a twentieth-century religion itself.

Any revolutionary regime which claims to take control of human destiny- in order to replace the unjust world of a dead 'God' with its own new world of human justice—must replace this dead 'God' with itself. It must therefore create its own

values, its own definitions of justice. Any means that serves its
cause are legitimate. So, innocent suffering may be inflicted
by the revolutionary elite on the masses in the present age for
the sake of the well-being of the masses of a future age. The
tyranny of the new order silences protest just as effectively as
'God' did in the monarchies of the old order. Every attempt
to wipe out the past and to 'start afresh' with autonomous man,
from the French Revolution to Pol Pot's Kampuchea, have
unleashed new gods made in the image of the revolutionary
elite. Theologies which justified human suffering have been
replaced in our modern age with anthropologies which justify
even greater human suffering . . .

Freud, too, is an interesting object of Freudian analysis. He
was driven by an overwhelming ambition to make a mark for
himself in history, modelling himself on his adolescent heroes
Hannibal and Napoleon. While appearing to reveal himself in
many allegedly autobiographical studies, he hated others investigating his early life and the origins of his ideas, even going
to the extent of burning all his letters and early manuscripts on
two occasions. What he is reported to have remarked when
standing before the complete works of the German poet
Goethe, 'All this was used by him as a means of self-conceal-
ment', is especially apt for himself.[17]

It was in the late 1890s that Freud developed the Oedipal
theory of neuroses. It came out of an intense period of self-analy-
sis following his father's death and rejection of his earlier theories
by the academic world. His exposure as a child to the emptiness
of Catholic ritual by a dour Catholic nanny, his passionate
devotion to his mother who fawned on him right through his
life, his contempt for a father who had accomplished little in life
and failed to provide adequately for the family, and his conviction
that the anti-semitism of Catholic Vienna was what had ruined
his chances of academic recognition . . . all these formed the
seething cauldron of emotions out of which the Oedipal theory
exploded. In other words, Freud made of his personal experience
a universal theory of emotional development and, later, generalized this further into an all-embracing 'explanation' of every
aspect of human life.

By locating all present guilt and abnormal behaviour in some
infantile experience inaccessible to the conscious mind, Freud
conveniently evaded taking responsibility for the many personal conflicts in his adult life (falling out bitterly with all his

friends and collaborators, committing adultery/incest with his wife's sister, and so on). One could argue that the theory, to which Freud was emotionally committed all his life, despite its shallow scientific pretensions, was his way of escaping from the reality of objective moral guilt and of appeasing his conscience. He made of the psychoanalytic movement his own religious cult, accusing anyone who disagreed with him of unacknowledged sexual repressions—so that his theory was never testable, as all arguments levelled against it came to be taken by its practitioners as proofs of the theory itself! He passed on the mantle of leadership to his own daughter after he had excommunicated the heretics. Despite its embarrassing dearth of therapeutic success, the psychoanalytic movement continued to proclaim the allegedly scientific dogmas of Freud with religious fervour.

It is also fascinating to observe that Carl Jung, one of the early students of Freud who later became a bitter opponent and the founder of an alternative school of psychology, believed that Freud had made of sexuality a pseudo-god: 'I had a strong intuition that for him sexuality was a sort of *numinosum* . . . it was something to be religiously observed . . . One thing was clear: Freud, who had always made much of his irreligiosity, had now constructed a dogma; or rather, in the place of a jealous God whom he had lost, he had substituted another compelling image, that of sexuality.'[18]

Freudian doctrine paved the way for the irrationalism of the twentieth century. It challenged head-on the dominant rationalist image of man in Freud's own day, an image of a being in pursuit of noble ideals, or alternatively (in the more prosaic form of utilitarian philosophy), a careful accountant of pleasure and pain. For Freudians, all this was bunkum. The real springs of human motivation flow from our instinctive needs and from the intense feelings that arise from intimate human associations. Reason is distorted by the dark subterranean forces of the psyche. Our rationality and morality are but a facade, deployed for deception and, especially, self-deception. We can never be sure that our inward convictions and compulsions are not self-deceit. Consequently, all we can do is place ourselves in the expert hands of the licensed therapist-priest, and trust his verdict on our condition.

Freud himself did not seem to perceive the implications of his doctrine. For, if valid, these insights undermine our com-

mitment to reason. He blithely continued to uphold rational-
istic values, and even to practise them. As the social philosopher Ernest Gellner shrewdly observes, Freud 'understood and
underscored the heavy psychic price which had to be paid for
the attempt to restrain the dark forces within us, but, being
willing to pay that price, failed to appreciate that he had
destroyed the logical necessity of doing so.'[19] Gellner continues: 'We believe what our Unconscious instructs us to believe,
and we are not privy to its motives or reasons. This doctrine
is applied primarily to beliefs about our own states of mind,
but strictly speaking it should apply equally to all our beliefs
without distinction.'[20]

Thus the authority of the professional Guild of interpreters
takes over from the authority of both reason and traditional
religion. In the Freudian world, as in the Marxist, humankind
is divided into the professional elite who 'know' (and therefore
can save), and the rest who can be saved if they show proper
deference to the interpretations of the elite. 'The notion of the
Unconscious is the equivalent of a doctrine of a kind of
universal cogntive Original Sin. Those in deep sin are not fit
to sit in judgement on their saviour.'[21] We have here the
emergence of a new atheistic religious orthodoxy, more totalitarian (because more covert) than its predecessors.

Quite apart from Freud and Freudianism, the general psychological orientation to life which has become very popular
in modern secular culture tends towards an idolization of itself.
Whenever someone counters another's truth-claim with a
comment such as, 'You believe that because it does so-and-so
for you', he/she is committing a logical blunder. Understanding a person's motives for believing statement A, or not
believing statement B, does not tell us whether either statement is true or false. That would take us beyond psychology.
For example, we may discover that a person has joined a
Marxist revolutionary group because he has been emotionally
deprived as a child and wants to identify with a cause that gives
him some self-importance. But that discovery still leaves us
with the question: is Marxism true in what it claims about
social reality? To use psychology in this way to avoid facing
up to the deeper questions of truth is to hide behind an idol
that sometimes goes by the ugly label *psychologism*. But to
demonstrate its futility, all we have to do is simply turn the
tables on those who hallow it: that is, as in the case of Freud

above, see if they would be satisfied with psychological explanations of their own psychological explanations!

Psychologism is rooted in the growing 'therapeutic culture'
which treats all social evils as if they were simply problems in
the individual psyche. It thus reinforces the privatization of
life, supports the valuations society places on men and women,
and plays straight into the hands of those at the top of the social
pyramid in whose interest it is to maintain the present social
order. The therapeutic culture is the flip side of the abdication
of political responsibility- the surrender of the public domain
to the rule of impersonal 'market forces' and 'technological
progress', to which we shall return in later chapters.

When we turn to truth-claims, both Freud's theory of
repression and the Marxist theory of false consciousness seem
designed to turn any contrary evidence around in their favour!
This is a feature of all therapeutic and political models of
human liberation which function as all-embracing systems of
thought. If people object that they feel neither psychologically
crippled nor politically oppressed, this awkward fact is used to
show just how bad things really are: things are so bad that
people don't know that they are repressed, exploited, oppressed etc! Now this may well be true, but by foreclosing all
avenues of possible criticism these theories become immune
to self-correction. They too become oppressive instruments
in the hands of fanatics.

2.6   Beyond Experience

We have observed that both Marx and Freud were greatly
impressed by Feuerbach's projection theory of religion. It is
significant that none of these three thinkers undertook any
serious investigation into any of the historical religions they
denounced so freely. Indeed Marx and Feuerbach generalized
about 'religion' with little more than Hegel's religious philosophy in mind. Marx, for all his emphasis on historical context,
was a very poor historian. Not surprisingly, he—and other social
scientists who followed in his tradition- were unaware of their
own captivity to the mentality which accompanies the modernizing process. We need to remember that so-called Modern
Secular Consciousness has no privileged access to reality. It is
itself a product of social and technological changes over the last
three hundred years, beginning in Europe and spreading across

the globe. If human beings project their own meanings onto the cosmos, then this human tendency is also a fact—and a fact that cuts across all human cultures and historical epochs. It may be the only universal aspect of all human existence. *This is a fact that itself cries out for meaning!* The human world, including all its symbol-systems (whether religious or secular, modern or traditional), may well be a signal, a 'clue', an intimation of another and more final reality. . . . [22]

That our deepest human emotions point us to a dimension of existence beyond space and time is a theme that recurs in the writings of the famous English literary critic C.S. Lewis (1898–1963). We all experience, at some time or other in our lives, intense feelings of 'inconsolable longing', which no earthly object or experience can satisfy. In one of his best-known sermons, preached before the University of Oxford on 8 June 1941, Lewis spoke of a 'desire which no natural happiness will satisfy', 'a desire, still wandering and uncertain of its object and still largely unable to see that object in the direction where it really lies'. When this human desire focuses itself on an object in the world, whether it be a work of art, a pleasurable experience or even a relationship with another person, the satisfaction of the desire leads, paradoxically, only to a deepening of desire. Lewis illustrates this from the experience of beauty:

> The books or the music in which we thought the beauty was located will betray us if we trust to them; it was not *in* them, it only came *through* them, and what came through them was longing. These things— the beauty, the memory of our own past— are good images of what we really desire; but if they are mistaken for the thing itself they turn into dumb idols, breaking the hearts of their worshippers. For they are not the thing itself; they are only the scent of a flower we have not found, the echo of a tune which we have not heard, news from a country we have not visited. [23]

Lewis called this yearning, unfocused on any finite object, joy, and he argued that it points to its origin and destination in God (hence the title of his famous autobiography *Surprised by Joy*). Joy, according to Lewis, is 'an unsatisfied desire which is itself more desirable than any other satisfaction . . . anyone who has experienced it will want it again.' [24] This bitter-sweet longing for something that will satisfy us in the deepest depths of our human being, points through those objects and persons which we think will satisfy it towards their real goal and fulfilment in God himself. There is a 'divine dissatisfaction' within human experience, which prompts us to ask if there is anything—or anyone—that can truly meet this need of the human heart. Similarly, that deeply sensitive French thinker, Simone Weil (1909–1942), reflecting on our human feeling for beauty and the longing that such beauty evokes, writes: 'The longing to love the beauty of the world in a human being is essentially the longing for the Incarnation. It is mistaken if it thinks it is anything else. The Incarnation alone can satisfy it . . . Beauty is eternity here below.'[25]

Couldn't all this be illusory? It could. But consider, for the moment, all our other human urges. The promptings of hunger and thirst correspond to the existence of real food and drink 'out there' in the world which can meet that need. Likewise, sexual desire exists because sex is real; the longing for love exists because love is real (and, as child psychologists have discovered, necessary for healthy human development). Lewis expresses the point with his customary clarity:

> A man's physical hunger does not prove that man will get any bread; he may die of starvation in a raft in the Atlantic. But surely a man's hunger does prove that he comes of a race which repairs its body by eating and inhabits a world where eatable substances exist. In the same way, though I do not believe (I wish I did) that my desire for Paradise proves that I shall enjoy it, I think it a pretty good indication that such a thing exists and that some men will. A man may love a woman and not win her; but it would be very odd if the phenomenon called 'falling in love' occurred in a sexless world.[26]

In all this Lewis echoes a traditional Christian theme about the origin and goal of life. Since we are created by God and for God, we naturally experience a deep sense of longing for him, which he alone can satisfy. In Augustine's famous words from his *Confessions*, 'Thou hast made us for Thyself, and our hearts are always restless until they find their rest in Thee.' In our alienated state of existence, we misinterpret our experience of longing— either by denying that it has any objective fulfilment or by redirecting it (usually subconsciously) on to some other object within experience. But, in any case, the Christian faith does not ultimately spring from reflection on subjective experience, least of all on some special domain labelled 'religious experience', however important personal experience is in the Christian life. It has always claimed to be anchored in events which occurred in the public arena of human history, accessible to the secular historian. It is this emphasis on historicity and concrete particularity that has always constituted the 'scandal' of Christianity in a world of religion.

2.7 Back to the Future

Thus, Christian faith is ultimately faith in a God who *speaks*. A God whose Word, historically disclosed, brings forgiveness for the past and hope for the future. A God whose Word detaches us from the status quo and empowers us to live in the light of what is to come; so that what men and women call 'reality' is not accepted as given and final but is brought into ever-growing alignment with that transforming Word. It is this God which distinguished Christian preaching and practice from all the monotheisms, atheisms, polytheisms and pantheisms of the Roman world. It grew out of the challenge to reflect on recent historical events which forced those who experienced them to think in new ways about their world and to work out a new kind of life in that world. This is a theme for exploration in subsequent chapters.

Atheism and philosophical theism are simply mirror images of each other. Often the protest of atheism in the modern world is directed against a god whom Christians should have no business defending, namely a god conceived in abstract categories of Being, Idea, Infinity, Goodness, Omnipotence and so on. This kind of god is easily hijacked to serve the interests of some special class, nation or institution. Biblical faith brings together what both philosophical theism and atheism force apart: God and the human, the transcendent and the immanent, unity and plurality, freedom and authority, history and eternity. It does this without lapsing into pantheism ('God is no more than the sum of all that exists') and monism ('all distinctions are but temporary manifestations of a single, undifferentiated, impersonal reality'). It also reminds the contemporary church that the demands of social justice are intrinsic to true worship, and shows us how idolatrous much of our theology can be. That the abandonment of a full-blooded trinitarian theology has been responsible for the church's vulnerability to the moral protests of modern atheism has been the burden of many distinguished theologians in recent years.[27] But enough has been said in the present chapter to suggest that failure to heed the much-maligned God of the Hebrew scriptures may well be the fundamental clue to the loss of spiritual authority in Christian public witness today.

Notes

[1] K. Marx, 'The Union of Believers with Christ According to John 15:1–14, Showing its Basis and Essence, its Absolute Necessity, and its Effects', in Karl Marx & Friedrich Engels, *Collected Works* (London: Lawrence & Wishart, 1975) vol 1:636–9

[2] J.N. Findlay, *Hegel: A Re-Examination* (London: Allen & Unwin, 1958) p. 139

[3] G.W.F. Hegel, *Lectures on the Philosophy of World History* (1837) (Cambridge University Press, 1975)

[4] Quoted in R.S. Peters, 'Hegel and the Nation-State', in David Thomson (ed), *Political Ideas* (London: Penguin, 1966) p. 139

[5] K. Marx & F. Engels, *The German Ideology* (1845) (London: Lawrence and Wishart, 1965)

[6] K. Marx, 'Contribution to the Critique of Hegel's Philosophy of Right: Introduction' (1844), in *Karl Marx: Early Writings* (tr. and ed. T. Bottomore, London, 1963) p. 44

[7] L. Feuerbach, *The Essence of Christianity* (1841) Ch. 1, reprinted in *Philosophers on Religion: a Historical Reader*, ed. P. Sherry (London: Geoffrey Chapman, 1987)

[8] Ibid.

[9] E. Fromm, *Sigmund Freud's Mission: An Analysis of His Personality and Influence* (New York: Harper & Bros.,1959) p. 94

[10] D. Bonhoeffer, *Letters and Papers from Prison* (London: Fontana, 1959) pp. 112–3

[11] J.K. Galbraith, *The Age of Uncertainty* (London: BBC, 1977) p. 22

[12] Quoted in C. Avila, *Ownership: Early Christian Teaching* (Maryknoll, NY: Orbis, 1983) p. 50

[13] John Chrysostom, *On Wealth and Poverty*, tr. Catherine Roth (New York: St Vladimir's Seminary Press, 1984) pp. 49–55

[14] Quoted in Avila, op. cit, p. 66

[15] Thomas Aquinas, *Summa Theologica*, Pt II-II, Q66, Art 7, tr. by Fathers of the English Dominican Province (New York: Benziger Bros, 1948)

[16] Charles Villa-Vicencio, *A Theology of Reconstruction: Nation-building and Human Rights* (Cambridge: Cambridge University Press, 1992) p. 265

[17] See J.N. Isbister, *Freud: An Introduction to His Life and Work* (Cambridge: Polity Press, 1985) p. 255

[18] Quoted in Ibid. p. 69

[19] E. Gellner, *Reason and Culture* (Oxford: Blackwell, 1992) p. 89

[20] Ibid. p. 95

21 Ibid.
22 See, e.g., P.L. Berger, *A Rumor of Angels: Modern Society and the Rediscovery of the Supernatural* (New York: Anchor Books, 1970)
23 C.S. Lewis, 'The Weight of Glory' in *Screwtape Proposes a Toast* (London: Collins, 1965) pp. 97–8
24 C.S. Lewis, *Surprised By Joy* (London: Collins, 1959) p. 20
25 S. Weil, *Waiting on God* (London: Fontana, 1959) p. 127
26 Lewis, 'The Weight of Glory', op. cit. p. 99
27 See, e.g., J. Moltmann, *The Trinity and the Kingdom of God* (Eng. trans. London: SCM, 1981); C. Gunton, *The One, the Three and the Many* (Cambridge: Cambridge University Press, 1993)

3

The World As Creation

'What is it that breathes fire into the equations and makes a universe for them to describe? The usual approach of science of constructing a mathematical model cannot answer the questions of why there should be a universe for the model to describe. Why does the universe go to all the bother of existing?'
— *Stephen Hawking, A Brief History of Time*[1]

The language of creation has made an amazing come-back in recent years, and in the unlikeliest of intellectual circles: that of physicists and astronomers rather than theologians and evangelists! It is curious that while an earlier generation of theologians abandoned biblical language for being supposedly incompatible with modern science, many of today's more famous scientists use biblical language freely in speculating on the implications of their work. But much caution is required. The concept of *creation* has come to mean different things to different people, both within and outside the Christian community. In order to sort out this semantic confusion, we need to pay attention first of all to the language of the Bible.

3.1 The Genesis Story

'In the beginning, God created the universe . . .' (Gen. 1:1). So begins the Hebrew Bible. It may be taken as referring to the beginning of God's creative activity or as a title summarizing the entire account of creation that follows. Either way, the 'beginning' is the absolute beginning of all events and of time itself. God is both the subject and the focus of the whole narrative. He is mentioned 34 times in 36 verses. The primary truth which it proclaims is theological: that the God who has acted in the recent history of the Hebrew people and entered into a liberating covenant-relationship with them is no less than the Creator and ruler of the whole universe.

In language of majestic simplicity, the writer portrays God's creative work in a series of pictures. The Spirit of God hovers over the world like a mother bird over its young, pointing to both the transcendence of God over his creation and also his intimate, caring involvement within it. Like any human craftsman, God 'speaks' and 'sees', 'works' and 'rests'. The Word of God, which is his self-communication, is uttered into the void— and events spring into being. The universe God creates is ordered and intelligible, because it has its origin in this rational Word. To use later Christian language, the activity of creation depicted here is a Trinitarian activity: God creates through the agency of Word and Spirit. In saying that the universe is created by God, the writer also indicates that the universe is open to God, not a closed system; it is open to new possibilities of transformation. God's relationship with his world is one of both loving intimacy and creative, commanding power.

The verb translated 'create' (*bara*) carries considerable force in Hebrew. In the Old Testament it is used sparingly and only of God, not of humans or pagan deities. It testifies to the freedom and power of God: he is not bound by necessity to create what he creates. It is this idea that gave rise to the classic Jewish and Christian emphasis on 'creation *ex nihilo*', bringing being out of non-being, clearly taught in such passages as Ps. 148:5; Prov. 8:22–27; Rom. 4:17; Heb. 11:3. He is not constrained (as in early Greek philosophy) by the rational and eternal forms of pre-existent matter.

It means that what the Creator brings forth—a *creation*—has to be understood on its own terms. Its patterns wait to be discovered, not deduced by rational speculation. But the freedom of God must not be interpreted as the expression of an abstract and arbitrary will. He creates because self-giving is his being; his love 'overflows' in bringing about a world that can share in the fulness of the divine communion. We shall explore in a later chapter the implications of this world-view for the development of science.

The literary structure of the narrative is a clue to its interpretation. We must not assume, in our modern arrogance, that the writer must answer the questions that we may ask out of our scientific interests: questions of when and how concerning the universe and the emergence of life. The purpose of the writer must be our guide in understanding the meaning of the text. The way the writer uses language tells us that his intentions are different. He makes use of symbolic numbers (e.g. 3,7,10,40) extensively: for example, 10 times 'God said' (3 concerning mankind, 7 the rest of creation); the verb 'to make' occurs 10 times; so does the phrase 'according to its kind'; the verb 'to create' is used at 3 places in the narrative and 3 times on the third occasion; we read 7 times the completion formula 'and it was so', 7 times the approval 'and God saw that it was good'. The names of God appear 70 times in chapters 1–4 of Genesis, 40 times Elohim, 10 times as Yahweh (the name of the covenant) and 20 times Yahweh Elohim. This is evidently a highly stylized, carefully constructed narrative.

The 'week' of creation is also built around a symmetrical structure. The following chart shows how the second half of the week parallels the first half— a familiar arrangement in Hebrew literature. So day 4 corresponds to day 1, day 5 to day 2, and day 6 to day 3. The first triad points to acts of separation or forming, the second to acts of filling. Or one can view them, from an earth-centred perspective, as the whole world arranged into 'spaces' (the first triad) and their respective 'inhabitants' (the second triad).

Acts of Forming	Acts of Filling
Day 1: Light/Darkness	Day 4: Lights of Day & Night
Day 2: Sea/Sky	Day 5: Creatures of Sea & Sky
Day 3: Fertile Earth	Day 6: Creatures of the Earth

This literary arrangement brings out the fact that God's world is an ordered structure (a cosmos), not a meaningless chaos. Also, the six-fold framework to describe epic events (written on six clay tablets, the commonest writing material of the period) was also a conventional literary style in the Sumero-Babylonian civilization of ancient West Asia. We also know that it was common practice to inscribe a 'colophon', the ancient equivalent of a title page of a modern book, on the last column of each tablet. The refrain 'there was evening and there was morning . . .' after each act of creation is an example of such a colophon. The study of ancient literary conventions has shed light on the way the text is to be appreciated. The value of Genesis as history has been amply confirmed by the accumulation of evidence from over 20,000 written texts that have survived from Babylonia since the time of Abraham.[2]

The 'days' then, are normal twenty-four hour periods but which the writer uses as a literary arrangement to serve a logical, rather than a chronological, purpose. Also, the expression 'there was evening and there was morning', though an unusual way in Hebrew to express a twenty-four period or day, is the normal idiom for describing human labour: a day's work ends at early eventide and is resumed at the first light of dawn (cf. Ps. 104: 23). By choosing to depict God's creative activity in the form of a working man's week, the writer is also able to affirm particular truths about the mutual relationships of God, the world and humanity—to which we shall return shortly.

Although most scholars endorse this literary interpretation of the week of creation (a variation of this view is to follow a Jewish tradition that the early creation account was revealed over seven days to Enoch, so that these signify days of divine revelation, each revelation written down on a tablet[3]), there are some who understand it differently. According to what is known as the 'concordist' interpretation, the creation 'days' represent vast epochs of time. The metaphorical use of day (as in Gen. 2:4) or the timelessness of God's perspective (e.g. 2 Peter 3:8) are often quoted in its favour. Its supporters argue that this brings it into concord with modern scientific accounts of origins. However, it ignores the phrase 'evening and morning' which occurs with the word 'day'; and its harmonization with geology or astronomy is only superficial. For, if we were to take it chronologically, however long the time periods involved, then the order of creation is flatly contradicted by modern scientific theories (for example, the sun being formed after the earth and its vegetation).

Any literal (as opposed to literary) reading of Genesis One, which argues that the events described are to be taken as literally occurring in that order within a seven twenty-four hour week, runs into all sorts of problems within the text itself, let alone with geology and astronomy! The sun and the moon are created three days after the light, though the Hebrews knew as well as we do that light comes from these heavenly bodies (cf. Ps. 104:19–22). And what are we to make of the lack of the 'evening and morning' refrain on the seventh day? Our reason for rejecting this literal approach is not due to any modern scientific considerations. Without bringing science in at all, we have simply paid attention to literary 'clues' within the text which help us identify the author's intentions and interests. This is a carefully constructed narrative, full of intricate artistry. A literal approach flattens the text and obscures its message. It is not the mechanisms and processes of creation that interest the author, but what creation tells us about the nature of God and his dealings with humankind.

This view is reinforced when we consider, as we must, the place of 1:1–2:3 (which is the real unit in the Hebrew text) in Genesis as a whole. The book falls into ten major sections. Each section has a title announcing what is to follow (usually in the form 'this is the family history of X'). Gen. 1:1–2:3 stands outside this organization. It is a grand 'overture' to the whole book of Genesis which traces the tragic spiral of human sin and God's plan of deliverance and restoration through Abraham and the patriarchal line. Although of little importance in the world of their day, the latter were incorporated into the redemptive purposes of Yahweh who was not a mere tribal deity but the God of the whole universe. Thus, the literary approach to the 'week' of creation does most justice to the integrity of the text and its background.

Returning to the unfolding creation narrative, observe that the world is created rich in diversity. The Creator blesses living beings with semi-autonomy, the capacity to 'pro-create' (v.22). Creatureliness, individuality, diversity and change are all pronounced 'good' by the Creator. He takes delight in what he brings into being. The sovereign Lord of creation speaks, and the creation responds (e.g. v.24). The earth must produce cattle, creeping things and wild animals. The waters must give rise to the swarming activity of sea creatures. In other words, the creation is equipped by the Creator to bring forth novelty in obedience to the Creator's call. Other biblical passages such as Psalm 104 and Job 38–41 expand the thought of Genesis 1, showing in delightful picture-language God frolicking with his creatures and calling forth their awesome powers.

The whole universe, then, is distinct from God yet dependent on God for its existence and sustenance. All its wonderful capacities for renewal, adaptation and development are built into it by the Creator, but all these complex systems and patterns work in response to the divine Word. Moreover, the fact that God not only creates time, but creates *with* time and *in* time would have had profound implications for ancient Israel, as indeed it does for modern society. Israel would learn to value time as the fabric of history in which God is involved. Redemption, unlike in other religious world-views (including Hindu and Buddhist thought), will function *within* time and not as a deliverance *from* time. The Creator personally engages with his creatures in their striving towards the goal of a perfected creation.

That an evangelistic/polemical intention lies behind the Genesis creation narrative becomes clear when it is read against the backdrop of the popular beliefs and practices of Israel's neighbours. While employing literary forms found in the creation myths of other cultures, the content of the narrative is deeply anti-mythical in its thrust, as we shall see. It repudiates many popular religious ideas of the first and second millenium BC. A seventh century Babylonian or a Canaanite in fourteenth century Ugarit (both centres of great civilizations) would have been shocked by the teaching of Genesis. It is a powerful witness to the uniqueness of Yahweh, the Lord of creation.

For instance, we note the following striking contrasts:-

(a) *Theism vs polytheism.* There are no rival gods nor helpers in the work of creation, as there are in every other religious epic about origins. The latter narrate the birth of the gods, their loves and their battles. No one is ultimately in control of the world. Its fortunes depend on which deity is currently in the ascendent. The gods (as in Hindu mythology) are personifications of various aspects of nature, and nature itself is deified as a living goddess who nurtures all living things and exacts a terrible vengeance on all who fail to worship appropriately.

Why does the writer put the creation of the sun and the moon on the fourth day, after the creation of light, when it would have been obvious to everyone that they were the sources of light for the earth? The reason becomes obvious when we recall that the worship of the sun and moon was very common in the writer's world (e.g. the great Chaldean city of Ur where Abraham came from was a famous centre of moon-worship). Also, then as now, many believed that human life was controlled by the motion of the moon and the planets. The sages of Babylonia kept detailed records of heavenly motions for the construction of astrological charts. Political decisions depended on the accuracy of such charts. It is not uncommon to find politicians, business leaders and even university teachers in Asia for whom horoscopes and 'auspicious days' are more real than anything in modern culture; and one suspects that this may also be true of some of their counterparts in the West. . . . The Genesis narrative 'de-bunks' this superstition. The heavenly bodies are simply creatures of God, lamps hung in the sky, with no divine power of their own. They are neither to be feared nor worshipped. Nature is but a fellow-creature with human beings: both are dependent on and nourished by the Creator alone.

(b)   *God's word vs cultic ritual.* In many societies, the powers of chaos and evil were warded off by the magical incantations of special religious 'manthras' (e.g. the popular *pirith* ceremonies in Sri Lanka and other Buddhist countries today). These human words, accompanied sometimes by appropriate actions, were believed to sustain the stability and fecundity of the world. But what does Genesis teach? It is the Word of God, not human words, which ensures the stability and continuing fruitfulness of the world. This radically 'de-mythologizes' the reigning religious world-views.

(c)   *A good creation vs a capricious, even evil world.* Once again, contemporary world-views would have understood 'salvation' as an escape from the sensory, empirical world of human existence. There was no value or purpose attached to the physical realm of space-time events. Meaning was to be sought in detachment from the external world which, in any case, was less real than the 'spiritual' realm. This view is contradicted by the doctrine of creation which sees the world as possessing an intrinsic worth and meaningfulness (though later corrupted and disfigured by evil—cf. Gen. 3) because it stems from the rational will of a good and loving Creator. Existence itself is declared blessed.

(d)   *Humans, the crown of creation, vs Humans, an 'accident'.* The teaching on humankind given in the opening chapter of Genesis is utterly unique. Unlike the common religious creation-myths which depicted man as an 'after-thought', an 'accidental' offspring of the gods, the entire narrative of Genesis 1 builds up to a climax in the account of human creation. That this is a turning point in the story is brought out by the author in three ways: (i) the language shifts from the repetitive 'Let there be . . .' to the more self-reflective 'Let us make . . .' (v.26); (ii) the self-deliberation is then followed by the act of creation (v.27), showing perhaps the deeper involvement of God in this aspect of his creative work; (iii) the fact of human creation, male and female, is repeated three times in the same sentence (v.27)—an example of poetic Hebrew parallelism.

Observe too that God commands human beings (v.28) to be fruitful. This stands in marked contrast to the fertility cults of the surrounding nations, in which the worshippers sought to persuade the gods to be fruitful. Life is a gift from God. His blessing confers both gift and task.

(e) *Humans, the Image of God.* What this chapter teaches concerning humankind is startlingly revolutionary. The stone or metal image that an ancient king set up was the physical symbol of his sovereignty over a territory. It represented him to his subject peoples. But here, it is humankind that consti-tutes the 'image of God' (vv.26,27). It is humans who represent God on the planet Earth. It follows that when human beings fashion images out of the created world and worship them, they worship something inferior to them and thus de-human-ize themselves. It also follows that the way we treat our fellow human being is a reflection of our attitude to the Creator. To despise the former is to insult the latter (cf. Prov. 14:31; James 3:9). And it is not only the kings and powerful lords of the earth who constitute the image of God, but all people every-where. Observe too that it is men and women together who are created as God's 'image', and so women are called to rule the earth alongside men. This high view of woman was unique among the cultures of the time, and has remained unique well into the modern age.

If we follow those Old Testament scholars who date Genesis during the time of the Israelite exile in Babylon, then the politically subversive (and hence liberating) character of this doctrine of humankind becomes especially apparent. For Babylonian society, like both other Mesopotamian and Egyp-tian civilizations, was hierarchically structured. At the top of the social pyramid was the king, who was believed to represent the power of the divine world. Just below him came the priests who shared his mediatorial function, but to a lesser degree. Below them were the bureaucracy, the merchants and the military, while the base of the pyramid was formed by the peasants and slaves. Thus the socio-political order was given religious legitimation by the creation mythologies of these societies. The lower classes of human beings were created as slaves for the gods, to relieve them of manual labour. And, since the king represented the gods on earth, to serve the king was to serve the gods. Consequently, the Genesis 'counter-myth' undermines this widespread royal ideology. It 'democratizes' the political order. All human beings are called to represent God's kingdom through the whole range of human life on earth. And, as we shall see later, God's rule is not the monarchical rule of a despot, but the loving nurture of a caring parent.

Thus men and women, according to the Genesis narrative, possess a dual nature. They are *creatures*, belonging to the rest of the animal kingdom: created on the sixth day, along with all the other creatures of the earth, and (in the following chapter) said to be formed 'from the dust of the earth', pointing to our human creatureliness (as if to say, 'they didn't drop from heaven like some immortal gods') and our relatedness to the earth. Modern science helps us to understand our connections with the rest of creation: our bodies are made up of chemicals that were cooked in the interior of stars a very long time ago, we share most of our DNA with other living organisms, we live on the exhalation of plants, and our well-being depends on the maintenance of sensitive balances in the biosphere.

But the other side of the truth about us is equally clear and vitally important: humans alone are stamped with the image of the Creator, called into a *personal* relationship with him which defines human life as more than merely biological. Human beings alone are addressed by God. To the Creator, we exist not only as his objects but as subjects. Human uniqueness consists not in the fact that we talk with each other, rather that God talks to us and invites us to reply. In other words, *we are invited to become part of the conversation that is the divine life*. Moreover, just as God has his being as a communion of Persons, so human being is constituted as persons (beings-in-relation). Just as God is related to us and at the same time remains other than us, so within the human community we are related in diversity. Personal freedom implies a space between each other that is to be respected, and yet we do not find our fulfilment as persons apart from God and one another.

Thus the 'other', far from being a threat to my unique identity, is the one without whom I would have no identity. It is this fact of personhood, established by creation, that confers dignity and value to every human life. We alone are treated as moral agents, commanded by the Creator and held morally responsible to him in our actions. Humankind is also called to be 'sub-creators' under the sovereign Creator in enabling the whole creation to flourish and reach its appointed fulfilment in time.

The revolutionary uniqueness of this view of human life is felt not least in our modern societies. We mentioned earlier Peter Singer and Helga Kuhse's assault on the Christian prohibition on infanticide. For them human beings are defined by what they *possess*: self-awareness, self-control, a sense of past and future, and so on. Simply being a member of the biological species *homo sapiens* is not enough to make one 'human' in the sense of a life that carries moral obligation. Thus human babies, and especially those who are mentally handicapped, do not count as human persons who have a moral claim on us. They conclude that 'to allow infanticide before the onset of self-awareness . . . cannot threaten anyone who is in a position to worry about it.'[4] Any argument that defines humanness in terms of what we *have*, rather than what we intrinsically *are*, can also be used to justify the killing of any adult suffering from the loss of the relevant function.

God is mystery, and man and woman in God's image are mystery. When we stand before another person, however destitute, disabled, diseased or degraded, we stand before something which is the vehicle of the divine, something which, in Martin Buber's classic terminology, is a 'Thou' and not an 'It'. Those whom we treat with reverence as persons become known to us eventually as persons.[5] We can acknowledge the gradualness of development into personal encounter, while affirming the reality of personhood from the moment of human conception. We can and do, of course, treat people like 'its', as simply physical objects— for instance, in pornography, in reductionist scientific theories (see, Chapter 6), through non-therapeutic experimentation, or by indiscriminate killing in warfare. We do so at loss to our own humanity. The death of God does not, as Nietzsche believed, lead to the glorification of man; but rather takes from men and women any claim they may have to be treated with reverence by their fellows. The Genesis story goes on to show how, when the man and the woman sought to become gods, rather than gratefully accept their unique dignity as the image of the only God, they perceived the other as both a threat to each one's autonomy and as an object to be manipulated in a world of manipulable objects.

Hence, Genesis presents us with an alternative vision to Singer, Kuhse and others who start with the human self and not with God. The moral implications of this vision is finely expressed in the words of the French biologist, Jean Rostan: 'For my part I believe that there is no life so degraded, debased or impoverished that it does not deserve respect and is not worth defending with zeal and conviction . . . I have the weakness to believe that it is an honour for our society to desire the expensive luxury of sustaining life for its useless, incompetent and incurably ill members. I would almost measure society's degree of civilization by the amount of effort and vigilance it imposes on itself out of pure respect for life.'[6]

(f)   *Universal vs chauvinistic nature of religious epics.* The creation epics of the surrounding civilizations were designed largely to explain why the local god of that city/civilization was currently in the ascendant (as, for example, the triumph of Marduk, the god of Babylon). But there is no mention of Israel or the Hebrew people in the creation account of Genesis. Uniquely blessed though they may be in receiving this revelation from the Creator, they are not inherently different from other peoples. All are creatures made to image God. There are no distinctions of language, race, caste or class mentioned in the text. The only distinction within humankind is that of male and female, but it is a distinction that is anchored within an equality of status.

Since the idea of humankind 'ruling over the earth' (v.28f) has been used by certain anti-Christian writers in recent years to accuse the Bible of encouraging environmental destructiveness, a few brief comments on this issue may be appropriate here. Typical of those who have made this charge is the late Arnold Toynbee who claimed that 'the recklessly extravagant consumption of nature's irreplaceable treasures, and the pollution of those of them that man has not already devoured, can be traced back to . . . the rise of monotheism . . . Monotheism, as enunciated in the book of Genesis, has removed the age-old restraint that was once placed on man's greed by his awe. The directive given in the first chapter of the book of Genesis . . . has turned out to be bad advice, and we are beginning, wisely, to recoil from it.'[7]

Such fanciful interpretations of history, especially when they come from a historian of the stature of Toynbee and are stated dogmatically with no shred of supporting evidence, can be due only to a prior antipathy to biblical Christianity on other grounds. Comments such as his may fuel the anti-Christian bias and the romantic view of non-Christian societies that have accompanied the disillusionment with science and the notion of progress in the post-Christian West. But they make strange reading for those of us living in non-Christian cultures which have not been tainted by the monotheism of Genesis and yet suffer the crippling effects of environmental damage—the pollution of air and water supplies, the disappearance of rain forests, desertification and soil erosion—whether due to poverty, neglect, civil war, political corruption or blatant commercial greed (not all of which can be laid at the feet of Western corporations and governments). The pollution and pillage of nature, whether as a result of ignorance, greed or selfishness has been characteristic of human cultures all over the globe and at all times in the past.

Joseph Needham's monumental studies on Chinese scientific and technological development[8] reveal how Chinese technology wreaked ecological destruction on a massive scale. Even Buddhists contributed to soil erosion and deforestation in the building of their temples all over Asia, and the eminent microbiologist and environmental campaigner René Dubos observes how 'the classic nature poets of China write as if they had achieved identification with the cosmos, but in reality most of them were retired bureaucrats living on estates in which nature was carefully trimmed and managed by gardners'.[9] Dubos' verdict is that 'If men are more destructive now than they were in the past, it is because there are more of them and because they have at their command more powerful means of destruction, not because they have been influenced by the Bible. In fact, the Judaeo-Christian peoples were probably the first to develop on a large scale a pervasive concern for land management and an ethic of nature'.[10]

Is it conceivable that the Creator, having repeatedly in the text declared his pleasure and delight over his creation, should

now turn to the crown of his work and command them to
destroy that same creation? The fallacy in the reasoning of
those who blame the environmental crisis on Genesis is simply
that they do not listen to the context in which the command
is embedded. We read into words like 'ruling' and 'dominion'
our fallen, self-centred experience of human rule: namely, one
of tyranny and exploitation. But humankind created as God's
image is to rule as God rules; and we have seen how God's
rule over the cosmos is depicted in this same chapter as one of
ordering, life-generating, life-preserving, servanthood and
personal enjoyment. In the following chapter, man is put in a
garden (representing the whole earth) and called 'to work it
and to care for it' (Gen. 2:15). He also names the animals, the
name in ancient thought capturing a creature's essential nature
or character and so implying intimate knowledge. So, the earth
and its creatures are entrusted to human care, and we have a
mandate from God for study, work and the enrichment of life
on the planet. We are neither its owners (to do with it what
we please) nor mere guests (to passively enjoy but not to
intervene in natural processes). The nature of our rule is
defined for us: it is one of enabling the earth to bloom.
Developing the earth's potential and conserving its fruitfulness
are twin aspects of responsible planetary stewardship.

I am tempted here to quote the great Swiss reformer John
Calvin (1509–1564), for it is often the Protestantism of Calvin
that is the villain of the piece in the writings of those critics
who blame the environmental crisis and the evils of capitalism
on the 'Protestant work ethic'. Whatever some of his followers
may have said and done, let us listen to Calvin's own comments on Gen. 2:15: 'The earth was given to man, with this
condition, that he should occupy himself in its cultivation . . .
The custody of the garden was given in charge to Adam, to
show that we possess the things which God has committed to
our hands, on the condition that, being content with the frugal
and moderate use of them, we should take care of what shall
remain. Let him who possesses a field, so partake of its yearly
fruits, that he may not suffer the ground to be injured by his
negligence, but let him endeavour to hand it down to posterity
as he received it, or even better cultivated. Let him so feed on
its fruits, that he neither dissipates it by luxury, not permits it
to be marred or ruined by neglect. Moreover, that this economy, and this diligence, with respect to those good things

which God has given us to enjoy, may flourish among us: let everyone regard himself as the steward of God in all things which he possesses. Then he will neither conduct himself dissolutely, nor corrupt by abuse those things which God requires to be preserved.'[11]

The evangelist Mark's image of Jesus 'with the wild animals' (Mk. 1:13) provides, as Richard Bauckham notes in a recent essay,[12] a particularly apt symbol for our ecologically sensitive age. It comes on the heels of Jesus' identification as the messianic Son of God (1:11, cf. Ps. 2:7) and his victory over Satan; and it needs to be read against the background of Old Testament eschatalogical hopes, as expressed in Is. 11:6–9 (following the description of the coming Davidic Messiah in v.1–5), Job 5:22–23 and Hos. 2:18. In Jesus the messianic reign has dawned, and this reign includes the healing of enmity between humankind and the wild animals. Human dominion, which was perverted into domination and mutual alienation by human sin, will be restored; and in Jesus' peaceful companionship with the wild animals we are given a foretaste of that eschatological restoration. Bauckham observes that Jesus neither terrorizes nor domesticates the wild animals. He is simply with them. And in that pregnant phrase 'with the wild animals' Mark gives us a powerful reminder of the value of the non-human creation in the eyes of God. Human dominion, restored in Jesus (the new Adam), enables the wild animals to find their place in the wilderness as creatures who share God's world with us.

Returning to the Genesis story, the 'week' of creation finds its ultimate goal, not in the creation of mankind, but in the 'rest' of God (v.31). Obviously this cannot be taken literally as God's non-action, for if God were to be inactive for even a moment the entire universe would cease to exist!

When asked why he healed on the day of sabbath rest, Jesus answered the Jewish leaders, 'My Father is always at his work to this very day and I, too, am working' (John 5:16ff). What then is the theological intention behind this language? Bearing in mind the focus of the writer on the inter-relationships between God, humankind and the world, we can suggest the following:-

(i) God's relationship with the world is not one of total *absorption*. Though involved in his creation and deeply entering into his work, nevertheless he is not defined by his creation (as in the philosophy of *pantheism* which speaks of God and the world as co-equal aspects of a single reality). God's being is not exhausted in his work. He can step back, so to speak, and behold his handiwork with the joy of the seventh day. It is the joy that all human sub-creators (to employ a term popularized by C.S. Lewis and J.R. Tolkien) share when we bring something of beauty and value into the world (whether another human life, a painting, a musical lyric, a mathematical theorem, a scientific theory, a book, and so on). Thus, the creation enjoys a certain measure of autonomy while remaining dependent on the Word of God. The basic processes and structures of the world have been so patterned that, in due time, they will perform the functions for which they were called into being. History, natural and human, has now begun.

(ii)   Human work too is *relativized*. We find our true identity not in our work of ruling the earth, but in God. We are created for relationships, primarily with our Creator. Work is an aspect of our worship of God, but it is not the whole of it. Pausing to enjoy the fruits of our labour with our fellow human beings and to give thanks to God for the gifts of life— this is what restores the true perspective on our work. So leisure is built into the created order. It is as much God's calling as is work. This was the basis of the sabbath law in ancient Israel. Its primary intent was to set human labour within the only perspective which gives it meaning: namely, the worship of God. It is still a revolutionary concept to follow in an age devoted to the frenetic, soul-destroying idolatry of work.

There are many more theological and ethical treasures one could quarry out of the opening chapter of Genesis. It is one of the world's most remarkable pieces of literature. It affirmed a radical theistic outlook in the face of empty religious systems, whether of polytheism, astrology and occult practices, pantheism, dualism and animism. Even today, its teaching stands as a bulwark against all those modern world-views which enslave human life: e.g. *naturalism* (that the universe is a closed system of causes and effects, with matter/energy defining all that is real), and its daughters *relativism* (there is no truth that is true for all, no moral values that are binding on all, because universal values derive from a universal purpose and there is no purpose to human life or the universe) and *subjectivism* (there is no truth outside one's own experience). There are rich implications for the modern world, whether in the areas of human rights, the basis for science and technology, the dignity of work, the care of the environment or the steward-ship of the earth's resources. Some of these will be explored in subsequent sections.

The main point I wish to make at this stage is simply that by asking the wrong kind of questions about the opening chapters of Genesis, namely questions to satisfy our scientific curiosity, we actually blind ourselves to the real questions the text puts to us: questions that challenge our world-views and our ultimate commitments in life.

3.2 Creation Language, Science & the World

The biblical doctrine of Creation asserts that every event in our space-time world owes its being (or, in philosophical language, its ontological origin) to the activity of a transcendent, wise and sovereign Creator who is also at work within that space-time world which he sustains. Creation language does not refer merely to an event in the distant past, whether of the universe or of human life, but rather to the ultimate origin of all events, past, present and future. The source and goal of all existence is in God. But this God is not a being in the ordinary sense of the word. He does not exist as a tree or a galaxy or even a human being exists. When we normally assert that something exists, we mean that it can be found within the space-time world. But clearly God does not exist in that sense. He is not found as an item within the mysterious and wonderful contents of the universe (likewise, even the universe as a whole, in this sense of 'exist', must be said not to exist!). He precedes all 'existents' by being the condition for their existence, so that his mode of being transcends the being that is exemplified by the objects we encounter in space and time. It is surely significant that the Bible does not begin with the claim that God exists, but rather that he brings beings into existence: 'Let there be . . .'

It follows that the world itself is not eternal; nor is it a self-existent, self-sufficient system. It is unceasingly dependent on the creative will of its Creator. 'In his hand is the life of every creature, the breath of all mankind' (Job 12:10). This sums up what the language of Creation seeks to convey. If God were to withdraw his presence from us for an instant, we would simply collapse into nothingness. We would cease to be. And what is true of us is true of every event and entity that we may encounter in the universe. God does not simply trigger off the initial impulse and then leave the universe to unfold according to some impersonal blueprint. That notion of a First Cause or Prime Mover is not a biblical one. It first came from the ancient Greek philosopher Aristotle and was popular in eighteenth-century Europe in the form of *Deism*, a 'natural religion' that often envisaged a Divine Architect or Mechanic, launching the whole process we call the universe, but active nowhere else. Unfortunately, many Christians as well as most non-Christians today think of creation in these terms, and it is this that leads to so much confusion.

We should also never think of God's activity as some kind of intrusion, an 'interference' in this world of space-time. Though we saw that the world is endowed with procreating powers and real capacities to bring forth change and novelty without some direct, 'special' act of God, both its being and its capacities so to act are gracious gifts from the Creator, and they are continuously sustained by his will and enabling. His activity undergirds all activity. Every event in the space-time fabric that we call the universe is linked 'horizontally' to other events within space-time and 'vertically' to the sustaining activity in eternity of the Creator. Every event—whether the birth of a flower, the death of a star, the flight of a bird or the firing of neurons in my brain . . .—owes its existence to the Creator's power. The world exists in God; he does not 'exist' as an object in the world. This is where all our thinking must begin. We have seen how the picture-language of Genesis 1 introduces us to a God who brings order out of chaos, so that the world emerges as a cosmos and not as a meaningless jumble of events.

God commands ('Let there be' . . .) and events leap into being. His word stamps the universe with order, it pronounces as 'good' the emergence of change and diversity, living and non-living matter. It expresses the Creator's joy over all that he chooses to bring into being.

So it is with all acts of creation. Think of a human novelist or poet. He begins with an idea, conceived in his mind, which he then embodies in written or spoken words. As he proceeds to speak ('Let there be such-and-such . . .'etc), events and characters spring into existence. As the story unfolds, its intelligibility is grounded in the intelligence of its creator. A great novel even assumes a life of its own. All creative writers testify to the way in which new (unplanned) situations arise from the work itself as they labour over it, and to which they respond. Similarly the Bible invites us to view the world in a sense as God's epic novel, involving human characters whose stories are still in the process of being written. It is an unfolding cosmic drama in which the Creator is intimately involved with his creatures.

This analogy of artistic creation serves to illustrate the biblical dynamic of *transcendence* and *immanence* in God's in-dwelling of his world. The artist puts something of himself into his work, so that although he transcends it in giving it a measure of independence, it can also be regarded (in a certain sense) as an extension of his personal being. Like all analogies, however, it does not do justice to the manner in which the divine author *humbly stoops to let himself be affected by the actions of his creatures and to invite them to share with him in the construction of their life-narratives*. From our perspective, as creatures within this cosmic drama, the story is open-ended: we are free agents whose thoughts and actions within this space-time world shape the future of that world. Made in the image of God, our freedom has not been taken away by the Creator despite the fact that it has been abused. The Creator still takes up our voluntary actions, whether good or evil, into his purposes for the world. We do not need to go beyond the book of Genesis itself to see examples of this mysterious interweaving of human responsibility with divine sovereignty.

For example, consider the Joseph stories which take up the last quarter of the book. The narrator traces Joseph's adversity to various complex sources: his own childish arrogance, his father's favouritism, his brothers' jealousy which prompted them to sell him as a slave to Pharaoh's court, Joseph's loyalty to Yahweh and to his employer Potiphar, the latter's poor judgement in choosing to believe his wife rather than Joseph, the thoughtlessness of the chief butler, etc. In Joseph's impris-onment and later exaltation, Yahweh is acting for the preser-vation of his people in accordance with his promises to Abraham, Isaac and Jacob (Gen. 45:8 & 50:19,20). It is only when we come to the end of the story that we can see how Yahweh achieves his sovereign purposes *through* the complex, inextricable causalities of human existence. The brothers of Joseph are not conscious of having been coerced or manipulated to act the way they did; indeed they recognize their culpability (50:15ff). But Joseph not only forgives them, but is himself humbled by the realization that, 'you intended to harm me, but God intended it for good to accomplish what is now being done . . .' (50:20). It is *not* that good is inherent in evil or emerges automatically from evil (for that belief would cut the throat of all human morality), but rather that the sovereign Creator, who is the Lord of history, can overrule the evil actions of his creatures to bring forth good.

God works simultaneously through, beyond, and in spite of his creatures' actions. So we need neither be idealistic about human history (as if all human actions were manifestations of the divine will) or cynical about human history (as if all human actions were insurmountable obstacles to the divine will). This confusion between the levels at which divine and human action operate, as well as a failure to grasp the ambivalent nature of all human achievements—for every human being is *both* created in the image of God *and* a fallen sinner—has led to meaningless conflicts between Christians and to tragic misunderstandings of the Christian message (as, for instance, among Marxists and Buddhists).

Evil itself is left unexplained in the Bible, for perhaps the very good reason that it *is* inexplicable. The moment we 'explain' it we have related it to a meaningful framework within which it now 'makes sense'. But the whole point of evil is that it does *not* make sense. It is insane, an absurd intrusion into God's good creation. To explain it is to explain it away. That is why every attempt to explain evil, as in Hindu and Buddhist doctrines of *dukka*, *karma* and rebirth, only ends up trivializing evil. When the category of *dukka* is employed to embrace everything from the sense of human finiteness to sorrow felt in the loss of a loved one to the brutalities of Auchwitz or Pol Pot's Kampuchea, the latter are robbed of their horror. In fact the feelings of shame, shock and revulsion that we experience when we see or hear of such atrocities (and which, in a biblical perspective, indicate a normal and very healthy response) are themselves part of the *dukka* from which we are told we need to be liberated.

While on the subject of Buddhist explanations of evil, I cannot help thinking that at the heart of Buddhism there lies a major confusion over the concept of creation. It seems that the Buddha understood creation as implying a fatalistic attitude to life. We read, for example, in the *Anguttara Nikaya* (III:61): 'So, then, owing to the creation of a supreme deity men will become murderers, thieves, unchaste, liars, slanderers, abusive babblers, covetous, malicious, and perverse in view. Thus for those who fall back on the creation of god as the essential reason, there is neither desire, nor effort nor necessity to do this deed or abstain from that deed.' It is against the doctrine of creation as taught by some Hindu schools of philosophy that the Buddha appears to be reacting. So, in order to safeguard human responsibility it was thought necessary to dispense with God altogether or, at least, to keep 'God-talk' to a minimum. Moreover, if 'God' is conceived simply as a First Cause, then, since Buddhist thought posits endless cycles of formation and dissolution with no beginning, such a concept is, at best, redundant, and at worst, meaningless. This remains the biggest obstacle to a Buddhist's understanding of Christian language about the Creator—and, sadly, most Christians have not helped to bridge the communication barrier because they themselves have been imprisoned in their thinking by Greek, Hindu or naturalist notions of causality.

3.3 Questions About Origins

We need to be careful, then, not to confuse the language of Creation, which speaks of *ontological* origins, with the language of scientific theories, such as Big-Bang cosmology or neo-Darwinian evolution, which are attempts to unravel the *chronological* origins and development of the universe and of life. Creation-language addresses different, more profound, questions: e.g. why is there a universe at all—and not nothing? Is there any meaning or purpose to this whole cosmic drama? How is science possible at all? What is humanness, and what, if any, is its significance?. . .

This is not to deny that scientific theories carry philosophical implications. They may also enlarge our understanding of how the Creator interacts with his creation and sharpen the language we use in discussing that interaction. But I can see no reason, on biblical grounds, for preferring 'Hot Big Bang' or 'inflationary' models to 'steady-state' models in cosmology or for rejecting any physico-chemical explanation of the origins of life on earth. We can criticize these on scientific grounds (and there are plenty of weaknesses in the Darwinian paradigm of evolution as well as in all present cosmological models), but both Christians and atheists make a logical blunder when they confuse the two types of questions that can be raised about origins.

The Big-Bang scenario was predicted by Einstein's General Theory of Relativity which depicted gravity as a curvature in the space-time fabric of the universe. When the equations were solved, what are known as mathematical 'singularities' appeared. These singularities represented points at which the curvature of space-time became infinite (or, in other words, the density of matter was infinite). Localized regions in the universe in which such singularities appeared were called Black Holes, while the singularity which gave rise to the expansion of the universe itself was picturesquely dubbed the Big Bang. Present calculations locate this event at fifteen billion years ago, give or take a couple of billion. It is this singularity, at which all the known laws of physics break down, which scientists such as Stephen Hawking and others refer to as the 'moment of creation'. It is at this point that 'God', or 'the Creator', is sometimes invoked. However it is important to note that this is simply the god of Deism (see above), though clothed in a more sophisticated scientific dress.

This is made clear by Hawking's argument that if the mathematical singularity could be removed from the model, then talk of 'creation' would be obviated. By combining quantum physics with General Relativity theory, Hawking believes that he has demonstrated that space and time can form a finite, bounded surface with no singularities or boundaries, like the surface of a sphere but in higher dimensions. This model could explain both the large-scale and small-scale features of the universe, including the arrow of time. Speaking of this 'no boundary' proposal, Hawking writes: 'So long as the universe had a beginning, we could suppose it had a creator. But if the universe is really self-contained, having no boundaries or edge, it would have neither beginning nor end; it would simply be. What place, then, for a creator?'[13]

The analogy of human creation which I used earlier reveals the philosophical error in this kind of reasoning. The author may be writing a novel on an August morning in 1995, but the events of his story may be spread over several decades, even centuries, and his characters may either make their appearance all at once or (what is more usual) at various stages in the narrative. But no amount of discontinuities in the story can be used to argue either for or against the existence of the author. The temporal origins of events in the story are (conceptually) distinct from the *ontological* origin of the story in the author's thought and will. It is the work *as a whole* that demands an explanation: is someone responsible for this or not?

Various New Testament passages bring out this coherence and dependence of the world on the eternal Word of God, identified now with Christ (e.g. Col. 1:15; Heb. 1:3). In his book, *The Clockwork Image*, the late Donald MacKay gave a very helpful, though limited, analogy of Christ's 'holding all things together'. He invites us to think of an artist painting a picture, but who uses, instead of conventional paintbrushes and a canvas, an electronic gadget with which he can throw any picture he desires on to a television screen. As in all TV receivers the picture is formed by electrons impinging on the screen and producing a flash of light. If the electron beam is controlled by a regular sequence of signals, the impact of electrons forms a stable pattern of light and shade. This is an example of dynamic stability. Billions of events are taking place, but they express an underlying order, a coherence that gives stability to the whole. This coherence depends on the artist's faithfulness to the idea he wishes to embody in the electronic signals that make up the whole picture. If he were an arbitrary, capricious creator, the picture would fluctuate chaotically from one moment to the next.

Let us suppose that the artist has chosen to depict the World Cup football final. If you have a scientific habit of mind, you would notice that every time the ball is kicked into the air it follows a parabolic curve. You may be able to deduce laws of motion, theories of gravitation etc. You can build up a chain mesh of cause-and-effect and, on the basis of that, make reliable predictions concerning the movements of the ball. If anything unusual happened you would be puzzled and look for an explanation. For, if a dependable artist is indeed 'upholding' the game in existence, then it is natural to expect that all events, however out-of-the-ordinary, should fall into some coherent pattern. In other words, it is your prior knowledge of the artist's trustworthiness (gained through intuition or personal 'disclosure', rather than your science) that gives you the expectations that make the practice of science possible. We shall return to this theme in a later chapter.

Let us remain with this model of the electronic artist.

Suppose that you are exploring, with a scientific habit of mind, the regular pattern of events that form the image of a football game. Imagine that something extraordinary happens: for example, the ball when kicked does not follow its customary parabolic arc but simply disappears into outer space! Can one deduce from this inexplicable event that there is an artist responsible for the picture? That would clearly be illogical. For *every* event on the screen, what we regard as the 'normal' no less than the 'abnormal', owes its being to the artist. He is sovereign over the ordinary events as well as the extraordinary. What we would call the 'normal course of events' is simply a description of the artist's normal mode of working. But if he is responsible for his creation, then he is free to do the unprecedented.

What Christians call the 'miraculous' (actually, the term itself is not a biblical one) are the out-of-the-ordinary acts of the Creator. But they are never irrational, meaningless events. They serve a higher purpose, but their meaning cannot be deduced by scientific theorizing. Rather, it is given to us by a word of explanation from the Creator himself (this is what some theologians refer to as 'revelation in word-acts'). So the 'miracles' of Jesus, for instance, were never meaningless acts to impress the gullible, but they are regarded as *signs* in the gospel narratives: acts of compassion and power which point beyond themselves to the way God's liberating rule which overcomes evil is taking shape in the person and ministry of Jesus. They are a foretaste of that new humanity, a new world that is coming into being through his death and the resurrection. The resurrection of Jesus itself is never portrayed as simply a 'man coming back to life', but rather as a *sign* of God's new creation and a reversal of human bondage to sin, evil and death. It would have been a meaningless event if part of any other man's life, but seen against the dramatic events of Jesus' life, and especially the claims he made concerning himself, it made perfect sense. So we should not fall into the common mistake of identifying the 'miraculous' with the 'irrational'. It's rationality can be discerned only within a wider conceptual framework than the scientific.

If God is the sovereign Creator, he is free to by-pass his 'normal' mode of activity whenever and wherever he chooses. We have seen that the order and stability we expect of our world, and without which it is impossible to live, are guaranteed by the Creator's trustworthiness. He is not capricious. He does not play fast and loose with his creatures. But within that order and stability, there is always newness: fresh surprises that enlarge our vision, disturb our complacency and humble our pride.

3.4 'The God of the Gaps'

Many people, including some very clever scientists who are philosophically illiterate, think of God as a rival to a scientific explanation of events. Where science cannot explain something (e.g. how living cells are formed from non-living macromolecules, why the early universe had the structure it did, and so on), 'God' is invoked; and where science can give a complete explanation, 'God' is jettisoned. This kind of God, whether believed in by Christians or anti-Christian atheists, is known as the 'god-of-the-gaps'. It occupies the gaps in scientific knowledge, so that as scientific knowledge expands, the area over which this god rules shrinks in size. The picture of the electronic artist shows the absurdity of this view, not only with regard to divine activity but also regarding science. Scientific knowledge itself, no less than the scientist himself, is part of the picture the Creator is drawing. The scientist cannot climb out of the picture to separate the agency of the Creator from that of an entity within space-time. Creation is an account of God's activity on a higher order than the account given by the natural scientist. So Hawking's God (discussed above) is not only deist in conception, but also a typical instance of the 'god-of-the-gaps'.

Perhaps the best-known example of such a deity in the history of science is to be found in the work of the great mathematical and experimental genius, Isaac Newton (1643–1727). Not only did Newton invoke God as the non-mechanical First Cause of his mechanistic world-system, but he argued that the dynamic instability of the planetary orbits (due to fluctuations caused by gravitational attractions between the planets and from passing comets) was counteracted by periodic divine interventions. The Frenchman Pierre de Laplace (1749–1827) later used Newton's own theory to show that Newton had underestimated the stability of the planetary system. He proposed, instead, a mechanistic explanation for the formation of the latter (the famous 'nebular hypothesis'). This may have been a vindication of the power of Newton's equations, but it only brought his theology into disrepute. There is an apocryphal but oft-recounted story of the emperor Napoleon, who, having listened to Laplace's exposition of his theory of the solar system, exclaiming, 'And what place has God in all this?'; and receiving the answer, 'Sire, I have no need of that hypothesis'. Laplace's words were not an assertion of atheism (though they were taken as such in subsequent history) but a rebuttal of the Newtonian god-of-the gaps.

Let us take a modern example, this time from biology. When the influential zoologist and writer Richard Dawkins, for instance, argues that 'Darwinism makes it possible to be intellectually fulfilled as an atheist' and that 'Natural selection is the blind watchmaker, blind because it does not see ahead, does not plan consequences, has no purpose in view. Yet the living results of natural selection overwhelmingly impress us . . . with the illusion of design and planning'[14], he is simply indulging in god-of-the-gaps style thinking. If talk of 'design and planning' in the universe is obviated, then it is assumed that God-talk too is unnecessary. But natural selection by itself tells us nothing either in favour of 'purpose' or against 'purpose'. The language of purpose is meaningful only when we start to relate the story that the natural sciences tell of the world to a higher story that involves persons, whether human or divine. But the story that science narrates cannot do that by itself, for it has chosen (for methodological, not philosophical, reasons) to leave out the category of purpose in its descriptions of the natural world. To use its results to 'prove' that there is no purpose to life and the universe is a mischievous sleight-of-hand. Dawkins is merely reading into his biology his own atheist outlook, which itself has been formed on other, extra-scientific grounds. The data of evolution are read through the grid of an atheistic (naturalistic) world-view. He is perfectly entitled to do this; but what is quite illegitimate is to argue that the blind watchmaker thesis now makes God superfluous.

We can discuss the purpose of the human story only if we know for sure that we are at the end of that story, just as we grasp the plot of a novel only when we have read it through to the end. But no science or philosophy can tell us whether we are at the end, the beginning or the middle of history. It is only if the Author of the story discloses the meaning of the

whole by giving us a glimpse of the ending that we can talk
with any confidence of 'purpose'. Now the Christian claim,
as we have seen, is indeed that. In the resurrection of Jesus of
Nazareth God has vindicated his creation, entrusting to us a
glimpse of the goal of history. Without that we are left to
empty speculation. It is important to assert this: we cannot
'read off' the purpose or meaning of history from events in the
natural or social worlds; we can only confess it in the light of
the resurrection.

But, leaving aside distinctively Christian arguments, there
is a remarkable irony in Dawkins' blind watchmaker thesis.
Writing of some of Darwin's twentieth-century followers who
have eliminated God from their world-view while still cling-
ing to the rationality of science, the historian and philosopher
of science, Stanley Jaki, makes the trenchant observation:
'Their work is a life-long commitment to the purpose of
proving there is no purpose. Every Darwinist is a living
refutation of a philosophy, Darwinism, for which purpose is
non-existent.'[15] Dawkin's own work as a scientist seems to be
undermined by his thesis. Within his naturalist perspective, the
only 'purpose' to life is to reproduce as much of one's DNA
as possible. Whither all intellectual and cultural achievement
in a society that truly embraces this as its dominant world-
view?

3.5 Evolutionary Red Herrings

Dawkins stands in a growing tradition of biologists who have
ventured beyond their field of expertise into grand theorizing
about human life. This would be unobjectionable if it were
not for the fact that they tend to impress their readers more by
the force of their professional reputation than by convincing
arguments. Consider, for instance, the oft-repeated assertion
by another famous biologist, stated with all the dogmatic
certainty of religious conviction: 'Chance alone is at the source
of all innovation, of all creation in the biosphere. Pure chance,
absolutely free but blind, is at the root of the stupendous edifice
of evolution. . . . The biosphere looks like the product of a
unique event whose chances of occurring were almost nil . .

The universe was not pregnant with life. . . . Our number
came up in the Monte Carlo game.'[16] This comment carries
the authority of a Nobel prize-winner, Jacques Monod, him-

self the grandson of the greatest evangelical preacher of nine-teenth-century France, Adolphe Monod.

Monod's invocation of Chance (with a capital C) is fraught with logical errors. The scientific notion of chance is an indication of our ignorance: 'chance' or 'random' events are unpredictable, either because the predictive schemes are too complex (as, for instance, when we try to forecast weather patterns) or (as in the subatomic domain of what is known as quantum physics) because no prior set of events existed from which they followed according to law-like precedent. Most physical laws are of a statistical kind: they speak in terms of probabilities of finding an entity or system in a given state at a given time. But 'chance' is not an agent that does things. It is not the source or cause of anything. Rather it stands for the absence of any assignable causal precursor.

The other notion of chance, with which Monod confuses scientific chance, is the ancient mythological concept of Chance (with a capital C), a capricious deity, the personifica-tion of chaos and meaninglessness. It is this latter pseudo-deity which biblical theism rejects. If we follow the concept of creation outlined earlier, then all physical events, with or without causal precursors in space-time, depend for their occurrence on the sovereign will of the Creator. Whether scientists classify events and processes as physically 'determi-nate' or 'indeterminate' (i.e. chance) is of no concern to the biblical writers. They assure us that God is the giver of being to both categories of events (e.g. Prov. 16:33). Thus chance, when used in a strictly scientific manner, is not an alternative to a theistic interpretation of physical events. (Interestingly, the recent study of chaotic systems in different branches of science have revealed an ordered structure even in processes classed as 'chaos'; but these arguments are irrelevant to the semantic clarification above).

The title of Dawkins' most famous book is intended as a refutation of the Divine Watchmaker model of William Paley and other eighteenth-century English writers ('God' winds up the universe like a clock and then leaves it to run its course). This kind of God served to give a sense of design to the world, but he himself was unfree, unlovable, unknowable, unin-volved and unconcerned! This was the God behind the eighteenth-century Enlightenment idea of 'natural religion', the God of Voltaire and Rousseau, the Underwriter of universal reason in Descartes' project of liberation from culture, and the Guarantor of universal human rights in the American constitution. It is not surprising that Darwin's theory of natural selection, first published in 1859, dealt a crippling blow to such 'natural religion' as well as to the god-of-the-gaps approach of more traditional theists. But Christians who were more biblical in their thinking were grateful for the fresh impetus it gave to re-examine their understanding of how God interacts with his world.

To what extent was Darwinian theory a challenge to Christian faith in the latter years of the nineteenth century? It is difficult to answer this question, because the introduction of any radically new theory provokes strong and immensely diverse reactions. Recent historical studies have shown up the wide range of responses, both among the scientific community as well as in the church.[17] Some scientists opposed the theory on purely scientific grounds, other scientists on religious grounds. There were others, Christian and atheist, who incorporated the theory into their world-view with little fuss. The historian Owen Chadwick points out, in his survey of nineteenth century secularization, that the 'onslaught upon Christianity owed its force . . . not at all to the science of the nineteenth century. It attacked Christian churches not in the name of knowledge but in the name of justice and freedom.'[18] Chadwick found only three British scientists who confessed to being led away from a prior religious faith partly by their scientific learning, one of whom was Charles Darwin. The intellectual 'crises of faith' on the part of prominent Victorians had little to do with science, let alone evolution.

In his impressive survey of Christian responses to Darwin in late nineteenth-century Britain and the USA, James Moore[19] has shown how the more evangelical (or biblical) a person's theological outlook, the more likely that person was to accept the theory and incorporate it into his world-view. This was because the more orthodox a person's theology (for example, trinitarian as opposed to unitarian) the further removed he was from the deistic outlook. Those who held to the sovereignty of God and his continuing interaction with his creation were less likely to be shocked by any thesis of 'common ancestry' between humankind and other creatures. The most bitter denunciations of Darwin in Britain were found among the High Anglicans, into whose theology deism and god-of-the-gaps type design arguments had made deep inroads. Moreover, a high view of biblical authority led to a refusal to use the Bible as a set of proof-texts from which to discover biological and geological data. Evangelicals stood in the Reformation tradition which taught respect for the 'book of nature' alongside the 'book of scripture': one knew God in a saving way through the latter, and could then discern his ways by exploring the former. If the same God stood behind both nature and scripture, there could be no final conflict between the deliverances of both. A cautious 'wait and see' attitude, which held that both current scientific theories and traditional interpretations are always open to correction, also seemed most honouring to God.

Among the evangelical scholars who did not see evolution as a threat to biblical faith were such prominent figures as B.B. Warfield, G.F. Wright, A.A. Hodge and James Orr. Indeed, Warfield, who was one of the greatest defenders of biblical authority against the liberal or modernist wing of the American Church, described himself as a 'Darwinian of the purest water', stating that 'for myself . . . I do not find that there is any general statement in the Bible or any part in the account of creation . . . that need be opposed to evolution'.[20] It was largely through the efforts of three evangelicals (Asa Gray, G.F. Wright and James Dana) that Darwin's theory was popularized in the US. It is ironic that several of the founders of 'fundamentalism' (which, in its original sense, sought to defend the fundamental doctrines of the Christian faith) were least troubled by the scientific aspects of the theory. Why is it, then, that many Christians today, and especially those influenced by the North American fundamentalist stream, tend to stigmatize evolution and evolutionary thinking as the greatest satanic deception that the church has to counter?

There are various reasons, sociological as well as theological, impossible to explore here. But a first step in sorting out the confusion must lie in a clarification of concepts that people use.

What do we mean by **evolution**? The term can refer to: (a) the general idea of change with time, so that the earth with its life-forms that we experience today is not the same as it was, say, ten million years ago; (b) the belief that all organisms are related through a common ancestry; (c) a theory setting out a specific explanatory mechanism for (b) above, as in the neo-Darwinian synthesis of natural selection with modern genetics; (d) a philosophical position that argues (from one or a combination of the above) that a theistic interpretation of life is outdated and contradicted by the 'facts' of science; and (e) an extension of one or more of the above to explain the origins of human morality, culture and religious behaviour, usually with the assumption that what comes later is an improvement on what preceded it. . . .

Of the above meanings of the term, (a) is, in my opinion, indisputable. Both (b) and (c) are acceptable if there is some empirical support for them and also no alternative theory to account for biological variation and change. As we have seen, science proceeds by building coherent patterns of explanation, so that a theory that can account for some observations is far better than no theory at all. In the words of a famous philosopher of science, Imre Lakatos, 'A theory can only be eliminated by a better theory, that is, by one that has excess empirical content over its predecessors, some of which is subsequently confirmed.'[21] Biologists like Dawkins have indeed shown the rich explanatory power of neo-Darwinian theory.

However there is still much in the theory that is based on speculation with little experimental evidence. For example, the severe paucity of transitional fossil forms and the lack of evidence for non-lethal random gene mutations are serious embarrassments to the theory. Also theories of chemical evolution (dealing with the transition from non-living to living matter) are trapped in an irresolvable dilemma: even the simplest building-blocks of life seem to require highly complex enzymes and DNA molecules for their synthesis, yet the latter are presumably—on the evolutionary picture—themselves constructed from these simpler units. Whether this 'chicken or the egg' situation can be resolved by invoking random fluctuations alone remains to be seen; but it seems far more likely that the 'new biology' which is emerging, based on more complex mechanisms and concepts (such as cybernetic feedback loops), will be needed to complement, perhaps even to replace completely, the neo-Darwinian scenario. Perhaps the biggest defect in the theory is its inability to account for the growth of complex organization. Adaptation to a changing environment cannot be the whole story. After all, some of the longest surviving entities such as viruses have a very simple biological structure. Other organizing principles seem to be at work in the universe.

But until we have a better understanding of such principles we are left with no option but to work within the neo-Darwinian perspective. It is interesting that Darwin himself seems to have been sensitive to these issues in dealing with doubts concerning the possibility of a highly complex and adaptive organ being generated by successive modifications, which in their early stages may not seem to confer any advantage. In *The Origin of Species*, he writes: 'He who will go thus far, if he find on finishing this treatise that large bodies of facts, otherwise inexplicable, can be explained by the theory of descent, ought not to hesitate to go further, and to admit that a structure even as perfect as the eye of an eagle might be formed by natural selection, although in this case he does not know any of the transitional grades . . . though I have felt the difficulty far too keenly to be surprised at any degree of hesitation in extending the principle of natural selection to such startling lengths.'[22]

It is positions (d) and (e) above which constitute the real threat to Christian (or any theistic) faith. But we have seen how empty and fallacious these arguments can be (Dawkins is an example of (d), while Freud was an example of (e)). These philosophical views, which essentially use biological ideas to promote a political agenda, have usually been labelled 'evolutionism' or 'evolutionary naturalism'. They make of nature and evolution new deities, often spelling them with a capital N and a capital E and ascribing to them personal agency. This again is ironic testimony to the inability on the part of humans like ourselves to practically (as opposed to theoretically!) embrace life in an impersonal universe.

One of the most sensitive Christian thinkers during the formative years of the modern world was the great scientist-theologian Blaise Pascal (1623–1662). Deeply sceptical of attempts to ground belief in God in either first principles of human reasoning or in arguments from design, Pascal pointed to the ambivalence of human existence: we are corrupt and wretched, subject to selfishness, guilt, boredom and anxiety, yet showing the vestiges of our created grandeur through our awareness of this condition. Humankind is suspended between the finite and the infinite, conscious of an inner void which nothing in nature can satisfy. No philosophy can make sense of this, no moral system can make us better and happier. Only the One who combined human greatness with human degradation on the cross can transform our condition and bring us to the knowledge of ultimate Truth. 'All of those who seek God apart from Christ, and who go no further than nature, either find no light to satisfy them or come to devise a means of knowing God without a mediator, thus falling into either atheism or deism, two things almost equally abhorrent to Christianity.'[23]

3.7 Celebration

At the entrance to the Cavendish laboratory in Cambridge, England, where many of the pioneering breakthroughs in nuclear physics were made, are inscribed the words of Psalm 3:2: 'Great are the works of the Lord, studied by all who take pleasure in them'. The Christian's attitude to the works of God is to be marked by study and delight. Hard work, but pleasurable work. 'You never enjoy the world aright,' wrote the young English poet Thomas Traherne (1637–1674), 'till the sea itself floweth in your veins, till you are clothed with the heavens, and crowned with the stars: and perceive yourself to be the sole heir of the whole world: and more than so, because men are in it who are every one sole heirs, as well as you. Till you can sing and rejoice and delight in GOD as misers do in gold, and kings in sceptres, you will never enjoy the world.'[24]

The knowledge of this God is not deduced from the study of the physical world. Rather, it is the knowledge of God which is given in the biblical revelation that provides the imaginative framework in which the physical world itself is recognized as a creation, affirmed in its goodness and beauty, explored and celebrated. It also keeps us from either lapsing into the worship of the world itself or denigrating and exploiting it for our selfish ends. Our exploration is only a *response* to the initiative taken by God in making himself known to us as our Redeemer and Lord. It is a rational response, prompted by the rationality of the divine self-disclosure. In the fine words of the Scottish theologian Thomas Torrance, 'If we are to engage in scientific exploration of the universe in response to the Word of God incarnate in Jesus Christ by whom it was made, we must learn to respect the nature of all created things, using pure science to bring their mute rationalities into such articulation that the praises of the Creator may resound throughout the whole universe.'[25]

The picture of the universe as a creation, permeated and guided by the Word of God, not only undergirds scientific activity but all language, music and the arts. No one today has expressed this insight with greater eloquence than the literary scholar George Steiner. Why should there be art, why poetic creation? The question is an exact analogue to that posed by Leibniz (1646–1716): why should there be being and substance, why should there not be nothing? Here is Steiner's answer (while acknowledging that every true poem, piece of music or painting says it better): 'There is aesthetic creation because there is *creation*. There is formal construction because we have been made form . . . The core of our human identity is nothing more or less than the fitful apprehension of the radically inexpressible presence, facticity and perceptible substantiality of the created. It is; we are. This is the rudimentary grammar of the unfathomable.'[26]

Steiner sees the aesthetic act, the conceiving and bringing into being of that which has no being, to be an *imitatio*, a replication on its own scale, of the inaccessible *fiat* of divine creation. He concludes, 'It is a theology, explicit or suppressed, masked or avowed, substantive or imaged, which underwrites the presumption of creativity, of signification in our encounters with text, with music, with art. The meaning of meaning is a transcendent postulate.'[27]

Notes

[1] S. Hawking, *A Brief History of Time* (UK: Bantam Press, 1988) p. 184

[2] See further K.A. Kitchen, *The Bible in its World* (Exeter: Paternoster, 1977) pp. 60ff; H. Blocher, *In the Beginning* (Leicester: Inter-Varsity Press,1984) Ch 2; D.J. Wiseman, 'Creation Time- What does Genesis say?' in *Science & Christian Belief*, vol 3, no. 2, April 1991

[3] E.g. Wiseman, op. cit.

[4] H. Kuhse and P. Singer, *Should the Baby Live?: The Problem of Handicapped Infants* (Oxford: Oxford University Press, 1985) p. 138

[5] See O. O'Donovan, *Begotten or Made?* (Oxford: Oxford University Press, 1984)

[6] Quoted in C. Everett Koop, *The Right to Live, the Right to Die* (USA: Tyndale House & UK: Coverdale, 1976)

[7] A. Toynbee, *Horizon*, vol xv, 1973, pp. 6–9

[8] J. Needham, *Science and Civilization in China*, 4 vols (Cambridge University Press, 1954–62)

[9] R. Dubos, *A God Within* (London: Sphere Books, 1976) p. 114

10 Ibid. p. 115

11 J. Calvin, *Commentary on Genesis* (1554) (trans. 1847, reprinted by Banner of Truth Publishers 1965)

12 R. Bauckham, 'Jesus and the Wild Animals (Mk 1:13): a Christological Image For an Ecological Age', in J. Green and M. Turner (eds) *Jesus of Nazareth: Lord and Christ* (Grand Rapids: Eerdmans/Carlisle: Paternoster, 1994)

13 Hawking, op. cit. p. 149

14 R. Dawkins, *The Blind Watchmaker* (London: WW Norton, 1986) p. 21

15 S.L. Jaki, *Angels, Apes and Man* (Illinois: Sherwood Sugden & Co, 1983) p. 63

16 J. Monod, *Chance and Necessity* (London: Collins, 1971)

17 See, e.g., J.R. Moore, *The Post-Darwinian Controversies: a Study of the Protestant Struggle to Come to Terms With Darwin in Great Britain and America, 1870–1900* (Cambridge University Press, 1979); D.N. Livingstone, *Darwin's Forgotten Defenders: the Encounter Between Evangelical Theology and Evolutionary Thought* (Grand Rapids: Eerdmans & Edinburgh: Scottish Academic Press, 1987)

18 O. Chadwick, *The Secularization of the European Mind in the Nineteenth Century* (Cambridge University Press, 1975)

19 Moore, op. cit.

20 Quoted in Livingstone, op. cit. p. 118

21 I. Lakatos, *The Methodology of Scientific Research Programmes: Philosophical Papers*, Volume I (ed. John Worrall and Gregory Curries, Cambridge University Press, 1978) p. 150

22 Charles Darwin, *The Origin of Species* (Harmondsworth: Penguin, 1968) pp. 218–9

23 B. Pascal, *Pensées, tr. by A.J. Krailsheimer (Harmondsworth: Penguin, 1966) no. 449*

24 T. Traherne, *Poems, Centuries and Three Thanksgivings*, ed. A. Ridler (Oxford: Oxford University Press, 1966) p. 177

25 T.F. Torrance, *God and Rationality* (Oxford: Oxford University Press, 1971) p. 164

26 G. Steiner, *Real Presences* (London: Faber and Faber, 1989) p. 201

27 Ibid. p. 216

4

Job & The Silence of God

'Talk to me about the truth of religion and I'll listen gladly. Talk
to me about the duty of religion and I'll listen submissively. But
don't come talking to me about the consolations of religion or I
shall suspect that you don't understand.'
—*CS Lewis (1898–1963), A Grief Observed*[1]

How dare we celebrate the Creator in the face of innocent
suffering? How do we speak of God from the midst of human
anguish? How do we dare affirm faith in a God of life and
justice when men and women around us die prematurely and
unjustly every day?

Of course, much of that suffering is the result of our human
solidarity, our being created as persons rather than machines.
Being persons, as we saw, involves us in each other's lives, for
ill as well as for good. Not only do we suffer directly the evil
that others do to us, but we share the pain of cumulative human
sin: we are born into an environment disfigured by the choices
and actions of our forebears, and we leave this world having
contributed (in varying degrees) to that tragic inheritance. But
that truth alone is cold comfort. It doesn't reduce the intensity
of distress caused by the seeming silence (and impotence?) of
God in the face of sin's rampage. And it is the suffering of
young children that raises most acutely the agonizing questions
about meaning and justice in human life. For it is here that all
our popular language of desert and retribution clearly floun-
ders, and many in non-western cultures resort to invoking
doctrines of past lives and rebirth as a way of 'explaining' what
seems so brutally inexplicable.

What we have come to call the 'problem of suffering'
focuses not on the experience of physical or mental pain as
much as on the experience of apparent meaninglessness.
Pain itself is an important aspect of our bodies' healthy
functioning. And we can all tolerate high levels of pain as
long as that pain can be understood to serve some purpose.

If we can somehow fit our experience of suffering into our life-story in a way that makes sense of it, the 'problem' of suffering disappears. But this is what we cannot do with the suffering of little children whose life-stories have hardly developed. And invoking past lives doesn't ultimately help dispel the cry for meaning, for we still want to know what they did in another life that merits such pain in this. If our notion of justice rebels against the idea of punishing people without declaring the charges against them, how could any cosmic process (whether we label it *karma*, destiny or the divine will) be deemed just if it has no spokesperson to interpret its workings to us? The harsh reality of unjust suffering is increasingly held up as the touchstone for any meaningful religious discourse, and it has often been the reason for unbelief in recent times.

However, is there not something ironic in this secular unbelief? For isn't the cry for ultimate meaningfulness to our life-stories itself a fundamentally religious impulse? Indeed there are good grounds for believing that most religions arose as attempts to give meaning to human life in a hostile and life-threatening universe. All religions seek to give to human beings and human experience a place within a cosmic order of things. The protest against meaningless suffering presupposes belief in the ultimate meaningfulness of reality: in other words, a religious, and essentially theistic, vision of life. The question of the innocent victim, 'Where are you, God?', itself springs from the lips of faith. If men and women believed themselves to be mere flotsam in an accidental universe, or that God was neither good, nor loving, nor powerful, there would, presumably, be no moral and spiritual torment to undergo. Their suffering would simply be a brute fact of the world, nothing more. But so-called secular men and women continue to experience bewilderment and even a sense of moral outrage in the face of innocent suffering. It seems their outrage arises precisely because they believe, at levels deeper than conscious thought, that their universe *is* fundamentally ordered, meaningful and good. The silence of God is hardest to bear for those who believe in a living God who relates personally to the human creation, and is not an amoral, inscrutable process.

4.1 Job's Anguish

The theme of unjust suffering recurs throughout the Bible, but no single book focuses our attention on it as poignantly as does the Book of Job. Job, an upright and God-fearing man, living a respected, happy and prosperous life, is suddenly plunged into sickness, deprivation and utter wretchedness. His friends find him seated on the garbage heap outside the city. He has been reduced, like so many in our modern world, to the status of a nonperson in the eyes of his wife, his friends and his former associates. His wife urges him to 'curse God and die' (Job 2:9). Will Job reject God? Was his faith and uprightness dependent on his material prosperity? If not, how will he now speak of God from the perspective of the garbage heap? These are the profound issues that the book unfolds. It raises the question whether there can be anything such as a disinterested faith, a faith 'for nothing'; or whether all religious behaviour is finally motivated by selfish concerns.

Job is not a patient man, and the book is not a call to patient endurance. Job is a rebellious believer. He protests his integrity and innocence to heaven. His rage is directed against a God who seems indifferent not only to his plight but also to the suffering of all innocent victims. He accuses God of arbitrariness in his dealings with humanity:

> If I say, 'I will forget my complaint,
> I will change my expression and smile',
> I still dread all my sufferings,
> for I know you will not hold me innocent.
> Since I am already found guilty,
> why should I struggle in vain?
> Even if I washed myself with soap
> and my hands with washing soda,
> you would plunge me into a slime pit
> so that even my clothes would detest me (9:27–31).

Such language shocks his friends who represent the conventional wisdom of the day. Theirs is a neat theological scheme which makes perfect sense of Job's miserable situation. The notion of temporal divine punishment is central to this scheme. Since wickedness is always punished by God and suffering is the form that punishment takes, then Job's suffering must be the punishment of God. It follows that Job has committed

wickedness. His suffering, therefore, is just. All his vain prot-
estations of moral integrity are not merely self-delusion on his
part, but the very height of blasphemy against God. If Job will
only admit his guilt and passively submit, perhaps God will
stay his hand and be merciful in his judgement. And so in the
name of theological correctness, they plead with Job to accept
his lot.

Job is familiar with such arguments. He does not deny that he
is a sinner like all other human beings, but he cannot detect a sin
in his life which merits such enormous suffering. His friends'
arguments, which are based on a particularly narrow concept of
justice, only intensify his consciousness of innocence. His experience has brought into question the self-contained theology of
his day. In the midst of his confusion and pain, made worse by
the accusations of blasphemy made by those to whom he turned
for support, and feeling persecuted by the 'hand of God' upon
his life, Job struggles to hold together these twin convictions:
that God is just and that he, Job, is innocent in his suffering. What
the religion of his society held to be self-contradictory propositions, Job embraces as true to his experience. But how is he to
speak of God from the perspective of his suffering?

As the book unfolds, we find the arguments of Job's friends
becoming more repetitious and monotous, while, in contrast,
Job's perspective is enlarged. The first enlargement arises
through Job's solidarity with all who suffer unjustly. His own
suffering makes him sensitive to the plight of the poor. In a
moving passage, reminiscent of the prophetic literature of the
Old Testament, Job describes the concrete suffering of the
poor—a suffering not decreed by destiny or due to inexplicable causes, but clearly the result of human wickedness:

Men move boundary stones;
they pasture flocks they have stolen.
They drive away the orphan's donkey
and take away the widow's ox in pledge.
They thrust the needy from the path
and force all the poor of the land into hiding.
Like wild donkeys in the desert
the poor go about their labour of foraging food;
the wasteland provides food for their children. . . .
The groans of the dying rise from the city,
and the souls of the wounded cry out for help.
But God charges no one with wrongdoing (24:2–5,12).

Job has launched a devastating attack on the 'windy arguments' of his friends. He dismisses the latter as 'miserable comforters' and 'worthless physicians' (16:2; 13:4). Their self-assured theology does not bear on the real world of human suffering, hopes and fears. They think they are being faithful to God by passing on the tradition of 'what the sages have declared, hiding nothing received from their fathers' (15:18), namely that the wicked live tormented lives and the upright are rewarded with happiness and prosperity. But this glib, abstract way of theologizing is the real blasphemy: they veil and distort the face of God. Seeking to justify God they only condemn innocent men and women. Job confronts them with the telling question: 'Do you mean to defend God by prevarication and by dishonest argument?' (13:7).

Job' rebelliousness is directed not primarily at the fact of his suffering but at the religious world-view that seeks to justify it. The God whom he is groping after in his suffering is a God who both listens and speaks to humanity. Job boldly demands that God confront him with the charges against him, and this demand is inspired by a firm trust in the ultimate righteousness of God. Job is sure that God knows him to be innocent and will declare that to his friends. We, the readers of the book, know that Job is innocent and that God has declared him to be so, for the author of the book has disclosed this to us in the prologue. But for Job the conviction that God alone knows the true situation is a conviction born of a living faith. He sees his struggle with God as a kind of lawsuit that he brings against God on behalf of wretched humanity. But through his tears he glimpses the presence of a witness and defender before the throne of God who will take up his case. Addressing the earth, which will receive the life that is now slipping away from him, he expresses his deepest hope in these words:

> O Earth, do not cover my blood;
> may my cry never be laid to rest!
> Even now my witness is in heaven;
> my advocate is on high.
> My intercessor is my friend
> as my eyes pour out tears to God;
> on behalf of a man he pleads with
> God as a man pleads for his friend (16:18–21).

This mysterious mediator, an approachable friend before the awesome face of God, appears again in a passage that marks the high point of Job's spiritual pilgrimage:

> I know that my Redeemer lives,
> and that in the end he will stand upon the earth.
> And after my skin has been destroyed,
> yet in my flesh I will see God (19:25,26).

Here Job refers to his *go'el*, his defender or avenger. The word arose out of the Israelites' sense of family solidarity, and it combined the thought of ransom with that of obligation. When someone fell into debt or suffered any misfortune, it was the obligation of the nearest relative to intervene. The law in Israel recognized the right of the *go'el*, the nearest relative, to redeem the property, freedom and life of those who were in no position to help themselves (e.g. Lev. 25:47–49; Num. 35:18–19). The term came to be used of Yahweh in his relationship with Israel as a whole. As a result of the covenant, God has become the nearest relative, the one who takes upon himself liability for his people, the one who rescues them and avenges them (e.g. Is. 43:14; 44:24; Prov. 23:10–11).

To whom is Job appealing? Much scholarly ink has been spilt in answering this question. I myself have no hesitation in saying that Job is referring to God and not to an intermediary distinct from God. In an earlier passage he has already appealed to God to protect him from God's wrath (14:13); and now he glimpses a profound insight— that the God he experiences as his adversary is at the same time his truest friend. God is both his judge and the one who will defend him on the day of judgement. The One who wounds him is also his healer. God will not let him be destroyed 'at the end' but rather 'I myself shall see him'—not as a stranger or as an enemy, but in a friendship closer than the superficial friendships he now experiences. It is this hope that causes his heart to break out into moments of joy in the midst of his trials. This dialectical approach to God is one of the most profound aspects of the Book of Job, and the Christian reader can sense here an anguished but courageous 'groping' towards the great themes of New Testament faith, especially the atoning work of the cross and a triune conception of the being of God.

The justice of God has been the main subject of the debate.

The companions of Job equate divine justice with temporal retribution. God gives to individuals according to their deserts. The outworking of divine government is, in their minds, crystal clear. In this perspective Job's sufferings are the result of his guilt. Job, on the other hand, begins not with theological principles but with his own experience. He declares his innocence and integrity. In the eyes of his companions, and to some extent in his own eyes, such a claim amounts to imputing guilt to God. Troubled by this seemingly blasphemous conclusion, Job desires to debate the matter with God personally.

4.2 Job's Vindication

Job receives his request. God answers him from 'the heart of the whirlwind' (38:1). This is a classic image in the Bible, forming the context for a 'theophany'—a disclosure of God's presence. The storm both conveys and conceals the fearsome majesty of God. And for the first time since the prologue to the book the author uses the covenant name of Yahweh in speaking of God. God is no longer distant and detached, but the gracious and faithful Lord of the covenant. He has been present all along, but now that presence is made known to Job.

At first sight there is something strange and disconcerting about the divine speeches. God does not rebuke Job for any sin (thus confirming his innocence) but neither does he answer the anguished questions that Job has fired at the heavens. He adopts the same confrontational posture that Job has assumed in his lawsuit against God. 'Brace yourself like a man; I will question you and you shall answer me' (38:3). There is no apology for God's long silence, no word of consolation for Job in his distress. But nor does God crush and humiliate him. He takes him instead on a whirlwind tour of the universe, educating him about stars and animals and monstrous creatures of the deep, in poetry that ranks amongst the most beautiful and evocative in world literature. But, however bewildered the reader may be, Job understands (see 40:3,4 and 42:1–6). Very few interpreters of the Book of Job seek to share Job's understanding. They assume that what God says is less important than the fact of God's speaking, the communication of God's presence to Job. Consequently they pay little attention to the content of the divine speech. In their view, the very presence of God is sufficient to satisfy the deepest desires of Job. While acknowledging the element of truth in this, I believe it to be seriously deficient. Instead I endorse the view of Gustavo Gutierrez that the 'content of God's speeches specify and concretize the response; the word of God gives the presence of God its full meaning.²′^

There are several themes which run through the two divine speeches (38:1–40:2 & 40:6–41:34), but prominent among them are the following:-

(a)   *The gratuitousness of divine love.* At the very beginning of the speech, Yahweh directs Job's attention to the very source of all existing things. The universe in all its wonder and mystery does not turn around Job or any other human being. The majesty of God is to be identified less with might than with creative freedom and the gratuitous initiative of love. It is this that enfolds the creation and gives meaning to God's work, whether in nature or history.

> Where were you when I laid the earth's foundation?
> Tell me, if you understand.
> Who marked off its dimensions?
> Surely you know!
> Who stretched out a measuring line across it?
> On what were its footings set,
> or who laid its cornerstone-
> while the morning stars sang together
> and all the angels shouted for joy? (38:4–7).

The teasing irony of God's speech exposes the childish pretentiousness of Job and his friends. They are not the centre of reality. And the doctrine of retribution, though it has a legitimate place in God's government of things, is not the key to understanding the universe. The free and gratuitous love of God is the hinge on which the universe turns. The world expresses the freedom and delight of God in creating. Utility is not the reason behind creation: not everything that exists was made to be useful to human beings, and therefore their true meaning can never be fathomed within an anthropocentric world-view.

> Who cuts a channel for the torrents of rain,
> and a path for the thunderstorm,

> to water a land where no man lives,
> a desert with no one in it,
> to satisfy a desolate wasteland
> and make it sprout with grass? (38:25–27).

What purpose does rain serve in places empty of human dwelling? Can Job and his friends celebrate with Yahweh the wonder and beauty of creation—without expecting that Yahweh's actions in the world of nature and history fit the predictive schemes of human reason? On what basis do they claim to know how God is going to act? What do you make of God's joke—the ostrich (39:13)! A creature bereft of good sense, flapping her wings but getting nowhere, leaving her eggs in the earth unaware that someone may step on them (39:15). Even those parts of creation which seem lacking in wisdom and purpose have their place in God's ordering of things. Perhaps the ostrich is a picture of Job himself— a paradoxical mixture of greatness and foolishness. They are both endowed with value by the gratuitous love of God.

David Atkinson discovers here a simple but profound pastoral application: 'God, we are told in Genesis, made the man and put him in a garden that was "pleasant to the sight". The context in which we live our lives contributes significantly to our sense of well-being. The ash heap may be an appropriate place on which to sit if we are in mourning, but it is no place to stay if we wish to feel better. Sometimes we will most help distressed people—help them draw nearer to God, from the depths of depression—not by teaching them doctrine, or by preaching our best sermon, or by showing them the error of their ways, but by walking with them around the garden, by taking them to see a waterfall or a sunset, by helping them recover an enjoyment in the world. Such steps are not always practicable, of course. But in so far as we can enable depressed people to see themselves in a new setting, and to recover a place of security and belonging within the rich panorama of God's creation, we are helping them. They need to know that they, too, *belong*. It is by enjoying the Creator's handiwork that we often begin to feel again the touch of the Creator's hand.'[3]

(b)   *The sovereignty of divine wisdom.* God has intimated to Job that there is indeed a divine plan unfolding in all of creation, but it is not one that the human mind can grasp so as to draw straightforward cause-and-effect patterns. But this should not be surprising when there is so much in God's world that eludes human control. If the creation cannot be domesticated, how presumptuous to think that the Creator's actions can!

> Who shut up the sea behind doors
> when it burst forth from the womb,
> when I made the clouds its garment
> and wrapped it in thick darkness,
> when I fixed limits for it
> and set its doors and bars in place,
> when I said, 'This far you may come and no farther.
> here is where your proud waves halt? (38:8–11).

The sea is a common biblical symbol of chaos, social and physical, restless and uncontrollable, its proud waves threatening to engulf the land and its inhabitants. But God has set limits to it, its fearsome power is subject to God's power. Likewise the monstrous, mysterious sea-creatures Behemoth and Leviathan, which make their appearance in the second divine speech, probably represent the terrifying forces of chaos and disorder that seek to overpower human life and the rest of creation. Powerful though they be, they are themselves held within the more powerful hand of the Creator. From the perspective of his suffering Job sees the creation as a chaos, a return to emptiness. Disorder and meaninglessness seem to have triumphed. God shows him that the divine power controls these chaotic powers even though they are not annihilated. There is evil in the world, but the world itself is not evil. There is chaos in the cosmos, but the cosmos is not a chaos.

No power on earth, however hideous and terrifying in its aspect, can separate us from the Creator's embrace.

> Who has a claim against me that I must pay?
> Everything under heaven belongs to me (41:11).

(c) *The 'weakness' of divine power.* As the broadside of ironic questioning continues, God invites Job to contemplate what he would do if he were in God's place!

> Have you ever given orders to the morning,
> or shown the dawn its place,

> that it might take the earth by the edges
> and shake the wicked out of it? (38:12,13).

To 'shake the wicked out' of the earth is what Job has been demanding of God. But God's light continues to dawn on them. Is the creation therefore flawed? All right, says God, you take over the running of the universe.

> Would you discredit my justice?
> Would you condemn me to justify yourself? . . .
> Unleash the fury of your wrath,
> look at every proud man and bring him low,
> look at every proud man and humble him,
> crush the wicked where they stand.
> Bury them all in the dust together;
> shroud their faces in the grave.
> Then I myself will admit to you
> that your own right hand can save you (40:8–14).

The irony employed in this passage brings home to Job the self-imposed limitations of the divine love. Insignificant though human beings may seem to Job, they are precious enough in Yahweh's eyes for Yahweh to heed their freedom, to bear with patience their wickedness and to seek their collaboration in the just government of the world. The divine freedom that Yahweh has revealed to Job has its correlate in human freedom. The latter is established by, and grounded in, the first.

Grace involves the communion of these two freedoms. Job's freedom found expression in his vehement complaints at God. God's freedom finds expression in the shocking generosity of grace that refuses to be confined within a system of predictable rewards and punishments. Until that terrible day of Final Reckoning, when evil and evildoers *will* be eradicated and all suffering innocents vindicated, Yahweh indicates that he does not take pleasure in the death of the wicked but wills that they turn from their wickedness to life (see e.g. Ezek. 18:23; Mic. 7:18; Hos. 11:8,9; 1 Tim. 2:3; 2 Pet. 3:9).

Job has travelled a long and tortuous road to his personal encounter with Yahweh. The answers he gets were not what he was looking for, but he has been liberated from his anxieties and found his hope fulfilled. That Job understands and is transformed by Yahweh's speeches is shown by his response:

I know that you can do all things
and no plan of yours can be thwarted. . . .
My ears had heard of you
but now my eyes have seen you.
Therefore I despise myself
and repent in dust and ashes (42:2,5–6).

God does have plans for his world, and that world is not a
chaos as Job had repeatedly suggested in his dispute with his
friends. His reasoning had then seemed to be: 'I do not
understand these plans. Therefore they cannot exist'. But the
integrity of his faith, expressed in his willingness to confront
the contradiction between experience and a doctrine of temporal retribution and to plead the issue not only with his friends
but with God himself, has led to another way of perceiving
and speaking about God. As Gutierrez puts it finely, 'What he
has now heard from the mouth of Yahweh has given him a
glimpse of another world, an order different from the one he
rejected but for which until now there seemed to be no
alternative. All this is still not entirely clear to him, but at least
he is no longer being suffocated by the religious universe of
his friends and indeed of his age.'[4]

What is the repentance that Job performs? Gutierrez points
out, following other commentators, that the verbs in the last
line have no object. NIV's 'despise myself' is misleading; the
New Jerusalem Bible is closer to the mark in translating it as
'I retract'. But we still face the question: what does Job retract?
Yahweh has not accused him of any sin, and indeed Yahweh
goes on to declare that Job alone has spoken correctly about
him (42:7ff). The verb *nahum* (translated here 'repent') usually
means 'to change one's mind', 'to abandon an opinion' (see
e.g. Ex. 32:12,14; Jer. 18:8,10; Am. 7:3,6). The image of 'dust
and ashes' describes the situation of Job before the dialogues
began, one of humiliation and lamentation. If we follow
Gutierrez in taking this to be the object of both verbs in the
sentence, we can then translate Job's response to mean: 'I
repudiate and abandon dust and ashes'.

This way of translating makes Job's response both coherent
and consistent with Yahweh's verdict about his servant. Job is
expressing not contrition as much as a decisive rejection of the
attitude of dejection and bitter complaint that had been his
until now. Job has now surrendered to love, a love that met

him in the heart of the whirlwind. His trust has been renewed, his horizons expanded, he now truly believes 'for nothing'. In recognizing God's freedom as well as his justice, *he has been released from the most subtle form of all forms of idolatry, namely, the desire to 'possess' God by imprisoning his dealings with humankind in a predictable, water-tight scheme.*

'What is it that Job has understood? That justice does not reign in the world God has created? No. The truth that he has grasped and that has lifted him to the level of contemplation is that justice alone does not have the final say about how we are to speak of God. Only when we have come to realize that God's love is freely bestowed do we enter fully and definitively into the presence of the God of faith. Grace is not opposed to the quest of justice nor does it play it down; on the contrary, it gives it its full meaning. God's love, like all true love, operates in a world not of cause and effect but of freedom and gratuitousness. That is how persons successfully encounter one another in a complete and unconditioned way: without payment of any kind of charges and without externally imposed obligations that pressure them into meeting the expectations of the other.'[5]

This is not the final word about suffering, least of all is it the final word about God. But it shatters our 'normal' human preconceptions, breaking open our hearts to await the message of a crucified saviour and an empty tomb . . . The God of the Bible gives us no theoretical answer to the mysteries of evil and suffering. I suspect that no 'answer' is possible, for evil in God's good world is a monstrous absurdity, an insane affront to One who is perfectly holy, true and loving. It is an enemy to be confronted and defeated, not a problem to be solved. Suffering and evil are so deeply embedded in our experience of human life that, in the attempt to turn them into intellectual problems for philosophical analysis, we may well lose a major key to their understanding, namely empathetic involvement in the suffering of others.

Epilogue

I began this chapter with the words of a Christian writer who married late in life, only to see his wife die a painful death from cancer within two years of their marriage. I close with another from an equally gifted compatriot of Lewis, Malcolm

Muggeridge, a journalist rather than an academic, who became a Christian late in life and used his formidable rhetorical skills to expose the shallowness behind much of our modern sophistication:

'Suffering crystallizes, as nothing else does, the dilemmas and nightmares of a life without God. It is an inflamed nerve which, touched, gives rise to howls of rage and anguish, especially today. Surely, when we can go to the moon, and ride through space faster than light; when our very genes are counted, and our organs replaceable; when we can arrange to eat without growing fat, to copulate without procreation, to flash a gleaming smile without being happy—surely suffering should be banished from our lives. That *we* should have to go on suffering, and watch others suffering, is an outrage; and a deity who, having the power to stop it, still allowed it to continue, would be a monster, not a loving God. So, Simone de Beauvoir, watching her mother die in agony of cancer, saw it as an "unjustifiable violation"; as something as "violent and unforeseen as an engine stopping in the middle of the sky". The image is significant. When machines jam and go wrong, we hate them utterly, and look round for a manufacturer or mechanic to curse. In the eyes of those who see men as machines, God is that manufacturer, and the mechanic his priest.'[6]

Notes

[1] C.S. Lewis, *A Grief Observed* (London: Faber & Faber, 1961) p. 23

[2] G. Gutierrez, *On Job: God-talk and the Suffering of the Innocent* (Maryknoll, NY: Orbis, Eng. tr. 1987) p. 69

[3] D. Atkinson, *The Message of Job* (Leicester: InterVarsity Press, 1991) p. 147

[4] Op. cit., p. 84

[5] Gutierrez, op. cit. pp. 87–8

[6] M. Muggeridge, *Something Beautiful For God* (London: Collins, 1971) p. 131

5

The Violence of Idols

'For every civilization, for every period of history, it is true to
say: "show me what kind of gods you have, and I will tell you
what kind of humanity you possess".'
    —*Emil Brunner (1889–1966), Man in Revolt*[1]

'Go on, have another', he urged, pushing a can of Foster's lager
towards me. The night was warm and the beer cost less than
a dollar, but I hesitated as Peter's salary was only twenty dollars
a month. Peter was a local church worker, but the university
professor I had met earlier in the day made only five dollars a
month more. Peter's wife had prepared a lavish meal, and a
TV set stood prominently in the living room like a shrine in
a Buddhist home. On most nights his two little boys would sit
transfixed, gazing uncomprehendingly at Oprah Winfrey and
Dynasty. I wondered where Peter got the money for all this.
'Oh the Lord provides', had been his pious answer. Later I
learned that, like most middle-class families, they were heavily
in debt to the loan-sharks.

After dinner I go for a stroll along the river, towards my
hotel. Huge billboards now deface the scenery, proclaiming
Scotch Whisky, American Cigarettes and Japanese Cameras. I
pass the old colonial hotel, once the only surviving monument
to the British Raj, recently renovated and now charging $220
per night. I had been there earlier in the day to ask the
receptionist and waitresses how much they were paid. $5 a
month, they had said, plus tips. Japanese and Hong Kong
businessmen, dressed in dark Amani suits and clutching their
Gucci attache cases, stream out onto the pavement and climb
into chauffeur-driven government vehicles. The military junta
has forcibly evicted people from the centre of the capital and
planted them in satellite towns, without any compensation, so
that prime land can be purchased by the new foreign companies that are being wooed into the country. An army jeep pulls
up. The driver siphons petrol out of the tank for passing

motorists (petrol is rationed, so this is a good way of making money). The military has bled this country dry. While the general hospital lacks essential drugs, the military hospital on the outskirts of the city boasts CT-Scans and Dialysis machines.

The next morning I read in the papers of young rural women being forcibly abducted by gangs for prostitution in the city, or sold to sex entrepreneurs in a neighbouring 'more developed' country. I also read of the dearth of seafood for local consumption as it is now all exported to hotels in Singapore and Hongkong to meet insatiable Chinese appetites. A cigarette factory is being set up by a Singaporean business venture. Arms are being sold to the junta by the Chinese, Singaporean and Thai governments. This country, I reflect, was once the rice bowl of Asia. I feel I am witnessing the opium trade of the last century, only now in reverse.

The historical allusions multiply as I run into a group of Singaporean and Australian Pentecostal Christians in my hotel. 'We are here to conduct seminars on church-planting', they inform me. The irony is just too much, and I crease up with laughter. '*You* want to teach *these* people church-planting?', I ask incredulously. (The churches here have produced more martyrs in the past decade than Singapore and Australia put together in their entire histories). Later that morning, I walk past one of the beautiful, golden pagodas that dot the landscape. Microphones blare out at the steady stream of devotees, exhorting the faithful poor to give money for the building of more pagodas. The more pagodas, the voice proclaims, the more peace in the country, and evil spirits will be warded off.

That night I reflect on Asia today: baffling, alluring, infuriating, exploited by its own people no less than by foreigners, preyed upon by the deities of the past and of the future . . .

5.1   Idol-formation

Idols, as we have seen, are creation substitutes for the God of creation. They elevate some aspect of the created order to the central place that the Creator alone occupies. They can take the form of mental concepts as well as physical objects. In fact, behind every physical image there lies a mental concept that gives the physical its alluring hold on us. Consider, for instance, one of the commonest examples we give when discussing idols: money.

I have before me a one-hundred rupee note. What is it that gives this piece of paper the value of one hundred rupees? Is it the price of the chemicals that have gone into it? Obviously not. It was a collective human decision to regard this particular piece of paper as carrying the value of one hundred rupees. It embodies a promise from the Central Bank that this piece of paper can be exchanged for a sum of goods worth one hundred rupees. In other words, it is we humans who define its value. It is our creation. (It is amusing to reflect that something as supposedly 'materialistic' as money can exist only through human trust and promise-keeping, that is on the moral realm which many businessmen and economists dismiss as irrelevant to the 'real world'!).

Let us follow what happens to money. After some time we forget that money is a human creation, that it is we who have defined it. Money now begins to define us, indeed to re-create us in its image. So my worth as a human being is now assessed on the basis of how much I earn, the amount of capital I have at my command. And whole human societies are assessed as 'developed' or 'undeveloped' on the basis of the level of capital accumulation that they have reached at a given moment in history. Instead of men and women controlling money, money now controls men and women. It dictates to us where we should live, what jobs we should do, how many children we should have, with whom we should mix and with whom we should not, what areas of knowledge should be developed and what should be neglected, and reaches into every nook and cranny of both public and private life. When men and women fall under the spell of money and cease to question its tyrannical hold on all human thinking, then they have become possessed by an idol— the god Jesus referred to as *Mammon* (an Aramaic term, the personification of wealth, representing the acquisitive spirit).

So it seems that behind every act of idolatry in human life, there lies a prior act of forgetfulness. In forgetting the true God to whom we belong and turning our backs on him, we end up forgetting that the works of our hands and minds are inferior to ourselves. By denying our nature—as creatures dependent on the Creator—we invite dependence on our own creations. This is why idolatry dehumanizes us. Our humanity is found in worship of the One who gives us life, life in all its fulness, and who calls us to share his glory as his image-bearers. Such worship enhances our humanness, but the worship of that which is inferior to us can only diminish our humanness by turning us into objects rather than persons.

We see this in the realm of science, for instance, when some influential theory (e.g. Darwinian evolution, the Gaia hypothesis) is misused to mount an assault on human dignity, to supposedly 'cut man down to size'; or when we stand in such awe before our technologies (e.g. AI systems) that we put them on pedestals and surrender our freedom to them. Or consider Marx's theory of historical materialism: it quickly forgot its origins in the fertile mind of a middle-class European, acquired an objective reality as 'scientific law' and was allowed to act back on human lives, controlling entire societies all over the world— with disastrous results!

Or take the concepts of *nation* and *ethnicity* which have come to dominate political life in modern times. When we forget that these are human creations, we give them a power over us which they do not otherwise possess, and we find ourselves indulging in actions on their behalf (e.g. lying, stealing, killing others) which we may not normally do as individuals. The nation-state, despite its declining influence in today's world, still expects me to put its interests before that of family, clan or the global human community. In return it promises me protection from violence against my person and property, equality of respect before the law, and a steadily improving standard of living. It is largely the failure of the nation-state to fulfil its promises that gives rise to the disintegration of states into ethnic blocs that we see all over the world. Such ethnic identities have a more powerful emotional hold on people, and the violence associated with them is often a mirror-image of violence perpetrated in the name of the nation-state. Paradoxically, such ethno-nationalisms are both counter-reactions to modernity and also attempts to seize the fruits of modernity by means of the apparatus of the state. This is no longer true of only Third World or newly modernizing countries. The recent 'separatist' identity among large sections of the Afro-American population in the USA is both a counter to, and a mirror of, the tribalism of white American society (though among the latter it has usually gone by the name of 'patriotism').

Similarly, the market mechanism for allocating resources was raised to a semi-divine status by Adam Smith's (1723–

1790) occult notion of an 'invisible hand' steering human self-interest to socially beneficent ends. He wrote of the entrepreneur that:

> he intends only his own gain, and he is in this, as in many other cases, led by an invisible hand to promote an end which was not part of his intention . . . By pursuing his own interest he frequently promotes that of the society more effectually than when he really intends to promote it.[2] For Smith, the 'invisible hand' was more than a figure of speech and more than an expression of the fact that human actions have unforeseen effects. It was the *deus ex machina* of his economics. Smith shared the optimistic eighteenth-century Enlightenment outlook on human progress, an outlook that often went hand-in-hand with a Newtonian model of determinate forces ordered by a benign divine Regulator. Smith and his most famous critic, Karl Marx, seem to have had more in common where their world-views were concerned than many of their disciples acknowledge.

Smith has been associated, rather unfairly, with the nine-teenth-century advocates of *laissez-faire* capitalism and their counterparts in the post-Thatcher/Reagan era in the West. Smith's concern was to defend free trade against mercantilist arguments that a strong government was needed to protect the interests of producers. Many of the mercantilist writers were themselves merchants who saw their own interests as best served by a nation-state which used economic policy as a means of reinforcing its own power. Smith rejected any action by government which discriminated against some citizens by supporting the interests of others. But while he opposed any government intervention in the operation of markets, he was aware of the responsibility of government to protect human welfare. Invoking 'the system of natural liberty' he defined three duties of government, the latter two proving a source of embarrassment to advocates of 'minimalist' government who look to Smith for support: namely, the 'duty of protecting, as far as possible, every member of the society from the injustice or oppression of every other member of it', and 'the duty of erecting and maintaining certain public works and certain public institutions which can never be for the interest of any individual or small number of individuals . . .'[3] Under the head of this third duty, he supported publicly-financed education. He also warned against 'the mean rapacity, the monopolizing spirit of merchants and manufacturers, who neither are, nor ought to be, the rulers of mankind',[4] and fiercely condemned eighteenth-century imperialism as a means of assisting home industries. (What Smith did not foresee was the degeneration of nineteenth-century liberalism into imperialism, the securing of 'open' markets and raw materials by military force, and that it would be a free trading country, Great Britain, which would become the biggest empire of all. Indians and Chinese remember 'free trade' as something imposed on them by coercion).

There are reasons, then, for believing that Smith would be horrified by the modern alliance of big business interests with political parties (in the most 'liberal' of states), and the combination of private wealth and public squalour that has come to characterize American and European cities at the end of the twentieth century. Smith may be the patron saint of capitalism and neo-classical economics, but like all such saints his texts are used selectively by his devotees. While commentators may disagree among themselves as to how Smith is to be read, there is no doubt that many modern economists and governments have made of 'market forces' a quasi-religious deity far more powerful than anything worshipped in pre-modern cultures. And, in the name of that deity, they have thrown men and women out of work, added insult to injury by blaming the poor for their own poverty, justified the ruthless accumulation of wealth by a few, and squandered the earth's non-renewable resources. As 'market forces' increasingly encroach on every aspect of human life, human beings are reduced to 'consumers', human behaviour to 'self-interest', human society to 'competitive individuals', and the worth of every human endeavour to 'cost-effectiveness' . . .

5.2 The New Demons

It is here that the biblical language of demonology may be appropriate for our modern societies. For, whether we take demons to refer to invisible sentient beings or as the 'spiritual ethos' of warped cosmic and human structures, it is evident that not only are individuals 'possessed' by such malignant powers but so are entire societies at various epochs in their history. Thus the Croatian theologian Miroslav Volf, reflecting on the recent conflict in the Balkans, marvels at how 'once the conflict started it seemed to trigger an uncontrollable chain reaction'. He writes: 'Of course, the big and strategic moves that started the conflict and that keep it going are made in the centres of intellectual, political, and military power. But there is too much will for brutality even among the common people . . . These were decent people, helpful neighbours. They did not, strictly speaking, *choose* to plunder and burn, rape and torture—or secretly enjoy these things. A dormant beast in them was awakened from its uneasy slumber.'[5] In a footnote in his paper Volf also quotes the words of Carl Gustav Jung, written on the eve of World War II: 'The impressive thing about the German phenomenon is that one man, who is obviously "possessed", has infected a whole nation to such an extent that everything is set in motion and has started rolling on its course towards perdition.'[6] When human beings give to any aspect of God's creation (for instance, sexuality and/or fertility) or to the works of their hands (e.g. science, the nation-state, the market mechanism) the worship that is due to the Creator alone, they call up invisible forces that eventually dominate them. When what is meant to be a servant is treated as a master, it quickly becomes a tyrant.

This is seen in every human project: once a project acquires a certain size and becomes invested with human dreams of 'progress' or of 'liberation', it attains a life of its own, dragging human beings and societies in its wake. It is also seen in the mega-corporations and bureaucracies of the modern world. No one is any longer in control. There is no one who bears responsibility when things go wrong. Having surrendered our hearts, individually and collectively, to idols, we become enslaved by demons. Such demons always demand human sacrifices: whether in the name of 'patriotism', 'revolution' or 'scientific progress'. So the cult of idolatry leads to the sacrifice of the weak and apparently useless members of society (from foetuses to other ethnic groups, to the infirm or the mentally handicapped), to the destruction of the earth's eco-systems and the abdication of human responsibility for the planet.

Idols are sustained and animated by belief-systems which disguise their role in human affairs. These belief-systems (or *ideologies*, which after Marx have acquired the pejorative sense of 'theoretical reason corrupted by self-interest') lend an air of legitimacy to every idol. Thus we may call *nationalism* the ideology that encourages uncritical allegiance to one's nation over other communities by fostering myths about ancestral heroes, sacred territory, a united past, the superiority of traditional customs and systems of knowledge, etc. It thus justifies acts of violence against all those deemed to be outside the nation and boosts the credibility of those who assume the mantle of 'leaders of the nation'. One of the persistent illusions of our time is that nationalism will die out with the spread of modernity. On the contrary, even as distances shrink and markets extend their global reach, national and ethnic divisions, far from attenuating in strength, grow ever more militant. We observed that the nationalism of the nation-state (which was characteristic of the early period of modernity) is giving way not so much to a new globalism as to the nationalism of ethnic identity (in the later phase of modernity). This movement lies at the heart of contemporary political life, from Quebec to New Zealand.

Similarly *scientism* becomes the ideology that puts scientific practice and theories beyond the reach of moral and philosophical criticism. By using a narrow concept of science to define what counts as knowledge and excluding all other truth-claims as not worth bothering about, it consolidates the power of scientists and technocrats in society. We have seen how religions have often been the most powerful ideologies in human societies, but the greatest suffering of the twentieth century has been inflicted by the militantly secular ideologies of Marxism, capitalism, scientism and nationalism. They are still rampant across the globe.

The dominant economic ideology now uncritically promulgated by American and European governments and schools of management is that the sole criterion for corporate decisions is return on investment capital. Any other consideration, such as corporate social responsibility or a 'social return' on capital, is arbitrarily ruled out of court as a distortion of economic rationality. Thus, in the name of this entrenched ideology, the wellbeing of millions in the present generation is destroyed for the sake of the putative wellbeing of future generations. This is one of the most bizarre features of the late twentieth-century: capitalism, in the form practised in America and Europe today and propagated throughout the world, seems to be behaving as Stalinism and Maoism did only a few decades ago.

Idolatries feed on one another. Nationalism and the cult of

violent revolution have often bred together. Today, in events such as the Olympics or the World Cups in football and cricket, Mammon, nationalism, and the idolatry of sport reinforce each other in global competition.

Impoverished Third World countries spend lavish funds on the construction of showpiece stadiums and the hosting of international contests. It is the usual practice for the police and city officials to sweep away beggars and shanty towns in the local environs so that an image of respectability could be projected on TV screens around the world. The shanty towns return once the cameras move away. Likewise, Scientism and Mammon come together in the huge armaments industries which fuel the engines of war. Sometimes they develop in reaction to other idolatries, as we saw in the case of Marx and Freud. In the bloody conflict in Sri Lanka, Tamil nationalism developed as a reaction to post-independence Sinhala–Buddhist nationalism which, in turn, was a reaction to the imperialisms of the European powers. Many former colonies still suffer from nationalist ideologies which are almost reflex reactions to the Western ideologies of scientism, consumerism and capitalism. They are all part of a search for self-identity and true community, but by isolating one aspect of reality and blowing it up into an all-embracing worldview they only become mirror-images of the very ideologies that they oppose.

We can never get away from the creation of idols and ideologies, for the human spirit hungers for meaning to life and does not find fulfilment with the merely material. Humankind, unlike the rest of the animal kingdom, does not live by bread alone. We live on meanings. It is only when the material world acquires some spiritual significance through an act of symbolic re-creation that it becomes the object of our attention: either as a servant or as an idol. An idol is usually some aspect of God's good creation. Its evil lies in the place it occupies in human thinking and feeling. It was never meant to be God and it cannot be God. Hence the cycles of disillusionment and despair that we go through, whether as individuals or whole societies.

In the prophetic mockery of idols and of idolatry that we find in the Bible, attention is often drawn to the dehumanizing effects, on individuals and on societies, of such false worship. For instance:

Their idols are silver and gold
made by the hands of men.
They have mouths, but cannot speak,
eyes, but they cannot see;
they have ears, but cannot hear,
noses, but they cannot smell;
they have hands, but they cannot feel,
feet, but they cannot walk;
nor can they utter a sound with their throats.
Those who make them will be like them,
and so will all who trust in them (Psalm 115:4–8).

Note the shattering conclusion: we become like what we worship.

The logic of this psalm follows from the biblical doctrine of humanness. We are created in the image of the God whose true likeness is disclosed to us in the human figure of Jesus Christ. Worship involves a restoration of our 'fallen' humanity to this true definition of what it means to be human. We may not notice this transformation into Christ-like humanness, but others will. Likewise, when we worship that in whose image we were *not* created it *will* show in our lives. It will show in the way we treat ourselves and the way we treat other human beings.

Consequently, it is not surprising that those who worship technology eventually develop machine-like personalities: emotionally under-developed, shallow in their relationships, driven by a desire to control and quantify every human situation, unable to appreciate beauty and value in anything outside the artificial. Those who worship sex, on the other hand, are incapable of trust and commitment in their human relationships and hide a lonely existence behind a mask of superficial 'adulthood'. A society in which sex is an idol is one that reaps huge social costs: for it leads to the abuse of children, violence against women, the breakup of marriages and family life, and the exploitation of the weak and vulnerable by the huge pornographic industry. Those who worship power live in a constant climate of suspicion, insecurity and fear. The only effective antidote to power is a vision of the One who having all power at his command, humbled himself, embracing the role of a lowly servant to unmask and dethrone the powers that have ravaged his world.

The created order, for all its splendour, is still transient, caught up in decay. That is the basic truth which the Buddha affirmed along with the Hebrew prophets (e.g. Is. 40:6ff). But the latter—and the rest of the Bible— sees this as only a relative, partial truth: if the creation does not possess the power to give life and meaning, it is because its own life and meaning depend on the word of the Creator. The worship of that which is transient only reinforces the awareness of our own tran-sience. The death at work in human life is far from being 'natural' or 'normal'. It is an abnormal intrusion, a sign of the Creator's judgement on human sin. In choosing to worship that which is subject to decay and death, we choose decay and death as our final destiny. But there is One who claimed to have come 'to give life, life in all its fulness' (Jn. 10:10). There is a new life that awaits those who, in their present state of decay and death, look neither to the created order nor to the works of their hands for meaning and self-identity, but rather to the life-giving Creator. The physical resurrection of Jesus is the Creator's vindication of the created order: it is his pledge of the renewal of all things under the rule of that same Jesus (e.g. Col. 1: 19,20; Phil. 2:9–11; 1Cor. 15:20ff), the final marriage of heaven and earth when the creation, made whole, will participate in his glory (e.g. Is. 65:17ff; 25:6–8; Rom. 8:18ff).

5.3   Development as Ideology

Words and images are more powerful instruments of domina-tion than armies, machines or bureaucrats. This is why every great social revolutionary has known that structural transfor-mation in itself is superficial. A semantic revolution, which transforms the meanings of words and images used by the ruling classes, is a fundamental pre-requisite for effective change.

Development is one of those words which, far from being innocuous, has served to reinforce the hold of modern idols over vast populations in the Third World (or, the South, to use a geographically appropriate term). It has become a source of propaganda for a particular way of life. In other words, it is an ideology. This should not come as a surprise when we remember its origins in the colonial enterprise of the last century. The Indian political and cultural analyst Ashis Nandy has spoken of two forms of colonization. The carriers of the first were 'people who, unlike the rapacious first generation of bandit-kings who conquered the colonies, sought to be helpful. They were well-meaning, hardworking, middle-class missionaries, liberals, modernists, and believers in science, equality and progress.' The second stage of colonization, 'the one which at least six generations of the Third World have learned to view as a prerequisite for their liberation—the colonizing of minds, based on the generalization of the concept of the modern West from a geographical and temporal entity to a psychological category'.[7] From 'westernization' to 'modernization' to 'development': images that turned the West, whether in its capitalist or socialist expressions, into the definer of the 'good life' for men and women across the globe.

Not surprisingly, 'development' became a neo-colonial project through which an aggressive, expanding Corporation Culture sought to establish a bridgehead among the political and commercial elites of the Third World. The attraction of 'development' is that it *has* brought substantial improvements in health care, education and general well-being to scores of people inmany countries. But it has, more often than not, given legitimacy to the acquisition and control of other peoples' resources, inevitably increasing poverty and distress under the guise of eliminating them. In the name of 'national development' (usually identified with 'the national interest') whole generations have been induced to accept enormous sacrifices in personal freedoms, the mutilation of their cultural endowments and the destruction of their physical and moral environments.

It never ceases to amaze me how many Christians, in the North and the South, continue to refer to the former as the 'developed' and the latter as the 'developing' world. When we in the South use this term to describe ourselves, we are evaluating ourselves by a set of cultural values that are alien to our own cultures, let alone to a biblical world-view! All our normative images and yardsticks of 'development' are ideologically 'loaded'. Who dictates that mushrooming TV ariels and skyscrapers are signs of 'development'? Who, apart from the automobile industry and the advertising agencies, seriously believes that a country with six-lane highways and multi-story car-parks is more 'developed' than one whose chief mode of transport is railways? Does the fact that there are more telephone lines in Manhatten, New York, than in the whole of sub-saharan Africa, mean that human communication is more developed in the former than the latter?

I have experienced greater generosity and sacrificial hospitality at the hands of poor peasants than I have from the very rich. The latter live barricaded behind high walls, are cocooned from reality in their air-conditioned Mercedes Benzes and BMWs, and even employ private armies to protect their family and property. Their lives are marked by fear, anxiety and boredom. By what criterion is a society that fosters the numerical increase of such people regarded as 'developed'? I do not hesitate to say that there is more genuine humanness—judged by biblical values of interpersonal relations, contentment, enjoyment of nature—in spite of all the cruelties and hardships, in a rural Indian village than in, say, a super-rich American suburb like Beverley Hills. Yet it is to the latter that urban people in the Third World are exposed in their media (even the blacks they see on their TV screens are all living in the lap of luxury!). It is not surprising that such images, which appeal to the acquisitive instinct in all of us, are the breeding ground for competitiveness, greed and violence.

The commonest measure of 'development' (on the basis of which entire societies are classified hierarchically) is the Gross National Product per capita. That improving levels of income are an important aspect of human well-being (for they raise the possibility of being free from material hardships), I do not deny. But GNP per capita tells us nothing about the *distribution* of income in a given society. It is a well-observed fact that, even as the GNP per capita increases by leaps and bounds, the purchasing power of whole segments of the population may decline and the levels of absolute poverty in the country actually increase. As we saw in Chapter 2, no *Christian* assessment of human well-being can ignore the issue of distributive justice, the access of the poor to the wealth that is generated. Moreover, a nation's GNP only indicates the volume of circulation of goods and services in the economy. It tells us nothing about the quality of those goods and services: are they beneficial or harmful, do they enrich or damage life, do they meet the actual needs of the community? It is perfectly possible to have a society with a high GNP per capita, thriving solely on the manufacture and export of armaments, heroin, tobacco and pornography. Would such a society be regarded as 'developed'? It would under the present ideology.

Those who subscribe to this creed of 'development-as-increasing GNP' also tend to be strong advocates of global population control. Unless obligatory limits are placed on the size of families in poor nations, they urge, not only will these nations lag behind in the 'development' race but the burden on the earth's environmental resources will grow at a catastrophic rate. This is a controversial and complex issue. But it is interesting to observe that such arguments always emerge only among the affluent nations and the pockets of affluence in poor nations. They fail to point out that the average American child consumes twenty times as much of the earth's resources as the average Chinese or Indian child. They also ignore the experience of the industrialized West and many parts of the Third World today that fertility rates come down with the expansion of basic education (especially for women), access to good medical care (thus reducing infant mortality rates), and income-generating employment. Large families are more often a result, than the cause, of poverty. Given a real opportunity to choose a smaller family without dire social and economic consequences, the poor do choose smaller families. Hence the doubly ideological character of an exclusive emphasis on population control as a means to 'development': it promotes the latter while protecting the living standards of the rich from being challenged.

In its reports since 1990 the United Nations Development Programme has sought to introduce another yardstick—a Human Development Index (HDI)—which gives equal weight to three factors: GNP per capita, average adult lifespan, and mean years of schooling. This is a welcome move away from the narrowness of earlier concepts of development. It recognizes that what men and women do with their lives is more important than their mere possession of income and commodities. The underlying philosophy of the reports seems to be the classical humanist approach (reaching back to Aristotle) that wealth is only an instrument towards the enhancement of the *quality* of human life. But the HDI is still imprisoned within a questionable framework of measurement. Life expectancy at birth continues to increase in many of our 'developing' countries, but so does the number of children born maimed physically and mentally through the growing incidences of harmful drugs, contaminated food and water supplies. Also, which would men and women prefer—to live fifty years of a full life, loved and wanted in a community of family and friends, or to live till eighty and die unloved and unwanted in a home for the aged? As for schooling, what is its content and quality? We have all met folk who are unschooled yet wise and cultured, and others who have many years of schooling behind them who are uncouth and ignorant.

Likewise with other common indicators such as doctors per 1000 population: does this really indicate the level of health care in a community? Improvements in health depend more on the provision of sanitation and clean public water supplies than on doctors and hospitals. Nor can it address the deeper questions of the nature of drugs dispensed and the suppression of indigenous resources in health care. I raise these questions, not to be perverse, but to show the ambivalence at the heart of these indices of 'development'.

The UNDP defines human development as a process of expanding 'the range of people's choices'.[8] The HDI is then to be seen as a measure of people's ability to live a long and healthy life, to participate in the life of the community and to have sufficient resources to obtain a decent living. It recognizes that these are 'not the sum-total of human life' and urges that human development must be 'development of the people *for* the people *by* the people'. 'Development *of* the people means investing in human capabilities, whether in education or health or skills, so that they can work productively and creatively. Development *for* the people means ensuring that the economic growth they generate is distributed widely and fairly . . . and development by the people [means] giving everyone a chance to participate.'[9] Their report admits that 'we are witnessing a new and disturbing phenomenon: jobless growth', and calls on policy-makers to pursue development strategies that will give people access to 'productive and renumerative employment'.[10]

There is much in this that, as Christians, we can endorse. The biblical concept of human stewardship (which we explored briefly in Chapter 3) demands that all people everywhere have the right not only to participate in the fruits of wealth-creation but in the process of wealth-creation itself. The expansion of private incomes is conducive to justice only if, at the same time, it expands the ability for public action in improving the living conditions of the worst off and thus contributing towards distributional equity. Also, the focus on human beings is a refreshing change from the opulence-oriented reporting of most 'development' economists. It is ultimately human persons who matter, not as a means of production and national prosperity (so-called 'human capital'), but as ends in themselves.

But the UNDP reports still operate within the discourse of 'development', and the latter is still defined by those who stand outside those societies that are to be 'developed'. If any process of 'development' recognizes the dignity of the poor, then governments and NGOs must listen to the views of the poor themselves as to what choices they would like to see expanded! When it comes to something as fundamental as food and drink, for instance, the rising incomes of the 'developing' poor may well mean that they now have a choice between Coca Cola and Pepsi. But they may still have no choice when it comes to drinking clean water! And what about the choice to reject completely the project of 'development'—how realistic an option is that in the present global political and commercial climate? Despite the emphasis on the 'empowerment' of the poor, a paternalistic attitude seems still to be perpetuated by the report's concept of 'development'.

Modernity *does* expand choice. Indeed this is often taken to be its chief defining characteristic. But it also forecloses others. When it comes to transport, for instance, in the modern cities of North America, I am compelled to own or hire a car and I *must* drive through large sections of the city with my doors locked and windows shut. Back home, in 'developing' Sri Lanka, I have a choice of walking, bicycling, taking a bus or auto-rickshaw, or driving a car . . . Seen from this perspective, much of the North must be considered 'developing' or even 'undeveloped'. The UNDP report recognizes that when the HDI profile is drawn up for ethnic communities rather than nation-states, the United States has an ambivalent status. Whites rank number 1 in the world (ahead of Japan), blacks rank number 31 (next to Trinidad and Tobago) and Hispanics rank number 35 (next to Estonia).[11] Similarly, there are marked inequalities between men and women in Japan. Women's average earnings are only 51% of those of men, and women are largely excluded from decision-making positions. They hold only 7% of administrative and managerial jobs. So, although the 1993 HDI puts Japan first as a 'developed' nation, when the index is adjusted for gender disparity, Japan slips to rank 17.

Perhaps the underlying problem here is the attempt to *quantify* and so calculate human 'development'. But only certain cultural definitions can be quantified (income level being the most obvious). How do we mathematically measure the climate of fear in a community? Or the breakdown of personal relationships, the vulnerability of the disabled and elderly, unhappiness among ethnic minorities, declining quality in education and health services, the loss of cultural heritage, the homogenizing of tastes, and the deterioration in natural environments? These are some of the ways in which, as a Christian, I would want to assess the health of a society. And, on these bases, I would want to affirm that in some ways I live in a much more 'developed' society than many in the North, and in other ways a much more 'under-developed' society than many in the North.

The quantification of 'development' is part of its ideological function. For it calls into being a new breed of 'development experts' and a new 'science' of 'development economics'. It has given not only employment but prominent social status to the directors of numerous 'development' institutions that have suddenly mushroomed all over the Third World. The international experts sell their services to Third World governments. They form the third component of the new triumvirate, alongside local politicians and wealthy industrialists. They live, move and have their being in the first-class compartments of aircraft and the business lounges of five-star hotels—from which they conduct seminars on the alleviation of poverty.

Most prominent among these experts are the men from the World Bank and the IMF. It is often forgotten that both these institutions are basically money-lenders. Those of us in the Third World who suffer under repressive or arbitrary political rule are grateful that the IMF and World Bank have recently begun to use Aid (an often misleading euphemism for a commercial loan) as a lever to hold national governments more accountable to their own people and to international opinion. The inclusion of environmental accounting in projects funded by the World Bank is also welcome, given the notorious laxity of most Third World governments in this regard.

However, there is another side to this coin. The IMF and

the World Bank themselves dangerously undermine the very struggle for democracy, in several ways. Firstly, these institutions represent power without corresponding responsibility. They are accountable to no one save themselves. They can impose unpopular policies on national governments and simply stand by and watch as these governments are toppled either by bloody *coup d'etats* or a disgruntled electorate. Despite their enormous influence on local populations, they have few mechanisms to receive intelligent feedback from the grassroots. Governments rise and governments fall, but like Tennyson's brook the World Bank and the IMF go on forever.

Secondly, the IMF has a standard 'development package' which it pushes as a universal panacea for all economic problems: simply privatize everything, reduce government spending (especially on welfare measures), liberalize trade, attract foreign capital. It seems more concerned with balancing books than alleviating poverty. Since these measures usually aggravate economic inequalities, and hence create social tensions, they can usually be imposed only by governments which have no moral scruples about suppressing dissent and using excessive force against their own populations. Little wonder that the largest dealings of the IMF and the World Bank in the Third World in the past have been with ruthless local dictators. So it seems that the standard formula runs counter to the expressed intention of these institutions to press for greater political freedoms in debtor countries. Either the formula or the intention will have to go. The formula itself is based on outdated economic theories which have been discredited again and again in Western societies.

Thirdly, the idea of a standard package that applies to all nations, irrespective of their widely differing histories, cultures and situation within the global order, is itself a denial of human dignity. It deals with abstractions and not human persons. As such, it fails to recognize the distinctively human elements in economic progress. It ignores the wisdom of those who have argued that a range of development strategies should be pursued by Third World nations, and that piecemeal changes to the economy are better than sudden and massive changes prompted by a political ideology. Given the failure of Reagan/ Thatcher-type 'economic miracles', it is refreshing to note that more and more economists in the West are coming round to admitting that they know less and less about the way modern economies work. Charles Goodhart, initially advisor to the Thatcher government, coined what has come to be known as Goodhart's Law: 'The moment some econometric correlation is taken as the basis for government policy, that correlation no longer applies'! This new-found humility, though, seems sadly to be lacking among both the foreign experts and high-paid 'consultants' who grace our shores and also local decision-makers.

Not only have the IMF/World Bank prescriptions for ailing economies rarely met with success, but they also appear to us as blatantly hypocritical. For instance, the USA is the world's largest debtor nation, with a budget deficit which is greater than the total Gross National Product of almost all African and Latin American countries put together. But it can simply pass on this deficit to the rest of the world as long as Japan and Europe keep buying the dollars it prints. Moreover, no Western society has been purely capitalist: they have been mixed economies, usually with legislation and welfare programmes in place which cushion the poor from the harsh aspects of the market. American and European governments subsidize their farmers and rush to prop up high-employment industries which may be in danger of collapse. Yet the US government and the IMF tie their Third World loans to demands that Third World governments cut back on their local food subsidies (a move that leads to a rise in malnutrition) and at the same time open its markets to Western transnational corporations, a move that often leads to the collapse of indigenous industries and the ownership of national assets by foreign businessmen. It has been estimated that the working of global markets represent an annual loss of opportunity to Third World countries amounting to $500 billion—ten times what they receive in foreign assistance.[12]

The argument that totally unfettered trade among societies (at all levels of economic, social, and political development) is an unqualified good, and will eventually lead to a better life for all, relies on the experience of the advanced industrial countries since the end of the Second World War.

All these countries protected their fledgling industries in the early years of their own economic growth, and Japan, an industrially backward nation in 1945, prospered through a policy of domestic protectionism and exploitation of open markets in the US and Europe. Moreover, despite its rhetoric of 'free trade', the US and the European Union continue to shield sensitive areas such as agriculture from foreign competition. In the words of Arthur Schlesinger, who served as a special advisor to the Kennedy administration: 'If the criteria of the IMF had governed the United States in the nineteenth century, our own economic development would have taken a good deal longer. In preaching fiscal orthodoxy to developing nations, we were somewhat in the position of the prostitute who, having retired on her earnings, believes that public virtue requires the closing down of the red-light district.'[13]

To oppose state and market, the public and private sectors, is obviously as foolish as it is unhistorical. In no currently affluent society has the private sector ever been able to provide, say, a good health service or an efficient transport service for the entire populace. In most Third World countries government spending on public enterprises—and especially in the crucial areas of primary health care and education—is proportionately much smaller than in the Western world. In the newly affluent countries of East Asia, governments have invested heavily in infrastructure development and the training of an industrial workforce. The provision of housing, basic health care and elementary education have been seen as falling within the purview of the state. The flourishing of private enterprise does not require the abdication of responsibility on the part of the political leadership. Rather the opposite: laws which curb property speculation and the abuse of the financial markets by a few powerful 'sharks' actually make good economic sense in addition to being morally compelling.

Of course it would be foolish to use the IMF, World Bank and Western governments as scapegoats for the economic mess in many parts of the Third World. While Christians in the West should be ruthlessly exposing the hypocrisy and complicity of their governments and financial institutions in perpetuating global economic injustice, we who live in the poorer countries of the world also have a responsibility to remind our political leaders, academics and business elites of their own hypocrisy and complicity in structural evil. Consider, for example, a country like Sri Lanka. Through a combination of short-sighted policies ('get rich quick'), ethnic and religious chauvinisms, corruption, nepotism and autocratic politics, we have succeeded in turning a lavishly endowed, highly literate and stable country into one of the poorest, most violent and crime-infested societies in the world. Our sorry dependance on the IMF and World Bank is a tacit admission of our own failures in leadership, in politics as much as in commerce.

Indeed, many governments of the South have an appalling record when it comes to meeting the basic needs of their people in priority areas such as health, education and shelter. Massive sums are spent on military expenditure in some of the poorest countries of Africa and Asia. Pakistan boasts of possessing some of the world's best fighter jets and anti-aircraft systems, and invests six times as much on its military as on health, education and agricultural extension *combined*. But Northern governments aid and abet such wasteful military expenditure and corruption in the South. Condemnation of autocratic rule in the South is hypocritical when it is America and Europe that supply the autocrats with the weapons of destruction, often used against their own people. That some of the most corrupt and brutal regimes have been the staunchest allies of the 'free world' is a well-known and scandalous fact of recent political history. Even that arch-fiend of the American media, Sadam Hussein, was installed in power by a *coup d'etat* which had the backing of the CIA. It was only when the puppet started pulling the strings, and American strategic interests in the region began to be threatened, that the US government embarked on its moral and military crusade against Iraq. There has never been a shortage of think-tank pundits and media personalities on hand to explain how these shifts of political alliance contribute to making the world safe for democracy and capitalism.

5.4   A Watery Chaos: Genesis 6–9

There are two well-known stories in the early chapters of the Bible which illuminate the spread of human violence and God's response to it. The first is the story of the Flood and the rescue of Noah and the animals in the ark (Gen. 6–9). The story is set against the spreading moral chaos in human life and God's purpose for the whole of creation. The earth which in Gen 1:31 was 'very good' is now seen by God as 'corrupt . . . and filled with violence' (6:11,12). The cause of the Flood is the wickedness of the human heart, for 'every imagination of the thoughts of his heart was only evil continually' (6:5). It is a wickedness which, like the blood of Abel (4:10), cries to the divine Judge for judgement. It is the culmination of humanity's refusal to recognize God-given limits, in other words to live within a structured world in which both physical and moral laws operate.

Sin has now become a reversal of the creation order. And so the sovereign God decrees judgement, and as is so often the case with the judgement of God, he allows the full-blown results of sin and wickedness to be their own judgement. Men who abandon God find themselves abandoned by God.

What is to be destroyed (6:13) has already destroyed itself (6:12). And the form that destruction will take is awesomely appropriate: a reversal of the creation pattern (compare 1:9ff). The creation will be 'unmade', returning to the primordial chaos. In other words, humankind's moral chaos results in a physical chaos which will sweep mankind way.

So the Flood is not the vengeful act of a capricious God. It is a picture of what happens when human beings abdicate God-given responsibility for each other and for the earth. The non-human creation was intended to blossom and flourish in harmony with humans who themselves were intended to live in loving obedience to God. Consequently, the return to chaos bears witness to the disobedience of humankind. The Flood story has been re-enacted many times in our own generation as the idolization of violence, technology and mammon have wreaked destructive wars and environmental disasters which, in turn, threaten to destroy all life on earth.

But there is another thread that runs through the story, and that is God's gracious and intimate concern for his own. We read that the sight of human wickedness and the corruption of the earth through violence 'grieved him to his heart' (6:6). The words convey both anger and anguish. The fact that this is figurative language should not blind us to the truth that God suffers in the face of what we do with ourselves and with the non-human creation. It is the 'risk' he bore in bringing into being a *creation* in contrast to a machine. It is the vulnerability of creative love. God himself feels the pain of a twisted world. In the words of the American philosopher Nicholas Wolterstorff, grieving over the death of his son in a mountaineering accident, 'Suffering is down at the centre of things, deep down where the meaning is. Suffering is the meaning of our world. For love is the meaning. And love suffers. The tears of God are the meaning of history.'[14] Indeed the wrath of God is the other side of his loving involvement with us. The opposite of love is not wrath, but indifference. To ask God to be indifferent to sin is to ask him to cease to love. Any other God, stemming from speculative philosophy rather than biblical revelation, is an idol.

The conflict between the 'God of the Philosophers' and the 'God of the Cross' was at the heart of the 16th-century Protestant Reformation. To Martin Luther (1483–1546), the God revealed in the humanness and death of Jesus Christ exposed the barrenness of the armchair theorizing of the scholastic theologians in the late medieval period. The latter were influenced by the great Greek philosophers, Aristotle being the most famous. God was the First Cause and the Final Cause in the chain of causality that makes up the universe, the Prime Mover of all change, all-powerful and untouched by the actions of his creatures. His existence could be proved by inductive argument from the works of creation, and his qualities could be inferred by analogy with those same works. Luther regarded such a God as an empty, if not boring, concept. What really mattered was the question: what does God think of *me*? The experiences of life repeatedly speak against the possibility of God really being interested in *me*. 'Reason plays blindman's buff with God; it makes all kinds of attempts to grasp him but always without success. It invariably misses him . . . Therefore it simply jumps in and gives divine titles and honour to what it thinks is God, while never actually hitting upon the true God . . . So there is a great difference between knowing *that* there is a God and knowing *who* he is and what he is like. Nature knows the first and it is written in all our hearts. The second is taught only by the Holy Spirit.'[15]

Despite humanity's sin, God will not let humanity go. Out of that sinful humanity his grace finds Noah. While the story of the Flood speaks of chaos and divine judgement, the story of Noah is the story of God's gracious love and Noah's response of faithful obedience to that love. Twice in the narrative we are told 'Noah did all that the LORD had commanded him' (6:22;7:5). On his obedience to God hangs the future of the animals too. Here the creation mandate (1:27ff;2:15–20) is being fulfilled: human life and animal life are bound up together in the future of creation. Thus the waters of judgement are also the means of preservation and continuity. Noah becomes a 'type' of the coming Saviour of the world: he passes through the watery grave, but by his willing obedience rescues those of his family who trust in him and in his God. He becomes the mediator of a covenant of unconditional blessing between God and all life on earth, human and non-human (9:8ff).

In a wise meditation on the Flood narrative and the modern threat of nuclear holocaust, Richard Bauckham observes that it is this Noahic covenant that enables us to see the full horror of nuclear weapons. They threaten to destroy the creation which God himself, despite his grief over its despoliation by human sin, has pledged himself to preserve. They threaten not only the human creation but also the animal creation for which God has made humanity responsible and which he made Noah responsible for preserving even through the Flood. 'In seizing the godlike power to destroy God's creation, which God himself in the Noahic covenant pledged himself not to use, nuclear weapons express humanity's refusal to fulfil the divine image in imitation of God and their determination instead to be gods in their own right.'[16]

Bauckham, however, also suggests that the Flood story can give us 'a new quality of awareness' of God and the world and ourselves: 'To read the Flood narrative with sensitivity to its original import is to acquire a renewed sense of the world in which we live as God's gift to us. As we see its destruction withheld only by God's patience and mercy, we find the world we take for granted becomes once again the world continually granted to us by God's grace. With Noah we lose the world and find it again, finding it the more valuable in its newly experienced relationship to God.'[17]

As the story unfolds, we see that the infection of sin has set into Noah's family too. As civilization spreads throughout the earth after the Flood, we are reminded again that 'every inclination of the human heart is evil from childhood' (8:21). But God wills history to continue. He himself is deeply involved in that story. Noah, the man who walked with God and trusted him when all around was chaos, ends up a sorry figure: humiliated through drink (another example of a gift of creation that quickly became an idol?). So it turns out that the experience of being saved through the Flood did not effect the deep-seated transformation that was required. The earth is washed, but not cleansed (cf. Jn. 13:8–11). It is human nature itself that needs to be transformed, and that transformation awaits a Saviour who can face the temptations of idolatry head-on and still emerge victorious. Meanwhile, the sad ending to the story of Noah is a vivid reminder of human frailty and the continuous struggle of men and women of faith against the ravages of a sin-drenched world.

5.5   The Unfinished Tower: Genesis 11

The second Genesis story on which I would like to comment briefly is that of the Tower of Babel (Gen. 11:1–9). It is a story of unity that ends in confusion and dispersion. But the confusion is the work of God: it is both an act of judgement and an act of mercy. To appreciate this, one must take note of the backdrop to the building project as well as the motivations of the builders. The land of Shinar was the site of the great city of Babylon which, in the second millennium BC, was the heart of the ancient world and its centre of power. Renowned for its military strength, occult religious wisdom and its splendid architecture, Babylon seemed the summit of human achievement. Thus *babel* for the Babylonians meant 'the gate of the gods'. They said it with pride. But for the narrator of Genesis 11:9 Babylon is—from the perspective of God's heavenly court—simply 'mixed up', sheer 'confusion' (applying the meaning of a Hebrew word that sounds very much like babel!). It is in this irony that the key to the story lies . . .

The builders are driven by a two-fold desire: 'to make a name for ourselves' and to avoid being 'scattered over the face of the whole earth' (11:4). The former conveys prideful ambition, the latter the quest for security in uniformity (for the creation mandate to 'fill the earth', Gen. 1:28, implied also the multiplication of human habitats and cultures). The tower whose top was to 'reach the heavens' is probably the famed religious ziggurats, artificial mountains which symbolized the merging of heaven and earth, a passage-way for the gods of Babylon. Interestingly the *stupas* of the Buddhists were modelled on the Babylonian ziggurats and had a similar cosmic meaning at the beginning.[18] So, here we see the marriage of the technological dream (to build a city that will be the envy of gods and nations), the religious dream (to divinize mankind by removing the creator/ creature distinction) and the political dream (to build a totalitarian system, based on technology and one unifying ideology, that will embrace all human beings and proclaim the autonomy of the human race).

The story of Babel is the story of Eden (Gen. 3) all over again, but the difference is that between the individual deed and the collective act. Here we are face to face with the communal expression of sin, the building of social and political structures that will shut God out of human reckoning and celebrate an illusory human autonomy. It is society organized in rebellion against God's kingship. Our human sin is simply that we refuse to let God be God, and we try, both individually and corporately, to seize God's place as the centre of reality. The holiness of God is repudiated by the technological myth that recognizes no moral limits to human technical possibilities, by the religious myth that promises mystical union with the divine Absolute through meditational techniques, and by the political myth that offers total security and a system to satisfy every human need. . . . As we have seen in our discussion of ideology, various combinations of these myths abound today.

When God, the rightful Lord, is deposed from the centre of social life, the seeds of disintegration and confusion are sown. Some substitute point of reference has to be created to bind people together. Terror can easily be unleashed by pointing to a common enemy and rallying folk together in a war effort that diverts attention from internal dissensions. Alternatively, all the resources of a nation can be channelled into some grand project, the equivalent to the Tower of Babel, that will give people a temporary sense of solidarity in power. Another common ploy, historically, has been to utilize the psychological powers of suggestion, propaganda and ideology to generate feelings of brotherhood (as, for instance, in Nazi Germany) and make people want what their rulers want them to want. But all these synthetic attempts at forging human unity are doomed to failure. For they are centred on idols, and idolatry, we have seen, opens the door to the demonic. At the end of the road lies the totalitarian Beast of the book of Revelation (Rev. 13). Seizing the authority of God himself, the Beast represents the monstrous power of the self-absolutization of the creature. It is chaotic, the final destruction of all human communication and human community.

For the Genesis narrator, the fragmentation of human society is not merely the inevitable outworking of human arrogance, but also the judgement of God. There is scornful irony in 11:5: the tower which was meant to reach the heavens is so small in heaven's perspective, that God 'came down to see' their efforts! Compare Psalm 2: 'Why do the nations conspire, and the peoples plot in vain? . . . The One enthroned in heaven laughs; Yahweh scoffs at them.' God scatters the proud in the imagination of their hearts (Lk. 1:51). The prophet Isaiah made the same point in his taunt against the king of Babylon:

> How you have fallen from heaven,
> O morning star, son of the dawn!
> You have been cast down to the earth,
> You who once laid low the nations!
> You said in your heart,
> 'I will ascend to heaven;
> I will raise my throne above the stars of God;
> I will sit enthroned on the mount of assembly
> On the utmost heights of the sacred mountain.
> I will ascend above the tops of the clouds;
> I will make myself like the Most High'
> But you are brought down to the grave, to the depths of the pit
> (Is.14:12ff).

The unfinished tower stands as a monument to the folly of human pride, both religious and political. It is significant that it is in their communication with each other that God's judgement begins. The rebellion in the garden (Gen. 3) began by humans listening to another creature rather than to their Creator, choosing to believe a lie rather than the truth. The lie led to disobedience, then to evasion and the shrugging off of all responsibility for one's actions (e.g. 3:12,13; 4:9). Language, which is one of the most distinctive expressions of our humanness, is thus corrupted, along with every other aspect of human thought and activity. The great lie 'You shall not die . . . but you shall be as God' (3:4) leads to the habitual lie, the eventual inability to distinguish truth from lies and the disintegration of all meaning in human speech.

It was George Orwell who, in his celebrated book *Nineteen Eighty Four*, coined the term *Newspeak* to describe the way language is sacrificed on the altar of our ideologies. So all dictators speak of 'safeguarding democracy', and all those who dissent are termed 'mentally ill'. What those who cling to power villify as 'terrorism' is called by those hungry for power 'a liberation struggle'. The compulsive addictions of the age— sexual promiscuity, alcohol, the drug culture, the occult—are proclaimed as 'liberating' and 'adult'. Abortion is routinely referred to by medical doctors as 'pregnancy termination'. The stockpiling of armaments becomes 'national security', the training of youth in armed combat becomes 'national service', and—perhaps most horrific of all—the massacre of whole populations becomes 'ethnic cleansing'. The nuclear age and modern warfare has introduced a whole new vocabulary to obfuscate the horror and brutality of war. So, for instance, civilian deaths constitute 'collateral damage', numbers of those dead are referred to as 'body counts', and death-dealing missiles are dubbed 'patriots'.

Thus, not only in totalitarian states but also in modern pluralist societies, language is often emptied of meaning and, consequently, human communication ceases. Divorced from any concern for truth, human language disintegrates into the yelling of slogans, the selling of images as opposed to ideas, the triviality of mass entertainment. Moreover, some modern philosophers go further: all we are left with, they claim, are multiple and incompatible 'universes of discourse' with no common framework of meaning. There are no more unified visions of reality, for reality itself is plural. Argument and disagreement are thus rendered void (a conclusion that seems to vitiate the passion with which this position is universally asserted!). This is where the road to Babel ends.

But a glimmer of divine mercy shines through the very act of divine judgement. The naivete of the language (11:6ff) must not be misunderstood. Like the narrative of Eden this is profound truth conveyed in childlike, pictorial language. The Lord God takes counsel with himself (as in 3:22ff) to draw out the implications of the human act: as long as the root sin is not dealt with, human unity is impossible—indeed, every attempt on the part of human beings to band together in ideological projects will only lead to the multiplication of evil. Misunderstanding and dispersion is not the worst thing that could happen to human collectivities. Far worse is the unspeakable terror that would follow the success of their project to unite in domesticating the absolute, to have total domination. 'By preventing the finishing of the tower, God shows mercy on those arrogant madmen.'[19] The scattering of the peoples also brings about, though in a now fallen world, an original

intention of God for the human race (1:28ff): the management
of the earth and the diversification of human cultures (for
cultures are different responses to different environments). But
the real message of hope in the story comes later, in God's call
to Abraham (11:27ff) of the family of Terah, from the heart of
the dispersed peoples, from Ur of Babylonia. From out of the
rebellious city itself, symbolizing everything that is a distortion
of true humanness, God calls a man and his family. They are
to journey with God in the wilderness, turning their backs on
the nations. But the future of the nations lies with Abraham
and, in particular, on his response to God's gracious promise
of blessing (12:2,3). He is called for the sake of all. His line is
chosen to be the means by which the God of the nations will
engage with idolatry in his world and bring about a new
humanity with its true centre in himself. So, Abraham, wandering in the desert with the Lord, and struggling often with
fear and doubt, becomes a bearer of hope for the nations.

This theme of divine election, of God calling out a people
of his own for the sake of the whole world, is central to the
unfolding story of the Bible. Election never meant that those
chosen are better than others, but rather that they are chosen
and entrusted, even burdened, with a message for the sake of
others. And in the sharing of that message they themselves are
bound to others in a process of mutual transformation which
is what 'salvation' is all about. The paradigm example is Jonah.
He was the prophet called by God to preach to the city of
Nineveh. In many ways he is the least attractive, morally and
spiritually, of all the characters portrayed in the book (the
pagan sailors, the people of Nineveh). Yet it is the reluctant
Jonah who is entrusted with God's word, and the future of the
people of Nineveh is bound up with Jonah's faithfulness to his
calling. It is his eventual obedience that brings the Ninevites
the blessings of repentance.

In the rest of the Bible, the city of Babylon came to
symbolize the anti-God society: pretentious, violent, superstitious, wealthy, persecuting the People of God, and doomed
to destruction (e.g. Dn. 3; Is. 47; Jer. 50; Rev. 17 & 18). It is
her sins that 'reached . . . to the heavens' (Rev. 18:5). She
represents the 'system', built on idolatry and injustice, seeking
to unite the world around her worship. As such she is the real
enemy of the hope held out by the line of Abraham. In the
book of Revelation she is contrasted with the holy city, the

New Jerusalem, which comes 'down out of heaven from God' (note the imagery, the deliberate contrast to Babel) whose open gates unite the peoples of the world (Rev. 21:10,24–27).

Notes

[1] E. Brunner, *Man in Revolt: a Christian Anthropology*, trans. O. Wyon (London: Lutterworth, 1939) p. 34

[2] A. Smith, *An Inquiry into the Nature and Causes of The Wealth of Nations* (1776), ed. Edwin Cannan (1904) (Chicago: University of Chicago, 1976), Vol. 1, p. 477

[3] Ibid. Vol. 2, pp. 208–9

[4] Ibid. Vol. 1, p. 519

[5] M. Volf, 'Exclusion and Embrace: Theological Reflections in the Wake of "Ethnic Cleansing" ', in W. Dyrness (ed.), *Emerging Voices in Global Christian Theology* (Grand Rapids: Zondervan, 1994) p. 34 (italics in text)

[6] Ibid. note 28

[7] A. Nandy, *The Intimate Enemy* (Delhi: Oxford University Press, 1980) pp. x,xi.

[8] *Human Development Report 1993* (United Nations Development Programme, Oxford University Press, 1993) p. 3

[9] Ibid. (Italics in text)

[10] Ibid.

[11] Ibid. p. 18

[12] Ibid. p. 11

[13] A. Schlesinger, *A Thousand Days*, cited in P. Vallely, *Bad Samaritans* (London: Hodder & Stoughton, 1990) p. 189

[14] N. Wolterstorff, *Lament For a Son* (Grand Rapids: Eerdmans, 1987) p. 90

[15] M. Luther, cited in P. Althaus, *The Theology of Martin Luther* (Philadelphia: Fortress, 1966) p. 16 (note 7)

[16] R. Bauckham, *The Bible in Politics: How to Read the Bible Politically* (London: SPCK, 1989) p. 140

[17] Ibid.

[18] E. Conze, *Further Buddhist Studies* (London: Cassirer, 1975) p. 13

[19] H. Blocher, *In the Beginning* (Leicester: InterVarsity Press, 1984) p. 211

6

Science and Anti-science

'Christian faith is needed today to restore a tolerable balance between the two competitive tendencies in Western culture: the tendency to make claims to final and ultimate truth, and a critical attitude that so undermines all claims to truth that we tend towards skepticism, relativism, and nihilism.'
—*Leszek Kolakowski, Polish Philosopher*[1]

That celebrated authority on Chinese civilizations, Joseph Needham, once made an interesting observation regarding the failure of science to flourish in a society that gave Europe many of the inventions, such as printing, which paved the way for its scientific and economic expansion: 'It was not that there was no order in Nature for the Chinese, but rather that it was not an order ordained by a rational personal being, and hence there was no conviction that rational personal beings would be able to spell out in their lesser earthly languages the divine code of laws which he had decreed aforetime.'[2]

What we have come to call modern science (with its emphasis on the experimental 'interrogation' of nature, theoretical analysis and prediction) has made rapid progress in twentieth-century China. Though most of China's out-standing scientists, several Christians among them, were either killed or imprisoned during the notorious Cultural Revolution of the 1960s, the present mood is one of 'catching up' at all cost with the West in every area of science and technology. Science, above all other Western products, is idolized among students in China, as indeed it is all over Asia. It is a central component of the package of modernity that sweeps the globe. Although Asia boasts an ancient technological tradition of enormous sophistication, modern technology is unique in that it is as firmly wedded to the scientific enterprise as to commercial power. A friend of mine who is invited by the University of Beijing to lecture on Christian philosophy has told me of the renewed

interest among scholars there concerning the relationship
of Christian faith and modern science.

The historical relationships between theology and science
are fascinating, not least because of the richly complex way
they have interacted over different periods. It is a story of
mutual support and also of mutual criticism. Many historians
have acknowledged the powerful effect that biblical convictions about God, humankind and the world had on the growth
of the scientific enterprise in the Protestant countries of Europe
following the Reformation.[3] While it is often difficult to
isolate intellectual factors from wider social-structural influences, it is surely significant that the early pioneers in every
branch of natural science (or 'natural philosophy' as it was
called) were deeply committed Christians who found their
motivation for their work in their personal faith (e.g. Kepler,
Ray, Boyle, Newton, Harvey, Lyell). It is interesting to note
also how so many of the nineteenth-century giants, whose
names adorn the standard introductory textbooks on physics
and chemistry (e.g. Joule, Rayleigh, Faraday, Kelvin, Stokes,
Maxwell) were men of orthodox and passionate Christian
convictions. James Clerk Maxwell (1831–79), the founder of
the electromagnetic theory of light and a pioneer in thermo-
dynamics, was convinced that 'Christians whose minds are
scientific are bound to study science that their views of the
glory of God may be as extensive as their being is capable of';
while his fellow Scot, Lord Kelvin (1824–1907) asserted boldly
that 'the more thoroughly science is studied, the further does
it take us from anything comparable to atheism'.[4]

The conflict/warfare metaphor of the relationship between
science and Christian theology was a product of the late
nineteenth century. Foremost among its proponents was Darwin's friend and popularizer, T.H. Huxley. Under the leadership of Huxley a small but vociferous band of professional
scientists (the term scientist itself was first coined by William
Whewell in 1834, indicating the emergence of a new, self-
conscious social grouping in Britain) organized themselves
into a 'Church Scientific', with the avowed intent of attacking
and undermining the credibility of the Church of England.
The latter was increasingly unpopular among the common
people, many of whom were attracted to the Methodist,
Baptist and other non-conformist churches (most of the Christian scientists mentioned above came from these latter

churches). The Church of England was declining in spirituality, its country parsons were wealthy farmers who were
alienated from the rural labourers, and the academic centres of
power were barred to non-Anglicans. So Huxley and his
friends had no difficulty in mobilizing discontent for their
assault on clerical cultural leadership.

Under men like Huxley, Herbert Spencer and Francis
Galton in Britain, and August Comte in France, science was
turned into a new religion. The Church Scientific organized
'lay sermons' on scientific subjects, dressed in gowns imitative
of the clergy, set up Sunday Lecture Societies to compete with
the Church of England Sunday schools, sang hymns to 'Nature' at mass meetings, and distributed pamphlets and tracts
which proclaimed scientific naturalism and denounced Christianity as the chief obstacle to scientific progress. Even buildings set up as monuments to science, such as the Natural
History Museum in London, were designed as secular cathedrals. A whole new 'history' of science was written, now
regarded as utterly worthless (save for the light it sheds on the
motives of the writers and their social setting), to show that
science and religion had always been bitter enemies, with
Mother Nature replacing God, and Copernicus, Galileo and
Darwin assuming a heroic status as the knight-saints of the
modern world. Thus a new mythology was created. The
idolization of science, with its new priestly class of professional
scientists, was now complete.[5]

But the new religion was short-lived. As Colin Russell,
Professor of the History of Science at Britain's Open University, observes, 'The euphoric haze of unlimited optimism
associated with Spencer and his followers was swiftly dispersed
by the two World Wars that followed. The contours of
Victorian scientific naturalism melted away in the face of
twentieth century science in its rejection of a closed, determi-
nate universe. In our own day the supreme irony is that the
very world-view from which naturalism sprang- a Romantic
view of nature—is amongst the most hostile opponents of
science itself.'[6]

Modern science is unable to fill the vacuum left by the loss of
traditional meanings, and the world-view that it offers in their
place would be utterly barren if taken as normative, all-embracing and self-sufficient. Consider, for instance, the influential
French writer Albert Camus' disillusionment with science:

. . . all the knowledge on earth will give me nothing to assure me that this world is mine. You describe it to me and you teach me to classify it. You enumerate its laws and in my thirst for knowledge I admit that they are true. You take apart its mechanism and my hope increases. At the final stage you teach me that this wondrous and multi-coloured universe can be reduced to the atom and that the atom itself can be reduced to the electron. All this is good and I wait for you to continue. But you tell me of an invisible planetary system in which electrons gravitate around a nucleus. You explain this world to me with an image. I realize then that you have been reduced to poetry: I shall never know. Have I the time to become indignant? You have already changed theories. So that science that was to teach me everything ends up in a hypothesis, that lucidity founders in metaphor, that uncertainty is resolved in a work of art. What need had I of so many efforts? The soft lines of these hills and the hand of evening on this troubled heart teach me much more.[7]

Antipathy towards science is rife today, especially in those countries which have drunk most deeply from the bitter wells of scientific naturalism. Universities in Britain and America find it difficult to fill their science classes with local students. But the ghosts of Huxley and Spencer still stalk the faculties of science, medicine and engineering in most Asian universities; while Comte continues to have a sizable following among the positivist economists and sociologists (to whom indeed he gave birth). Most professional scientists, perhaps like their counterparts in the West, have little awareness of the historical development of their disciplines, leave alone the presuppositions that undergird them. The motivation for a scientific career is largely pragmatic: social status as a professional in science runs high, and political and commercial inducements play a significant role in channelling the brightest students into the applied sciences. Governments understandably see investment in applied science and technology, rather than fundamental science or the humanities, as the way to rapid economic 'development'.

If, however, one were to hop across the typical university campus to the Humanities department, one would encounter Lyotard and Levi-Strauss, Derrida and Foucault, on the lips of intellectually chic students and their professors. That those who have barely begun to experience the benefits and the miseries of modernity should be indulging in the rhetoric of 'post-modernist' authors must surely strike the Western observer as distinctly ironic. But it is only as ironic as those Western critics who, while enjoying the comforts of modern scientific technology, make it their life's work to denigrate science and to undermine its intellectual foundations. We shall explore some of the causes for disenchantment with science in this chapter.

One must not, of course, exaggerate the degree of disenchantment even in the Western world of late modernity. Whatever may be the tendency in some vocal intellectual circles, the psychiatrist and social critic David Smail is surely right when he says that 'Our attitude to scientific and technical matters is soaked through with awe, and the uninitiated will drink in the banalities and fake profundities of, say, television scientific acolytes with a credulity quite as blind as that of any newly converted religious zealot'. He continues, '"Scientists think . . ." and "scientists have shown . . ." etc, form the preamble to countless statements of almost infinite implausibility, to which, because of their apparent scientific legitimation, the layman is expected to give immediate credence. This, moreover, is not simply the result of a popular corruption of matters surpassing lay understanding, but a clear reflection of attitudes held by many scientists themselves.'[8]

We are still in the presence of an *idol*.

6.1   The Faith of Science

Doing science is primarily an act of faith. To embark on scientific work requires a basic assumption: there is a real world outside our minds and it is structured in an orderly and intelligible way. We have seen (in Chapter 3) that this is implied in the biblical understanding of the universe as a *creation*. Moreover, this created order is contingent, not necessary. In other words, the universe does not *have* to be the way it actually is. There is no logical necessity either for God to create the world or to create it the way we experience it. God is not constrained by anything outside of himself. He is free to create any kind of universe he wills. We saw, in an earlier chapter, how this is a consequence of the biblical doctrine of creation *ex nihilo*.

What are the implications of this view for scientific enquiry? Simply, that the rational structure of the universe needs to be *discovered*. It cannot be specified in advance. Rationalists believe that the laws of the universe are logically necessary; so they can be inferred by pure reasoning. For instance the Greeks argued that because the circle is the perfect geometrical shape, and God is by definition the perfect Being, the heavenly bodies he creates (the planets) must move in circular orbits. Actual observation, however, showed that they move in distorted circles called ellipses. In Aristotle's system, the planets could not have satellites. When Galileo, in the seventeenth century, built a telescope and discovered the satellites of Jupiter, his claim was denounced by the rationalists of his day (many of whom were eminent church authorities) who had been brought up to believe that this was as impossible as for two plus two to equal five.

It is because God's creation has a contingent order that it has an infinite capacity to surprise us. That order is discovered by a combination of imagination and controlled experimentation. Our cherished beliefs, in science no less than in other areas, are having to be continuously revised. The biblical worldview encourages men to be open to new evidence, to follow where the facts may lead, and not to hide behind closed rationalist systems. Another important aspect of the faith of a scientist lies in the significance he gives to the human person. To embark on a career of scientific research one has to assume that the human mind is capable of unlocking the secrets of the universe. Have you ever paused to think what a radical assumption this is?

Physically speaking, humans are microscopic specks of dust on a very ordinary planet revolving around an average-sized star in a remote corner of a galaxy which comprises a hundred billion stars and which itself is only one among a similar number of galaxies. And, if the geological and neo-Darwinist theories concerning the formation of the earth and the emergence of life on earth are a reliable picture of what has happened on our planet, then human life is very recent on a universal time-scale. Some astronomers and biologists boast that their discoveries have 'put man in his place' and they pour scorn on the biblical emphasis on a human being's intrinsic value and dignity. Thus the eminent astrophysicist, Chandra Wickramasinghe, in an attempt to show that modern astronomy is a vindication of Buddhist philosophy, writes: 'The sobering lesson of astronomy, a lesson that still continues to unfold, is that our planet and humans upon it are truly insignificant on a cosmic scale. Our egocentric, ethnocentric and anthropocentric interests must surely pale into total insignificance in a cosmic context.'[9]

However, those writers who delight in belittling human life are not only committing the childish error of confusing size and age with value or significance; but they also fail to see that astronomy and evolutionary theory themselves are products of that same insignificant human mind! To use human theories to attack human significance is to destroy the very foundation of those theories. Surely the very success of science itself bears eloquent testimony to the significance of human life. As Pascal put it in the 17th century: 'Through space the universe grasps me and swallows me up like a speck. But through thought I grasp it.'[10] Listen, too, to the philosopher-theologian Thomas Torrance: 'Behind and permeating all our scientific activity, whether in critical analysis or in discovery, there is an elementary and overwhelming faith in the possibility of grasping the real world with our concepts, and, above all, faith in the truth over which we have no control but in the service of which our rationality stands or falls. Faith and intrinsic rationality are interlocked with one another.'[11] Another scientist who has spoken eloquently on the faith of the scientist and the awe and sense of wonder that science invokes is the greatest physicist of this century, Albert Einstein: 'Without the belief that it is possible to grasp reality with our theoretical constructions, without the belief in the inner harmony of the world, there can be no science. This belief has and always will be the fundamental motive for all scientific creation.'[12]

The fact that science is possible is itself a fact that points us beyond science. Even when we use mathematics to unlock the secrets of the physical universe, something very strange is happening. For these mathematical patterns are abstract human creations, conjured up by human thought. Time and time again the breakthroughs in fundamental science have occurred because someone has chosen to trust a theory simply because of its elegance and simplicity from a mathematical point of view, and then discovered that it does indeed generate empirically successful results in the physical world around us. This 'unreasonable effectiveness of mathematics' (a famous phrase of the Nobel laureate Eugene Wigner) is a source of wonder to many philosophically-inclined mathematicians and physicists.

Thus, for example, the solid-state physicist AJ Leggett, writes: '... just about everything we know, or think we know, about the universe and its history is based on extrapolation of the laws of physics as discovered in the laboratory to conditions different by many orders of magnitude in density, temperature, distance, and so forth. That we can get in this way a provisional picture which has even a reasonable chance of being self-consistent is little short of amazing.'[13] He continues, with a modesty untypical of popular accounts of modern physics, 'Even given this, the list of fundamental things we don't know about the universe is daunting. Among other things, we don't know what it is (mostly) made of, whether it is finite or infinite, whether it really had a beginning, and whether it will have an end. It is clear that we have a long way to go.'

The science journalist Timothy Ferris concludes his marvellously comprehensive survey of the growth of modern science with the question, 'Why then does science work? The answer is that nobody knows. It is a complete mystery— perhaps *the* complete mystery- why the human mind should be able to understand anything at all about the wider universe . . . Perhaps it is because our brains evolved through the working of natural law that they somehow resonate with natural law . . . But the mystery, really, is not that we are at one with the universe, but that we are so to some degree at odds with it, different from it, and yet can understand something about it. Why is this so?'[14]

As Ferris observes, evolutionary biology will not help. It may well be true that if there was no consonance between the workings of our minds and the way things are we would have perished long ago. But what counts for survival in the world is everyday experience (of, for example, gravity and pain, rocks and trees) and everyday thought (at the most, Euclidean geometry, arithmetic, simple mechanics). But we are not talking at this mundane level. We are dealing here with the counter-common sense behaviour of the subatomic world and the creation of vast galaxies at distances we cannot even imagine, with strange entities such as 'black holes', 'gluons' and 'quarks' all predicted by abstract and sophisticated mathematical ideas. How can gauge field theories and string theories be spin-offs from the evolutionary struggle for survival? Even the dream of men like Stephen Hawking to have a mathematical 'theory of everything' simply begs the question. A theory of everything, if it is to be truly a theory of everything, must include within it the most intriguing question that we are discussing: whence the desire of Hawking-like creatures, accidentally thrown up like flotsam in an obscure part of the universe, for an explanation of 'everything'—and their confidence of success? (I leave aside till later the other fallacy behind Hawking's quest: namely, the failure to appreciate that there are other levels of explanation whose categories cannot be reduced to physical and mathematical concepts. So even if a physical theory can, in principle, 'explain everything' within its frame of reference, it may be remarkably deficient when viewed from another level).

Now, if we are creatures made in the image of the Creator, called by God to responsible stewardship, it is not presumptuous of men and women to seek to understand their Creator's world. We would naturally expect some sort of a correspondence between the human mind and the physical universe which that mind explores. Both the contingent rationality of the universe and the rationality of the explorer are grounded in the ultimate rationality and faithfulness of the Creator's will.

This is not a knock-down argument for belief in a Creator, for in the realm of our fundamental religious or philosophical commitments there is no logically compelling argument for either belief or unbelief. Unbelief too is based on acts of belief that can never be demonstrated logically, while any system of logic is itself based on axioms that can never be proved within that system! Moreover the attempt to argue for the reality of God in this way runs the danger, as we have seen earlier, of ending up with a god-of-the gaps and a deistic Designer. My argument is rather as follows: given many other grounds for faith in a God who is the Creator of the world, and whose character and relationship with humankind is disclosed in the biblical revelation, the entire scientific enterprise becomes perfectly reasonable. It also accounts for the historical observation that modern science originated— and was nurtured—in a cultural environment deeply influenced by these biblical convictions. Outside of those convictions, science itself cries out for meaning; and men like Hawking are hard pressed to justify their commitment to the very work that they often use (or, more accurately, misuse) to attack those same biblical convictions.

One could carry this discussion further by pointing to recent developments in cosmology (that branch of astronomy dealing with the evolution of the universe) which seem to show a remarkable connexion between the emergence of human life on the planet Earth and the large-scale structure of the universe. The most popular theory today of the origins of space-time is called the Big Bang scenario: the universe is presumed to have begun in a super-dense, super-hot state that cooled to form the universe which we see today. The process has been going on for about fifteen billion years. The numerical values of certain fundamental physical constants (e.g. the gravitational constant G, the electric charge of the electron, the ratio of the proton and neutron masses) would have been determined in the first few microseconds of the early universe. These values are discovered through experiments and are found to be extremely 'fine-tuned'. In other words, the calculations show that if any one of these had been different by one part in several millions, it would have led to a very different kind of universe—specifically, one in which galaxies could not have formed, solar systems never have emerged, and life on earth would have been impossible.

This discovery, which goes by the name of the *Anthropic Principle* (from the Greek word for human), revolutionizes our view of the universe by linking cosmic physics with human biology. The stronger version of the Anthropic Principle states that the physical constants *had* to have their present values, and the universe had to have certain features in its earliest phases, in order that carbon-based life forms, culminating in human observers of the universe, might emerge in that universe after a suitable length of time.

Since this principle seems to bring back ideas of 'purpose' and 'final causes' into science, it is vigorously resisted by those scientists who still cling (for other, non-scientific reasons) to their view of human life as an accidental phenomenon in an impersonal universe. How could life have been the very goal towards which the early universe was moving? The thought is staggering. One way of getting around any theistic implications is to postulate the existence of 'many worlds' or 'multiple universes', so that every conceivable numerical value for the physical constants is realized in some hypothetical universe. These universes would form an infinite mathematical set, and we would just happen to live in the one member of that set where the constants took values which made our existence as observers of that universe possible. But since these universes cannot communicate with each other, the theory is utterly untestable and therefore unscientific. It stretches our credulity to breaking point. But this is the extent to which otherwise reasonable men seem willing to go to evade any possible theistic implications that may attach to scientific discovery . . .

6.2   Research and Responsibility

It is helpful to think of a scientist as a map-maker. There is a real world of events and entities whose relationships the scientist tries to grasp through concepts, models and theories. The latter are not be confused with reality itself, but they are helpful guides for finding our way around reality. However, a scientific map, unlike a road or railway map, is more than merely descriptive. It also attempts explanations and predictions of events. Scientific laws are prescriptive, not in the sense that they specify what can *never* take place in the world, but rather in the sense that they tell us what reasonable expectations we *should* have. A reliable scientific theory says what is reasonable for us to expect in an unfamiliar situation, based on what we have experienced in other situations. But theories are always fallible, flawed and limited in scope. Hence the combination of confidence and humility that is the hallmark of all good science.

Map-making carries moral responsibility. In the biblical notion of 'knowing', knowledge and responsibility go together. To know something is to be responsible. If I claim to know something and yet do not act on the basis of what I claim to know, I do not really know it. Consequently, as one's area of map-making widens, so does one's area of personal responsibility. Fields such as brain research, nuclear energy and molecular biology bring with their increased understanding a corresponding increase in human responsibility for what we claim to know.

The scientist, unlike most other professionals, is a producer of knowledge; and, so, he carries a greater moral responsibility than other professionals. Since he is the creator of awesome potentialities (for good or for evil), he cannot wait till those potentialities are actualized before he begins to explore their implications. For instance, a lawyer might have chosen to defend Hitler because of his belief that the law should be given full scope to function; or a doctor might have chosen to treat Hitler, even to save his life, because she has sworn to treat all men alike irrespective of their moral character. But a scientist who has been devising, say, more efficient gas chambers or more advanced missile systems for the Nazis cannot, at the end of the day, disclaim responsibility for what Hitler did with those devices. The scientist shares in the responsibility for evil.

One of the effects of the Fall (Genesis 3) and of human sinfulness is the divorce between knowledge and responsibility. The separation between theory and action is taken for granted, and often boasted about, in academic institutions. Scientific journals, research papers and books are filling the world's libraries at a staggering rate. Yet a relatively small proportion of the world's population benefits from this 'knowledge'. As self-centred human beings, it is easier to delight in the technical aspects of our craft than to face up to tough, challenging issues which may call for a spiritual maturity which as scientists we may lack.

This is why science has become an instrument of great violence today. Ironically, side by side with its great benefits, in the name of science more violence has been inflicted on human beings and other living creatures in this century than in the entire history of humanity. Science is no longer a quest for understanding, a humble delight in the creation of God. It is tied to military power and huge commercial interests. The distortions of human sin are reflected in the misplaced priorities of scientific research. As Professor Richard Bube, formerly of Stanford University, has written: 'Much of scientific research today is motivated by one of two simple questions: (1) does the research promise financial profit in the near future (the industrialization of science) or (2) does it promise contributions to the military program (the militarization of science)? . . . This means that the choice of research topics and the directions of research efforts tends to be more or less directly influenced by military needs in a proportion out of balance with overall human needs.'[15]

This is true not only in the United States and Europe, but also in poor countries such as India, China and Pakistan. The 'cream' of Third World scientists are skimmed off and put to work on military-related research either in the United States or in their own countries. It is estimated that there are more scientists and engineers alive in this generation than have existed in all of human history— and almost half of that number are involved in research connected to military interests. This represents a terrible waste of human talent, let alone of the earth's natural resources. We now possess the satellite technology to survey every square metre of our planet, but we are still unable to provide the cities of the world with safe and reliable electric power or a pollution-free public transport system.

The practice of science has to be weighed in the context of today's global realities. Eighty per cent of the world's population who live in the South (or the Third World) consume only twenty per cent of the world's wealth. The US alone, with only five per cent of the world's population, uses nearly a quarter of the world's energy, half of which is discarded as waste heat. All the fuel used by the South for all purposes is only slightly more than the amount of petroleum the North burns to move its motorcars.

The world is becoming increasingly unequal. Today, taking into account loans, outright aid, and repayments of interests, the poor countries send about $30 billion a year to the affluent countries in excess of what they receive from the latter. If the falling prices of the agricultural commodities of poor nations are brought into the calculation, the net South-to-North flow of capital would be around $60 billion a year. But to obtain a more accurate figure, one should also include the fortunes of Third World politicians and businessmen that are 'exported' to banks in Europe and America, and the profits of multinational corporations which are sent back to their parent base in the North. How many people in the North realize that their extravagant living standards are being maintained largely by income from the poorest nations of the world?

Whatever aid is given to the South is a mere drop in the ocean of what flows from South to North, and even this is tied to conditions which benefit the donor much more than the receiver! It is well known that the US government gives aid as an instrument of foreign policy and not in response to human priority concerns as identified by the United Nations. Of all official development assistance given by the North to the South in 1992, only 7% was targetted for priority areas. Most of the $15 billion given as 'technical assistance' went towards the purchase of equipment and payments for technical experts from the donor nations. Little wonder that the incomes of the richest 20% of the world's population is 150 times the income of the poorest 20%.[16]

The unjust distribution of global wealth also determines the nature of goods that are manufactured. A large proportion of the affluent nations' GNP is devoted to consumer goods and the production of technologies to make these consumer goods. Since there are also gross inequalities within poorer nations, the same high-tech consumer products (motorcars, computers, video-recorders, cameras etc) are enjoyed by elites in countries where the basic needs of nutrition, sanitation and shelter for the great majority of its citizens have still to be met. Thus only a small portion of the world's resources flow towards the processing of basic goods required by half the world's people (and especially the world's children) for their survival.

The North's control of technology has contributed to the plight of many poor nations. Rich countries use their industrial and agricultural technologies to produce surplus goods which they are unable to use themselves. Surplus crops, cereals or materials are dumped on the world market, causing prices of Third World commodities to collapse, and thus further reduce incomes and living standards among the poor. Export earnings in the Third World are falling dramatically at a time when they have to cough up more and more funds to service foreign debts. At the end of the 1980s total Third World debt stood at $1,300 billion, 90 per cent of it owed directly to institutions in rich nations, or indirectly through international organizations. This figure amounts to nearly half the Third World's total GNP. Latin America's debts are currently four times the size of its total annual exports. For every one per cent rise in Northern interest rates, a four per cent rise in export earnings is needed simply to keep up payments. In order to pay interest on debts, nations must continue to borrow. There seems to be no end in sight to this downward spiral.[17]

One global industry that continues to make huge profits even in times of economic recession is the **pharmaceutical industry**. World sales of the larger pharmaceutical companies exceeds the GNP of many Third World nations. It is an unusual, if not unique, industry in that it requires someone outside it to promote its manufactures: neither 'market forces' nor 'consumer sovereignty' operate, because it is the medical doctor who decides which drug the consumer should buy. So, the medical profession has become the major target of the sales-promotion drives of these companies. Medical research, educational institutions, seminars and symposia are very often sponsored by pharmaceutical companies. Although over twenty per cent of its total sales derive from the Third World, less that one per cent of its total research and development expenditure is orientated towards Third World health priorities.

The promotional activities of the drug companies shape not only the direction of medical research in the North, but also the prescribing habits of medical practitioners all over the world. Most doctors, especially in the poorer nations, have little access to information about drugs apart from the promotional literature of the drug companies. A recent study of advertisements in the premier medical journal of Sri Lanka showed that 49% of the pages contained drug advertisements (more than the twice the number in equivalent Scandinavian journals), only 25% of the drugs advertised were in the list of essential drugs drawn up by the government health ministry, and only 16% of them carried the minimum scientific information that a medical practitioner should know.[18] In the medical curriculum of most faculties of medicine around the world, pharmacology is taught without any reference to the costs of individual drugs. It is often the practice to prescribe drugs under their commercial brand names rather than the generic name. Thus medicine becomes, unwittingly, an instrument in the exploitation of the poor.

In her well-documented survey of the operations of pharmaceutical companies, *Bitter Pills: Medicines and the Third World Poor*,[19] Diana Melrose, pointed out (among other things) the following:

—Approximately twenty percent of all drug sales at the manufacturers' level goes for promotion, which include free samples to doctors, the sponsoring of medical meetings, advertisements in medical journals and direct advertisement to the public.

—Although the World Health Organization has identified approximately 200 drugs in 27 broad groups as 'essential, basic, indispensable and necessary to any nation's health needs', many of these drugs are in short supply in most Third World nations, while non-essential drugs outnumber essential drugs 10:1. As much as 70 per cent of the pharmaceutical products on the world market today are non-essential or even undesirable.

—The over-prescription of drugs by the medical profession and the prescription of glamorous and costly drugs with limited medical potential have seriously set back efforts by public health workers to educate people in health education and so alleviate poverty. Pressure from the industry also distorts the direction of pharmacological research.

The world has now entered the much-heralded **Age of Biotechnology**. With recombinant DNA technology it is now possible to manipulate the genetic blue-print of living organisms to suit our own cultural, political and economic aspirations. Pharmaceutical and agri-business companies are staking out exclusive rights to patent genetic material taken from the Third World's forests. They are heavily lobbying governments to allow the patenting of all human, animal and plant tissue. This raises profound ethical questions which reach beyond the scientific community. The use of this technology in human reproduction and genetic screening opens up the prospects of discrimination against those we consider 'unimportant', even 'useless', according to our warped scale of values (this is the real aspect of 'playing God' in genetic engineering) and the exploitation of women in a commercial eugenics. The synthesis of new viruses and bacteria for use in biological warfare could lead to a genetic arms race every bit as horrific as the nuclear arms race. Cross-species genetic transfers go far beyond traditional breeding of animal and plant species, reducing genetically engineered animals to the status of manufactured products. Are human body parts and even a major portion of the human genome soon to become the patented property of a private company? That would indeed be the culmination of the consumer society, human inheritance itself turned into a saleable commodity.

The TV/entertainment industry is now being tied in with the major newspapers, telephone and computer companies in the much-vaunted global **information superhighway**. A few huge conglomerates bid to control this vast empire. Already Rupert Murdoch's Asian Star network broadcasts American 'soaps' into the homes of unsuspecting Chinese and Indians. Far from expanding freedom of choice, it represents a new economic and cultural imperialism. Local, independent film-makers cannot hope to compete with such giant companies. The relentless concentration of media power in the hands of a few men and a few companies shrinks public choice. Formerly independent newspapers and publishing houses are

now swallowed up by the conglomerates, leading to an emul-
sification of television, books and newspapers into one bland,
conservative pulp. The alliance of conservative politicians and
mega-businessmen serves to drive the press into right-wing
ideological positions. So, paradoxically, even as the channels
available for communication expand, the actual content of
communication contracts.

The fault lies not with the satellite and new fibre-optics
technologies, but rather with the human context (economic,
political, ideological) in which they are developed. Scientific
and technological research *by themselves* do not lead to the
enrichment of human life. It all depends on who has *control*
over the fruits of research. Research and development that
takes place within a grossly unequal economic order and/or a
repressive political order will tend only to exacerbate those
inequities and/or repression. The powerful consolidate their
power, usually at the expense of the weak.

As an example of this tendency, consider the famous **Green
Revolution** of the 1960s. Certain high-yielding 'miracle
seeds' were developed by agrarian research institutes in Mexico
and the Philippines and introduced to other agricultural societies. Here was a technology designed to increase local food
production and so alleviate malnutrition and rural poverty.
However, these seeds, being artificially nurtured, required
high doses of pesticides for protection against pathogens; they
also needed good irrigation and high inputs of fertilizer. Most
agricultural countries are economically poor and have to
import fertilizers and pesticides. They also had to rely on
foreign experts for advice and on seed banks owned by
multinational institutes. So the import bills increased more
rapidly than did agricultural exports. Moreover, the vast majority of subsistence farmers could not afford fertilizers and
pesticides, nor did they have adequate irrigation facilities for
their small-holdings; so they sold their land to the wealthier
farmers. This resulted in more landlessness and worsening rural
poverty. The much-heralded Green Revolution fell flat.

To whom did the Green Revolution bring a lucrative
harvest? The Indian writer Claude Alvares is blunt in his
answer: 'To those who designed the project, including American private foundations like Ford and Rockefeller; multinational corporations, who manufactured the seeds, equipment
and nutrients; the banks who provided the credit and certain

categories of very large farmers.'[20] It is with hindsight that we realize that the alleviation of famine and rural poverty has much more to do with land reform, co-operative ownership of technology and the purchasing power of the poor than with the raising of national food productivity.

The introduction of new technologies in societies with grave disparities of income—and backed up by aggressive modern marketing techniques—serves only to generate envy, frustration and social violence. They become, unwittingly, instruments of human exploitation rather than of human participation and stewardship. This is why, contrary to the beliefs of many managers and technocrats around the world, technology can never be a substitute for imaginative and courageous political leadership. It is only when science and technology are seen as servants of a higher human vision that they can become truly liberating instruments.

In biblical terms, the idolatry of science as an end in itself and the shrugging off of moral accountability for one's work are a denial of stewardship. Science, like every other human activity, participates in the alienation that rebellion against the Creator brings in its wake. Young people entering the fields of science and engineering must be aware of the social, political, and economic contexts of those fields. Science is not an autonomous discipline conducted in a vacuum.

As a Christian I believe that the scientific enterprise must be ruled by love: love of God and of neighbour. Where love is absent, science becomes demonic. It enslaves rather than liberates. Love of God includes respect for truth. It leads to integrity in work, so that fame, reputation and wealth (whether personal or national) are not the motivators in research. Love of neighbour means that global human need takes priority over personal 'self-fulfilment'. It also means that sometimes the demands of human compassion will override human curiosity. Thus, certain areas of investigation have to carry legal restrictions because they can easily be abused or directly threaten human personhood: for example, non-thera-peutic research on embryos, the elderly or the handicapped. The benefits that accrue through this kind of research need to be sought by other means which do not violate human dignity.

The justification for the pursuit of 'knowledge for its own sake' is really quite hollow, for knowledge involves the ability to relate and integrate ideas with one another across the span of intellectual disciplines. And knowledge co-exists with other ends such as justice and human flourishing, however variously defined. It is only in a culture where knowledge has degenerated to the accumulation of isolated 'facts' that people can argue for 'knowledge for the sake of knowledge'. The single-minded assertion of scientific autonomy in the West is now giving way, hesitantly but surely, to a recognition of society's claims on science. No profession exists in isolation from the wider community of fellow-citizens. The history of science since the 1930s has given ample and painful evidence of the way scientific curiosity has shaded into lust for power and the exploitation of the powerless. And, as democratic participation hopefully increases throughout the world, scientific curiosity too will be held accountable to society's norms.

The danger, of course, is that society's norms will become more and more distorted— just as democracy itself is often subverted and distorted by the power of huge commercial interests. Already the spectre of scientists having to justify their work in terms of the crude consumer values of the market is rampant across the globe. This is not the kind of 'accountability' that I am espousing. What is called 'pure science' is, I have argued, a response of respectful obedience to the intelligibility of a world that we as Christians recognize as coming from our Father's hand. But it is that emphasis on obedience, with its attendant values of love and wonder, and respect for the created order and for human community, rather than mere curiosity, which prevent pure science from degenerating into a Nobel-prize seeking monomania.

The British philosopher, Mary Midgley, though not a Christian herself, has argued persuasively against such monomania by using what may seem a strange illustration— the parable of Jesus concerning the merchantman who sold all he had to gain one pearl of great price. For what is bought is not just stored (as is so much 'knowledge' today, in libraries and computer banks). She writes, 'Unless the merchantman merely wants that pearl to sell again, he wants to do something with it. He wants, it seems, to enter into relation with it, to wonder at it, to contemplate its beauty. But wonder involves love. It is an essential element in wonder that we recognize what we see as something we did not make, cannot fully understand, and acknowledge as containing something greater than ourselves . . . Knowledge here is not just power; it is a loving union, and what is loved, cannot just be the information gained; it has to be the real thing which that information tells us about . . . The student will learn the laws and practice the customs belonging to the kingdom of heaven or of nature, trying to become more fit to serve it. But first comes the initial gazing, the vision which conveys the point of the whole. This vision is in no way just a means to practical involvement, but itself an essential aspect of the goal.'[21]

Conceptual revolutions need to occur if the scientific community is to rediscover its reason for existence. Midgley is scathing in her exposure of academic pretentiousness: 'Sanctimonious obsessiveness needs to be publicly unmasked. It needs to be spelt out why an attempt to understand desertification in Africa in order to resist it is not, just as such, at some deep level academically inferior to an advance in theoretical physics. Something needs to be done here about the tendentious current use of words like "basic" and "fundamental" to describe any research which is not intended to be useful. Trivial questions are still trivial, even when their answers are useless. Their uselessness cannot of itself transform them into fundamental ones.'[22]

6.3   The Assault on Objectivity

The traditional picture of science as a quest for objective, universally valid knowledge has come under heavy fire in recent times. There are many streams that have converged into this torrential assault on objective knowledge. One early source of criticism came from within physics itself, namely quantum mechanics and relativity theory, both of which have demonstrated the impossibility of describing a set of events without reference to the observing system. This has served to re-kindle idealistic philosophies which emphasize the role of human consciousness in the 'construction of reality'. Typical of this approach are the popular writings of physicists like Fritjof Capra, one of the prophet-gurus of the New Age movement. For Capra it is an 'accepted fact' with many scientists that 'the basic structures of the world are determined, ultimately, by the way we look at the world; that the observed patterns of matter are reflections of patterns of mind'.[23]

The more significant criticisms have come from developments within the philosophy of science itself. Contrary to the popular picture of science, a scientist is not a neutral observer of 'facts out there' waiting to be collected and fitted into a theory of the world. Even our simplest acts of perception are mental interpretations. For example, if I say I am observing a 'red chair', I am interpreting a set of external stimuli within the framework of theoretical concepts ('redness', 'a chair') which are social constructions I have learned from childhood—language, after all, is the supreme social construct. So we do not have direct access to physical reality, but all reality is mediated to us through our interpretative schemes.

Scientific activity can be regarded as perception on a much more sophisticated scale. The physical reality which the scientist explores is grasped only through a conceptual scheme. What a scientist observes will be shaped by the theory (and models of reality) he already holds. Whereas a student will see only broken and confused lines when looking at a bubblechamber photograph, a trained physicist will actually *see* a record of sub-atomic events. Theories decide what we select as 'facts', and our interpretation of those facts is also based on theory. Whenever a student learns science he first learns a tradition (sometimes called a paradigm) handed down by those who have practised his field before him. The paradigm forms the framework for his thinking. It defines the subject matter of investigation, trains him in interpreting data through the 'spectacles' of the reigning theory and sets the agenda for future research: namely, what constitutes a 'problem', which questions are legitimate to ask and which are not, etc. So all scientific learning is a complex interplay of tradition, experience and criticism. This will be explored in a little more detail in the next chapter.

Also, a *sociology of science* has developed as a branch of a more general sociology of knowledge (treating 'knowledge' as a social product). This has highlighted the way that scientific paradigms have been influenced by prevailing cultural thought-forms, social prejudices, and even political arrangements. We have already observed the dependence of modern science on huge commercial and military interests. The kind of questions science thinks worthy of investigating will reflect the values, priorities and world-view of the wider society in which scientific activity takes place. And the popularity of theories also reflects wider social interests. So, for example, historical studies on Charles Darwin and public responses to

Darwin's book *The Origin of Species* (1859) have shown that the idea of natural selection in biology, with its emphasis on competition and the survival of the 'fittest', found a ready niche in the value-system of *laissez faire* capitalism and Victorian attitudes towards non-white races who were considered intellectually and morally inferior (a view that Darwin himself held).

So, scientific activity does not occur in a cultural vacuum. We have already seen that the presuppositions on which science is based were themselves derived by the pioneers of science from a Judeo-Christian world-view. We have also seen how Dawkins and others committed to a naturalist world-view tend to describe scientific theories in ways that make them more conducive to that particular world-view than to others. Similarly, Chandra Wickremasinghe, who with Fred Hoyle remain the most passionate defenders of the Steady-State theory (the older rival to the Big-Bang model in current cosmology), unconsciously betrays the underlying reason for his commitment to this theory: 'Consistent with Buddhist belief the universe, comprising countless minor, intermediate and major world systems, each undergoing cyclical changes within them, has an overall quality that is boundless and eternal.'[24]

Some sociologists of knowledge, especially of the older Marxist school of historical materialism, have seen causal connections between the *contents* of individual theories— and not merely social support for them—and prevailing social and economic conditions. In a classic study of the origins of quantum physics in 1920s Germany, Forman argued that the uncertainty principle of Heisenberg and the a-causality of the quantum world were the offspring of the social upheavals and political uncertainties of the Weimar republic. The social rootlessness of the Jews in Europe was the reason why Jewish physicists were most prominent in the development of the new ideas.[25]

We have also seen how the 'conflict' metaphor to describe the relationship between science and theology was developed by Huxley and others in the context of a struggle for social supremacy by the emerging scientific professional class over the Anglican establishment. The amateur scientists, many of whom in England were clergymen or gentlemen of private means were now replaced by a new professional class. Science became a specialized, well-organized, full-time profession. Like all new social groupings it had to carve out for itself a distinctive niche in the intellectual environment. The differences in methodology between the different physical sciences were blurred and all were subsumed under an abstract procedure labelled 'the scientific method' which was credited with the brilliant success of science. The rising prestige of science meant that other branches on the tree of human knowledge felt the threat of being lopped off. All these other disciplines, including theology, sought to remodel themselves on the lines of 'scientific method' in order that their practitioners could avoid being marginalized and perhaps unemployed.

This older ('Positivist' or 'strong empiricist') vision of science—which sees scientists as people dealing with a world of 'pure observations' uncontaminated by 'theory' and 'subjective values' (which belong to the realm of religion and philosophy)—has long been exposed as naive and dangerously misleading. The term 'positive' here carried the sense of what was given or laid down, that which had to be accepted as we found it and beyond which we cannot go; so it carried a warning against all metaphysical and theological enquiry. All knowledge is given in sense-experience alone and codified in scientific laws. All theoretical terms must be translated into statements about sense-observations and logical relations; otherwise they were (at best) 'useful fictions', heuristic aids that did not make assertions about the real world. Positivists dreamed of a science, built up from an axiomatic set of formally defined propositions, which would yield successful predictions and empirically verifiable laws. Positivism went hand-in-hand with an optimistic view of the benefits that the extension of scientific method would bring humanity. This positivism was the dominant image of science through the nineteenth century in Europe and well into the mid-half of the present century. Unfortunately, it still shapes the view of science held by many, including professors of religion and theology who have felt burdened to reshape their professional disciplines to meet the stringent demands of this tradition.

This bizzarely restrictive view of knowledge found one of its most lucid and influential spokesmen in Bertrand Russell. In the closing chapter of his widely popular book *A History of Western Philosophy*, Russell contemptuously dismissed all moral and political philosophy as empty 'sophistry'. Only logical analysis of scientific propositions concerning the physical world was to count as real philosophy. While acknowledging that 'there remains a vast field, traditionally included in philosophy, where scientific methods are inadequate' and that 'science alone, for example, cannot prove that it is bad to enjoy the infliction of cruelty', he continued: 'Whatever can be known can be known by means of science; but things which are legitimately matters of feeling lie outside its province.'[26]

Note how the whole range of human interests, all the questions we can ask and think about, are reduced to either 'science', which is identified with real knowledge, or 'matters of feeling' which are not objects of knowing. Anything that cannot be located within the purview of 'science' is just expressive of emotion. But surely, the fact that our feelings come into our moral judgements does not mean that there is no thought involved in the latter. The example Russell gives of a moral value is actually a case in point: for the German philosopher Nietzsche did indeed hold that the enjoyment of cruelty was a deep universal feeling and therefore acceptable, while there are philosophers of the behaviourist school who would argue that moral judgements do not attach to mental states but only to actions. In other words, these are 'feelings' that can be—and are—discussed, and they themselves arise out of broader world-views which can be articulated and argued rationally. Why positivism is such a strange doctrine is that it took such a long time for people to see its self-contradictory character. Consider Russell's own book on history from which the above quotation was taken. By his own recommendation we should not take books on history seriously (or, at least, those which do not yield scientific 'laws'), because they fall outside the scope of 'science' and are simply emotional exercises on the part of the authors!

The tendency to identify science exclusively with knowledge is nonsensical even within the so-called 'hard' sciences. People don't acquire knowledge for the first time when they start to study science. There is a whole background of knowledge, implicitly accepted, which undergirds their study. We have already seen that many of the presuppositions of physical science- including the reality of the external world and of other minds, the value of intellectual enquiry, the trustworthiness of their memories and the reports of other colleagues both past and present, and much else besides—all count as knowledge, and it is only by treating this as knowledge that it becomes possible to do any science at all. Moreover, by reducing scientific knowledge to the study of observable regularities and their prediction (and thus bracketing the issue of Truth in science) the strong empiricist tradition, paradoxically, converges with idealistic philosophies in subverting the *objectivity* of science. For if we regard theoretical terms (e.g. genes, neutrinos, viruses, black holes, etc) as merely 'useful fictions' in our predictive schemes, and not referring (in however inadequate a way) to real entities and states of affairs in the world, we fail to account for the success of the scientific enterprise and the conviction on the part of most working scientists that their models and theories are about a real world which exists independently of how they think about it.

Such positivism is now largely of antiquarian interest, but it has a disconcerting habit of still turning up in some university departments, especially outside Europe. In the light of the intellectual strait-jacket that it arbitrarily imposed on European philosophy and theology in the name of science for almost a half-century, it is hardly surprising that today we are witnessing a violent swing towards the other extremes of a cognitive supermarket. (Indeed, it may not be that great a swing; for, as indicated above, it is ironical that an overblown empiricism may have actually paved the way for the new 'anti-realist' intellectual temper!) We are now encouraged to be sceptical towards all claims to truth as well as towards all talk of an objective moral order. There are no truths nor values which are binding on all human beings. There is no way, we are told, that we can demonstrate that one man's theory is better than any another or that one set of moral beliefs is superior to another—for all such demonstrations will depend on assumptions which the other will not accept. The only theories that survive are those which have social power on their side.

In what has come to be called the *strong programme* of the sociology of knowledge as developed, for instance, by the Edinburgh school of Barry Barnes and David Bloor, all distinctions between 'knowledge' and 'belief', 'truth' and 'falsehood' are removed. Attention is shifted away from traditional epistemological questions concerning how knowledge of reality is possible to the sociological question how 'reality' itself is socially constructed. Knowledge is now whatever a particular social group takes to be knowledge. Truth is whatever a group regards as true. Reality is what is reflected by the beliefs of a society. Whatever we know/believe (the distinction—which was based on earlier 'realist' assumptions that reality was independent of human conceptions—has now disappeared) is socially conditioned, and explicable *wholly* in terms of the social institutions in which we find ourselves. The ambitious scope of this programme can be gauged by the fact that Barnes and Bloor think that even the 'truths' of logic and mathematics are matters of social convention and custom. What grounds are there for intellectual authority? It all comes down to social persuasion. They write:

> As a body of conventions and esoteric conditions the compelling character of logic, such as it is, derives from certain narowly defined purposes and from custom and institutionalized usage. Its authority is moral and social, and as such it is admirable for sociological investigation and explanation. In particular, the credibility of logical conventions, just like the everyday practices which deviate from them, will be of an entirely local character.[27]

Thus, within the space of one generation we have moved from a predominantly empiricist conception of science to an anti-realist, sociological conception of science. Science is now seen as simply one among many social practices, no different from astrology or witchcraft or the rain-dances of some aboriginal tribe. We shall explore this shift within the philosophy of science itself in a little more detail in the next chapter.

6.4 Towards a Christian Response

I believe that there is much in these arguments that is not only historically valid, but also an echo of biblical teaching about the nature of human sin and the ways in which sin distorts all human structures of knowing and relating. All the assumptions of the Enlightenment (for example, human reason is unaffected by culture; humans are good by nature and perfectible through knowledge and improved living conditions; morality and a just world can be constructed by the autonomous human reason; science gives us a direct and certain knowledge of the world, etc) were deeply anti-Christian, and it should come as no surprise that those who drank so deeply from them should now feel themselves to have been poisoned! The irony is that these very assumptions are still being inculcated in the minds of science students all over the Third World through books and TV programmes which spread this outmoded philosophy in the name of 'science' or of 'modernity'.

So, while welcoming the anti-empiricist shift in (postmodernist) thinking about science and the belated recognition of the ideological captivity of institutional science, Christian students (whether in the West or the Third World) must, nevertheless, expose some of the ideological underpinnings of the assault on science. Owing to the introductory character of the present book, I can only sketch in outline what a Christian critique could look like (though the following chapter will also take up some of the points discussed here):

(a)   The anti-science scepticism of some brands of postmodernism is simply the logical consequence of the idolization of science and reason which has shaped Western society ever since the eighteenth century. Science itself, as we have seen, was based on a Judaeo-Christian vision of the world as a creation of God. When this vision is lost, science becomes simply a quest for power. Human reason, which is designed to function in humble response to God's self-revelation, goes hopelessly astray when it sets itself up as its own judge. Reason cannot justify itself by reason. If all thinking is to be critical reasoning, then sooner or later we shall have to think critically about reasoning itself. And if we are alone in the universe, a mere accidental by-product of an impersonal material process, and all our reasoning is to be based on that presupposition, then reasoning too evaporates. So the preoccupation with 'reason-bashing' that is so much part of the contemporary Western academic and cultural scene is understandable from a Christian perspective.

(b)   It is the Creator who guarantees the objectivity of knowledge. All our formulations are at best tentative and approximate; and they come under his wise judgement and scrutiny. It is thus perfectly reasonable to affirm *simultaneously* that there exists an objectively true account of the universe, including an account of ourselves, and that all our accounts are partial and distorted—and, in some cases, will rightly vary from person to person (for what person A would be correct to believe may, in certain instances, be different from what person B would be correct to believe because he stands in a different relationship to the event or process: but neither person would be correct to believe just anything, and the difference would be an objective fact to the Creator who sustains the flux of events that forms our common experience). Moreover, the degree of objectivity possible in any situation will vary from one field to another, depending on the nature of the enquiry. The Christian has grounds for being both humble and confident in his scientific map-making. Atheistic philosophies of science oscillate between an arrogant positivism and a counter-reaction of confused subjectivism.

(c)   The content of theories and ideas must be assessed as to their truth value, independent of the actual process of discovery or formulation. The latter may be culturally or psychologically unique. For example, is the statement 'Gravitation is a curvature of space-time' true only for German Jews because it was first formulated by a German Jew at a certain period of European history? Similarly, whatever may have been the reasons for the popular acceptance of Darwinian evolution in nineteenth century England, we still need to ask whether the theory does account for species variation and the fossil record better than any other theory currently available.

(d)   There is in existence a large body of reliable scientific knowledge which does claim *universal* assent. The problems of measurement in the sub-microscopic world do not invalidate the rational expectations we have on the basis of this knowledge. For example, each time we fly in an aircraft we are entrusting our lives to fallible theories of aerodynamics and solid-state physics. Despite the fact that this knowledge is not 'provable' by 'universal canons of reasoning', we trust it; and our trust is justifiable only in so far as we do not argue that all theories or views of science are equally valid.

(e)   Even in Einstein's Theory of Relativity, although measurements on events in space-time depend on the observer's frame of reference, the laws of physics which describe those events are themselves *invariant*—that is, true for all observers and frames of reference. The speed of light is also invariant.

Indeed Einstein was led to develop his Special Theory out of a desire to make the electro-magnetic laws of James Clerk Maxwell have the same mathematical form in all frames of reference (which is why Einstein's own name for this theory was actually Invariance Theory!). So, any argument that uses Einstein's theory to argue against the notion of absolute truth or objective values is simply playing with words.

(f)   Likewise in quantum physics, although the values of individual physical variables may not be 'fixed' apart from the process of measurement, there exists an objectively true description of the state of the system, known mathematically as its *wave-function*: so that it *does* matter whether or not one has derived the correct wave-function. There are also other ways of interpreting quantum-mechanical indeterminacy which do not lapse into subjectivism. In fact, it is misleading to argue that human consciousness determines the experimental result obtained in quantum measurements, for it is the observing apparatus (e.g. a photographic plate) and the phenomenon under investigation that make up one indivisible quantum system. Louis de Broglie, one of the early pioneers, warned against such monistic interpretations: '[It has been said that] quantum physics reduces or blurs the dividing region between the subjective and the objective, but there is . . . some misuse of language here. For in reality the means of observation clearly belong to the objective side; and the fact that their reactions on the parts of the external world which we desire to study cannot be disregarded in microphysics neither abolishes, nor even diminishes, the traditional distinction between subject and object.'[28]

(g)   Human values are not wholly subjective. They can be argued over and be compared with one another. To the Christian, those values which are consistent with the Creator's revealed will and character are universally applicable. The scientific community shares many common values: for example, truth-telling (in work and reporting of results), right of free expression and access to information, team-work, patience, honest debate and mutual criticism, and so on. Whenever these values have been flouted (and they have, as anyone familiar with the history of science knows) the scientific world is deeply shocked. Moreover, those who criticize science for its captivity to military or commercial interests and, at the same time, deny the objectivity of moral judgements are simply undermining their own criticism. For the latter is a moral argument. It assumes that the use of science to repress, torture or exploit is wrong—not just for them, but for all people everywhere.

(h) The sociology of knowledge is itself a social practice with its own socially-conditioned rules and criteria of explanation. By its own presuppositions it invites sociological explanation: What is it about the social conditions of the late twentieth-century Western world that makes many of its intellectuals incline towards sociological, rather than philosophical, explanations? Why do some sociologists find it plausible to claim that science is not the pursuit of truth but the will to power?

What will to power is concealed within the sociology of knowledge itself, at least in its strong version, when it aspires to embrace all human knowledge-disciplines in purely sociological terms? These are important questions, and they threaten to lock us into an infinite regress. Even if we were to come up with reasonable answers to these questions, we are faced with the next question of why they seem reasonable to us now when they would have been considered strange to intellectuals living a generation ago. We get sucked into a sociology of the sociology of the sociology of knowledge, *ad infinitum*. This is a vicious regress for the sociologist of knowledge, since the latter purports to offer *total explanations* of why beliefs are held. But such explanations are only what one particular social group, namely sociologists conditioned to argue in a certain tradition-specific way, hold to be valid. The reason they do so can itself be 'explained', and this explanation can itself be 'explained', and so on . . .

(i) No one would deny that social contexts exercise a powerful influence our beliefs, but the issue is whether they tell the *whole* story. If our beliefs are not really *about* anything, we are confronted with the well-known problem of 'reflexivity'. No theory that denies the objectivity of truth can be objectively true. The only way non-sociologists can be persuaded to accept anything that sociologists say is if the latter are prepared to assert that certain things are *true*, that certain social states-of-affairs *do* obtain in the world and *are* causes of wrong beliefs . . . But such assertions would undermine the attempt to shift attention away from what is the case to what people hold to be the case. If the strong programme were shown to be true, it would thereby be shown to be false. If its 'truth' is no different in logical status from all other human beliefs, why should anyone outside that particular group accept it?

Contra Barnes and Bloor, it cannot be a matter purely of local convention that it is undesirable for me both to assert and deny a statement at the same time. For I would be withdrawing the very thing that I am putting forward, and so saying absolutely nothing. Morever, any denial of the principle of non-contradiction cannot avoid invoking the principle itself. Thus the linguistic disapproval that lies behind the principle is grounded in more than simply moral or social constraint: for the only alternative is not a different set of social customs, but total silence. Here the strong programme of the sociology of knowledge has clearly subverted itself. Its use of language to communicate to others presupposes certain 'givens' such as the need for coherence and consistency. Without these, argument is rendered impossible.

Indeed, any person who wishes to *argue* a position (and not merely assert it) in order to convince or persuade others to accept it, cannot avoid distinguishing between what is and what is not the case. Once we accept this distinction we also accept the possibility that many of our beliefs may be mistaken. Thus any argument presupposes that we (and our beliefs) are more than the social influences that shape us. It takes for granted the distinctions between subject and object, between what a person believes and the reality which that belief purports to be about.

6.5   Reductionist Science

Another source of contemporary disillusionment with science has to do with its perceived assault on human dignity. The mentality associated with positivism tends to be reductionist not only in methodology (taking complex wholes apart so that we can investigate the simpler components) but also in philosophy (implicitly or explicitly denying that the whole is anything other than the sum of its parts). Camus' protest (see the introduction to the present chapter) at the reduction of this 'wondrous and multi-coloured universe' to a story of 'atoms and electrons' is an illustration of the way many people fear that everything that makes life worthwhile (for instance, the sense of wonder, human loving, aesthetic beauty, moral judgements) is 'explained away' by the analytical methodology of science.

That there is ample justification for this fear is seen from many cases of popular science journalism. A good example is provided by the blurb on the back cover of Richard Dawkins' best-selling *The Selfish Gene*. We are informed, with splendid assurance, that 'Our genes made us. We animals exist for their preservation and are *nothing more* than their throwaway survival machines.'[29] The logical error involved in this type of reasoning takes the form: 'Since, scientifically speaking, X can be described as Y, X is nothing but Y'. It often accompanies another logical error known historically as the Genetic Fallacy which argues: 'If A has come from B, then A is nothing but B'. We have already seen this form of argument arising many times in discussions about biological evolution.

Let us take some less sophisticated examples. A physicist may legitimately 'explain' a Beethoven symphony as 'longitudinal patterns of molecular vibrations in the air', but this is of no interest to any non-physicist and especially to a musician or musicologist. Indeed the latter will remind the physicist that he/she has quite simply missed the point of the work as a whole. This is not, however, a fault of the physicist, for the appreciation of music is outside the scope of physics. The concept of a symphony is not found in any physics textbook. But, granted that the physics-level description is true, there is a higher-level description which requires *new* concepts to do justice to all that is happening in the room. If, however, the physicist were to deny the musicologist's account simply on the grounds that musical concepts cannot be expressed in terms of physics, he/she would be committing the error of 'nothing-buttery' (a colourful term coined by the late Donald Mackay to describe this logical fallacy).

Another example, this time from computers. A physicist or engineer may explain the behaviour of a computer in terms of transistors and other components of its 'hardware'. The mathematician may say that the computer is behaving in a certain way because it is being controlled by a programme ('software') which, let us assume, is working out the income tax returns of a company's employees. The income tax laws which determine the output of the computer cannot be reduced to the laws of electro-magnetism which determine the computer's circuitry.

The two descriptions *complement* rather than contradict one another. Both are required, but for different purposes.

The physical scientist's *methodological* reductionism is a valid, useful and often necessary approach. It is normally how a scientist works. Each aspect of a complex phenomenon is analyzed separately. But if he/she were to go on to claim that the adequacy of his/her story at its own physical level requires the musician and the mathematician to deny the validity of their higher-order stories, that would be downright silly. To do so would make him/her guilty of *metaphysical* reductionism: namely, the failure to perceive the hierarchical character of reality which requires description and understanding at several levels of meaning. Even within science, while it may be valid to reduce a complex whole to its component parts in order to discover underlying causal mechanisms, it is usually the case that the whole is much more than the sum of its parts. As we move to higher levels of complexity, new properties emerge which require new explanatory concepts and theories which cannot be reduced to lower-level accounts. Thus human sociology cannot be reduced to psychology, psychology cannot be reduced to biology, biology cannot be reduced to chemistry, and chemistry to quantum physics.

We have already seen that the story told by the biblical theologian is a higher-order explanation of reality than the Big-Bang or evolution-story of the natural scientist. The reason we say it is a 'higher-order' account is simply because, even as the musicologist's analysis of music assumes that the physics-level analysis is true (there would be no music if there were no molecular vibrations in the air), so to say that we are persons created in the image of God assumes that the biological-level description is valid. Our personhood is embodied in physical and biological structures, just as Beethoven's symphony is *embodied* in the complex patterns of sound waves in the air or a mathematician's computer programme is embodied in the integrated circuitry of the machine.

What would happen if the computer were wrecked or the air sucked out of the room? The software could still be run on another computer and the symphony played in another place. Likewise, even when our bodies are destroyed in death, our Creator can re-embody our personhood in new structures of his choosing. That is his freedom, and it is the basis of our Christian hope.

There is a close connection between reductionism and ideology. Successful ideologies are based around a single, vivid image which captures one aspect of a wider truth, but by hammering away at that truth blows it up into an all-embracing 'explanation' of reality. Common examples (some of which have been mentioned in earlier chapters) are: the image of class struggle in Marxism, repressed sexual desire in Freudian psychoanalysis, the selfish gene in sociobiology, the conditioned reflex in behaviourism, and male patriarchy in feminism. Facts which do not fit are simply ignored. Those who are hypnotised by such images are under compulsion to reduce everything else to their special terms.

There is a further tendency among professional scientists, and especially those who have strayed into the limelight of the media, to adopt both a pessimistic attitude towards the rest of human thought and an exalted opinion of their own scientific work. Thus, the astrophysicist Steven Weinberg concludes his best-selling book on the origins of the universe, *The First Three Minutes*, by predicting that all earthly life will one day become extinct, a fact which seems to him to mean that consequently all the values we now espouse are invalid and illusory. But the one exception he finds to the general meaningless of life is his own life's work: 'The more the universe seems comprehensible, the more it also seems pointless. But if there is no solace in the fruits of our research, there is at least some consolation in the work itself. Men and women are not content to comfort themselves with tales of gods and giants, or to confine their thoughts to the daily affairs of life; they also build telescopes and satellites and accelerators, and sit at their desks for endless hours working out the meaning of the data they gather. The effort to understand the universe is one of the very few things that lifts life a little above the level of farce and gives it some of the grace of tragedy.'[30]

What are the assumptions which lie behind this purple prose? First, there is the equating of temporality with meaninglessness. This brings to mind the ancient Gnostic/Manichean doctrines of the evil of physical existence-doctrines which the early church refuted with its celebration of creation, the incarnation and resurrection. Is a book meaninglessness because it has a last page? Is a piece of music meaningless because it doesn't last forever? There is something paradoxical about an author asserting the meaningless of a

world whose rational structure he has been brilliantly eluci-
dating for his readers in the preceding pages. Secondly, it is
clear that for Weinberg the task of 'understanding the universe'
basically refers to his own subject, astrophysics (hence the
reference to the instruments of his trade). This alone is sufficient for humankind. But how can this be? It needs to be
argued, but argument is what is lacking. In a world drained of
all value and meaning, how can astrophysics alone have value
and meaning? It would be more reasonable for Weinberg to
conclude that it is the astrophysicist who has value, and thereby
confers value on the work he does. But this, of course, is not
what he says. His words stand as a monument, not to science,
but to a reductionist *ideology of science*.

There is another curious fact worth observing, but this time
in the criticisms of reductionist science by those who advocate
a synthesis of science with the ancient *gnosis* of Hindu, Buddhist or Taoist mystical traditions. Such advocates also argue
that these gnostic world-views have been vindicated by the
results of sub-atomic physics. The 'quantum logic' that applies
to the micro-world is said to be more true than the 'classical
logic' which works in the everyday world, because the former
appears to be consistent with Buddhist philosophy. Also the
physical energy fields of the quantum theory are identified
with the psychic or spiritual energy (or universal consciousness) that the mystics spoke about. But this is simply metaphysical reductionism of the worst kind! On what grounds can
we assert that the quantum world is 'more real' than the
macro-world of everyday experience? Isn't it more likely, as
we saw above, that as we move to more complex levels of
reality new 'entities' appear (such as individual consciousness)
which cannot simply be dismissed as 'less real', leave alone
'illusory'?

Moreover, no true Hindu, Buddhist or Taoist will ever
accept that the mystical insights which are accessible only
to sages, *arahats and rishis* (and that after a lifetime of
rigorous discipline) should be identical to the results of
rational and empirical investigation. To do so would be to
subvert the transcendent truth-claims of the major Indian
and Chinese religious traditions! It would be to reduce
mystical experience to mathematical analysis and physical
experiment. It seems, then, that the attempt (embarked
upon by Capra and others) to marry Indian and Chinese

religions with the latest fashionable theory in the physical sciences can only backfire, hastening the eclipse of the former by the latter.

I leave the final word with Donald MacKay, neurophysicist and philosopher, who has done more than any other scientist to rebut the absurdities of reductionism:

> Even in science it is to the conscious experience of other observers that we appeal in order to resolve questions of objectivity and reality. Thus the practice of science itself is built on a recognition that *people have ontological priority over things*: our fellow scientists as conscious beings, are more indubitably "real" than anything we may collectively believe about the world around us. Nothing could be more fraudulent than the pretence that science requires or justifies a materialist ontology in which ultimate reality goes to what can be weighed and measured, and human consciousness is reduced to a "mere epiphenomenon". Even apart from biblical considerations, this is to stand reality on its head.[31]

6.6 Epilogue

In the traditional Christian approach to issues of faith and science, the prevailing scientific view of the world is taken for granted and science itself is assumed to rest on unchallengeable foundations. The task of the apologist was then to show that the claims of biblical Christianity are essentially compatible with the scientific picture of things.

In this chapter I have reversed the traditional pattern, which I believe to be seriously flawed and also very dangerous. My aim has been two-fold: first, to strengthen the argument of Chapter 3 that the scientific enterprise itself emerges from the world-view of biblical theism as a natural expression of obedience to God; and, secondly, to argue that when science is divorced from this biblical world-view it either leads to an irrational idolatry (what is sometimes labelled 'scientism' or 'positivism') or else provokes denigration and rejection. These two extremes are very evident in all cultures that have been influenced by the spread of modern science and technology; and I believe their intensity is in direct proportion to the decline of biblical influence.

For Christians, whether engaged in scientific research or seeking to understand and explore the biblical revelation and the traditions of their faith, there is a powerful sense of

ultimate accountability in all that they do: accountability to
the God of truth, justice and compassion who will call us
to answer for what we have done with his works, performed
in our midst.

Notes

[1] L. Kolakowski, *Modernity on Endless Trial* (Chicago: University of
Chicago Press, 1990) p. 73

[2] J. Needham, *Science and Civilization in China* (Cambridge: Cambridge
University Press, 1954-) Vol 2, p. 581

[3] See, e.g., R. Hooykaas, *Religion and the Rise of Modern Science* (Edinburgh:
Scottish Academic Press, 1972); S. Jaki, *Cosmos and Creator* (Edinburgh:
Scottish Academic Press, 1980); C.A. Russell, ed., *Science and Religious
Belief: a Selection of Recent Historical Studies* (London: Open University,
1973)

[4] Cited in C.A. Russell, *Cross-Currents: Interactions Between Science and Faith*
(Leicester: InterVarsity Press, 1985) pp. 210, 212

[5] For further details see, e.g., Russell, ibid. Ch 9; O. Chadwick, *The
Secularization of the European Mind in the Nineteenth Century* (Cambridge
University Press, 1975)

[6] Russell, op. cit. p. 195

[7] A. Camus, *The Myth of Sisyphus* (London: Penguin, 1975) p. 25

[8] D. Smail, *Illusion and Reality: The Meaning of Anxiety* (London: J.M. Dent
& Sons, 1984) p. 108

[9] Prof. C. Wickramasinghe, 'An Astronomer's View of the Universe and
Buddhist Thought', *Ceylon Daily News*, May 15 1992

[10] B. Pascal, *Pensees*, trans. AJ Krailsheimer (London: Penguin, 1966) no.
113

[11] T.F. Torrance, *Christian Theology of Scientific Culture* (New York: Oxford
University Press, 1981) p. 63

[12] A. Einstein, *The Evolution of Physics* (New York: Simon & Shuster, 1938)
p. 313

[13] A.J. Leggett, *The Problems of Physics* (Oxford: Oxford University Press,
1987) p. 110

[14] T. Ferris, *Coming of Age in the Milky Way* (New York: William Morrow
& Co, 1988) p. 385

[15] R. Bube, 'Crises of Conscience for Christians in Science' in *Journal of
the American Scientific Affiliation*, March 1989

[16] Source: *Human Development Report 1993* (United Nations Development
Programme, Oxford University Press)

[17] Source: UNICEF, *State of the World's Children: 1990 Report* (Oxford
University Press)

[18] G. Tomson & K. Weerasuriya, 'Codes and Practice: Information in drug
advertisements-an example from Sri Lanka' in *Sociology, Science &
Medicine*, vol. 31, no. 7, 1990 pp. 737-47

[19] D. Melrose, *Bitter Pills: Medicines and the Third World Poor* (Oxfam, 1982)

[20] C. Alvares, *Science, Development and Violence* (Delhi: Oxford University
Press, 1994) p. 43

[21] M. Midgley, *Wisdom, Information & Wonder* (London and New York: Routledge, 1991) p. 41

[22] Ibid. p. 58

[23] F. Capra, *The Turning Point* (London: Fontana, 1988) p. 85

[24] Wickremasinghe, op. cit.

[25] P. Forman, 'Weimar Culture, Causality and Quantum Theory 1918–1927 . . .', *Hist. Stud. Phys. Sci.* 1971, 3, 1–116, reprinted in *From Darwin to Einstein: Historical Studies on Science & Belief*, (eds.) C. Chant and J. Fauvel (UK: Open University, 1990)

[26] B. Russell, *A History of Western Philosophy* (1946, London: Routledge reprint. 1991) p. 788

[27] D. Bloor and B. Barnes, 'Relativism, Rationalism and the Sociology of Knowledge', in M. Hollis and S. Lukes (eds), *Rationality and Relativism* (Oxford: Blackwell, 1985) p. 45

[28] L. de Broglie, *Matter and Light* (New York: Dover Books, 1946) p. 252

[29] R. Dawkins, *The Selfish Gene* (1976, Oxford University Press paperback edition 1989) (my emphasis)

[30] S. Weinberg, *The First Three Minutes: A Modern View of the Origins of the Universe* (London: Flamingo, 2nd ed. 1983) p. 149

[31] D. MacKay, 'Brain Science and Human Responsibility' in *Behavioural Sciences: a Christian Perspective*, ed. M. Jeeves (Leicester: InterVarsity Press, 1984) p. 57 (my emphasis)

7

Idols of Reason and Unreason

' . . . as far as all the opinions I had accepted hitherto were
concerned, I could not do better than undertake once and for all
to be rid of them in order to replace them afterwards either by
better ones, or even by the same, once I had adjusted them by
the plumb-line of reason.'
                   —*René Descartes (1596–1650), Discourse on Method*[1]

Much of what has been written so far can be regarded as a
commentary on the biblical concept of sin. One of the
best-known definitions of sin in recent times is that of the
American theologian Reinhold Niebuhr: 'Sin is . . . the
unwillingness of man to acknowledge his creatureliness and
dependence upon God and his effort to make his own life
independent and secure. It is the vain imagination by which
man hides the conditioned, contingent and dependent character of his existence and seeks to give it the appearance of
unconditioned reality.'[2] Sin is, primarily, a theological concept
rather than a moral one. It speaks of the refusal or failure to
acknowledge the truth about ourselves and to trust the living
God (cf. Rom. 1:21). It leads to the vain effort to establish an
independent and secure basis to our lives (what we have called
'idol-formation'). This illusory quest on the part of one
generation only leaves succeeding generations disillusioned.
But the latter, trapped as they are in God-denying social,
cultural and intellectual formations, only perpetuate the idolatry of their forebears. Thus sin leaves a trail of evil in its wake.

The effects of sin are seen in all areas of human activity, from
the religious to the economic. We have explored some of these
in earlier chapters and humbly acknowledged the challenge
they pose to Christian discipleship in the closing decade of the
second millenium. Sin cuts across all human cultures, traditional and modern. It is embodied in multiple forms of
idolatry, both without and within the Christian church. But
since the present book is concerned with the idols of moder-

nity, we have found it necessary to look a little more closely at the worship of science and some of the backlash it has generated since the 1960s. In the present chapter we continue that story. But, first, to see how sin finds philosophical expression in its quest for an 'independent and secure' basis, we need a quick historical orientation.

7.1 Building on Quicksand

The movement known as the European Enlightenment in the eighteenth century contributed significantly to the distinctive self-consciousness of modern culture. Complex as it was, one of its central features was the attempt to emancipate human reason from the authority of all tradition and custom. Immanuel Kant (1724–1804) summed up the central theme of the Enlightenment in his famous phrase 'Dare to Know'. It was a summons to have the courage to think for oneself, to test everything in the light of reason and conscience, to dare to question even the most hallowed traditions. In his famous essay, *What is Enlightenment?*, he offered the following definition:

> Enlightenment is man's release from his self-incurred tutelage. Tutelage is man's inability to make use of his understanding without direction from another. Self-incurred is this tutelage when its cause lies not in lack of reason but in lack of resolution and courage to use it without direction from another. *Sapere aude!* Have the courage to use your own reason! That is the motto of enlightenment.[3]

Note the important phrase 'without direction from another'. For Kant and the other advocates of Enlightenment, their philosophies were intended to bring about human liberation. The human individual was autonomous, answerable to no one save the dictates of his reason and conscience. He was a self-thinker and a self-legislator. That goal remains the central thrust of modern secular culture. Any attempt to live the Christian faith and to bear missionary witness within that modern worldview has necessarily to face up to the Enlightenment questioning of tradition and of authority.

One of the great precursors of the Enlightenment was the Frenchman René Descartes. Although he died more than a century before the heyday of the French Enlightenment, his influence on that age was considerable. Descartes believed he possessed a New Method which would, at one stroke, sweep away all the accumulated dust of centuries and provide a fresh beginning for human thought. Interestingly, he was urged to develop and publish his method by the Roman Catholic authorities in Paris, concerned as they were by the rising tide of scepticism about knowledge of the physical world and the atheism that attended such scepticism. The Church's official scientific dogmas, which the sceptics queried, were founded on the physics of Aristotle. So Descartes was enlisted as an ally to combat the anti-Aristotelian (and, hence, anti-ecclesiastical) temper of the times. Descarte's own aims remains a matter of some controversy.

Descartes' project begins with scepticism towards any claim to knowledge. He resolves to treat as false any belief that was capable of being doubted: 'I thought I ought to . . . reject as being absolutely false everything in which I could suppose the slightest reason for doubt, in order to see if there did not remain after that anything in my belief which was entirely indubitable.'[4] All our received social inheritance (what he called 'custom and example'), including the knowledge of other minds, God, and the natural world, cannot be an adequate basis for true knowledge, for all these are not beyond the shadow of doubt. The only thing that it would be perverse to doubt, however, is the reality of the doubting subject. Knowledge of the existence of one's self or soul is thus the clearest and most fundamental idea we have: 'I think, therefore I am'.

The subject's next task is to link the doubting self it knows with other objects in the world in a way that will allow them to become known too. 'I shall continue always in this path until I have encountered something which is certain, or at least, if I can do nothing else, until I have learned with certainty that there is nothing certain in the world.'[5] In this way Descartes proceeded, step by step, to demonstrate the existence of God (a Supreme Being, omnipotent and perfectly good) and, from the existence of God, the existence of an external world. Note that God, in this system, played the role of underwriter, serving to guarantee the legitimacy of other steps in the procedure. Descartes' confident hope was that, on the lines of mathematics, a universal system of indubitable knowledge would be constructed on the basis of 'clear and distinct ideas' which were compelling in their cogency. He is thus a typical *rationalist*, one who believes that the human reason is the primary source of our knowledge of reality.

The British *empiricist* approach to knowledge which emerged in the eighteenth century was a refinement of the Cartesian (the adjective deriving from Descartes) model. Here Descartes' 'clear and distinct ideas', which were the basis of all knowledge, came to be replaced by strange new entities called 'sense data', believed to be the raw units of experience. All human ideas are constructions out of sense data. Sensory experience thus became the basis for knowledge and, in the more dogmatic forms of empiricism, the *only* arbiter of any knowledge-claim. But this immediately ran into a predicament for, as David Hume showed very early on in the Enlightenment project, the basis on which these sense-data were put together was itself problematic, so that a risk-free foundation for knowledge remained elusive. The acids of doubt that Descartes dredged up turned out to be corrosive solvents of every system erected to replace traditional sources of knowledge. But, despite the Humean warnings, the ideal persisted: knowledge seen as impersonal, detached and free from doubt. Faith was what people fall back on when knowledge is unavailable.

This model of knowledge has come to be seen as an illusory and, indeed contradictory, quest. On the one hand, it sought to extract knowledge from the inner recesses of the individual subject—whether as 'sense data' or 'clear and compelling ideas'—and, on the other hand, to have this knowledge refer to a real world beyond the individual subject. The image of the thinker as a solitary astronaut in a hermetically sealed cabin and communicating with the outside world only by means of an array of screens and controls in front of him, is ultimately a sterile one. On what grounds does one accept the input appearing on the screens, especially if the astronaut has never been outside the cabin to check if there is anything at all 'out there'?

It is logically impossible to doubt all one's ideas at the same time. Whenever we doubt a truth-claim, it is on the basis of other truth-claims which, at that moment, we do not doubt. For instance, the insight which Descartes regarded as basic—the reality of the thinking 'I'—is not basic at all. We would have no concept of the self at all if we did not think of it as part of a world of others. And, as the later Wittgenstein and other linguistic philosophers have pointed out, such concepts presuppose the use of language, and language implies a society. We cannot speak of the 'I' except in a language that presupposes the existence of others who are able to communicate like ourselves and living in a public world which could be talked about. The language of self-knowledge makes sense only because it is already part of what Wittgenstein called 'a form of life': comprising social practices, publicly established concepts of knowledge and what constitutes standards of acceptable 'evidence', and so on.

Another powerful (if ultimately self-subverting) assault on the Cartesian-Kantian project stemmed from the ideas of the Freudian psychoanalytic school which we noted briefly in chapter two. For, as Ernest Gellner, observes pungently: 'The concept of the "Unconscious" devalues both the individual's autonomy and all inner rational compulsion, *and* the authority of evidence. He can never tell whether his inner conviction is not the voice of the Deceiver, nor can he be sure, whilst unaided, whether the evidence of actual behaviour is not merely "superficial" and a piece of clever deceit. Only the licensed Practitioner (at best) can tell him, and *ex hypothesi*, there is no appeal against his verdict. Nothing could be less Cartesian in spirit than such self-surrender and leap of faith.'[6]

The fundamental error which underlies both the Cartesian and empiricist enterprises has come to be known as *foundationalism*. The foundationalist project centres on the notion that there exists a body of foundational (or basic) propositions which are absolutely certain. Their truth is indisputable and self-validating: simply thinking about them makes their truth apparent. (Softer contemporary versions would speak, not of certainty, but of a 'high intrinsic probability'). More complex (nonbasic) propositions, however, need justification: specifically, they need to be *inferred* from these basic propositions, either deductively or inductively.

This vision of knowledge has been in philosophical retreat during the second half of this century, and in its place have come all kinds of epistemic relativisms. The radical versions of the latter, as we noted in the previous chapter, tend to be self-refuting. In order to avoid these extremes, it is important to note what a valid, non-relativistic critique of foundationalism does *not* say. It does not say that our knowledge has no foundations, that there are no rational grounds for believing anything, that we are all imprisoned within our cultural and linguistic systems, that truths change all the time and differ from person to person and society to society. What it *does* say is that the picture of human thinking given by the foundation-alist model is false and misleading: false, because no system of thought can be validated by principles which are themselves self-evidently true; and misleading, because human thought does not, in any case, proceed by ranking ideas of increasing certainty in a sort of one-dimensional array.

The Enlightenment belief that there exists a neutral and universal vantage-point, independent of culture or tradition, from which the rationality (or otherwise) of any tradition can be evaluated is naive. It is only a little less naive than their confident view that the Enlightenment itself happened to occupy that masterly position. The thinkers of the Enlighten-ment failed to see how, like the rest of us, they themselves were culturally-conditioned, caught up in the flux of historical existence. Moreover, they themselves were not as united in their projects as is commonly supposed. As Alasdair MacIntyre expresses it,

> Both the thinkers of the Enlightenment and their successors proved unable to agree as to what precisely those principles were which would be found undeniable by all rational persons. One kind of answer was given by the authors of the *Encyclopedie*, a second by Rousseau, a third by Bentham, a fourth by Kant, a fifth by the Scottish philosophers of common sense and their French and American disciples. Nor has subsequent history diminished the extent of such disagreement. Consequently, the legacy of the Enlightenment has been the provision of an idea of rational justification which it has proved impossible to attain.[7]

7.2 The Post-Kuhnian Perspective

The foundationalist dream underlay much of the philosophical discussions about science well into the middle years of the twentieth century. It still survives in popular accounts and perceptions of science, but it was dealt a body-blow through a book by the American Thomas Kuhn, which explored how scientific changes actually occurred.[8] Kuhn's work has been the most influential of recent discussions of science, and his ideas have stirred up powerful currents in other branches of academic learning. His work may best be appreciated as an attack on the individualist mythology that permeates most accounts of science. According to this mythology, the scientist is a solitary hero who tries to make sense of the data he encounters by constructing theories. In the older 'inductivist' model, the individual inquirer first assembles his data and then extracts from them a theory. In the anti-inductivist, Popperian school of thinking (associated with the eminent Sir Karl Popper)[9], one first begins with a theory, which is an act of creative imagination, and then bravely sets out to seek the empirical data which can blow it to pieces. On the latter model, science is seen not as the *generator* of reliable truths, but as the reliable *eliminator* of falsehoods.

But this, as many critics pointed out at the time, led to a vision of scientific activity that ran counter to the way science was actually perceived in society and also among the scientific community— namely, as a body of beliefs close enough to the truth to warrant the risking of lives and huge national fortunes. Popper had sought to succeed where Descartes and Kant had failed: to vindicate the rationality of science, to rescue it from mere culturally-inspired opinion. But his 'falsification by counter-example' has the ironic effect of subverting our confidence in the practical *application* of well-established scientific ideas, for such confidence now appears irrational.

A more serious charge concerns the historical plausibility of his portrait of science. Scientists cling tenaciously to their theories; and if they followed Popper's bold proposal of 'conjecture and refutation' and abandoned a theory which was rich in explanatory power simply because it conflicted with a few observations, many famous theories would never have seen the light of day. Popper's falsificationist view of science seems naive. It fails to appreciate the complexity of the relation between theories and experimental evidence. But, be that as it may, the only point I wish to make for my present purpose is that both the inductivists and the Popperians stood in the Cartesian tradition of assuming that there exists a straightforward, rational cognitive procedure which leads to reliable knowledge when applied by any individual inquirer. The path out of ignorance lay neither in a transcendental realm nor with the human investigator, but rather in the ruthless application of a correct epistemological method.

Kuhn demolished all that. He pointed out that scientists live in communities. They think, for the most part, in terms of a shared cluster of concepts, models, historical examples of what counts as 'good work', standards of evidence and so on, all of which constitute a scientific *paradigm*. This paradigm is more important than a mere theory, for it generates research programmes which can develop the theory in various directions. The paradigm introduces a measure of order into the manifold, chaotic and ambiguous world of 'data'. It thus makes orderly inquiry possible. These paradigms have developed historically, and a scientific training involves being socialized into the reigning paradigm in one's particular field of study. Under the conditions of what Kuhn called 'normal science', members of a research community do not question the reigning paradigm. They remain loyal to it, interpret everything through it, and seek to extend it by accommodating an increasing amount of data within its explanatory power.

But the paradigm is not immortal. There comes a time when it experiences a crisis as more and more data accumulate which cannot be accounted for within the paradigm. But unless there is a serious contender—that is, a new paradigm—on the horizon, normal science continues. 'Revolutions' in science, such as those which occurred under Copernicus or Darwin or Einstein, usher in new paradigms: the old 'facts' are now seen in a new perspective and new data emerge as fresh 'facts': 'The historian of science may be tempted to exclaim that when paradigms change, the world itself changes with them. Led by a new paradigm, scientists adopt new instruments and look in new places. Even more important, during revolutions scientists see new and different things when looking with familiar instruments in places they have looked before.'[10]

According to Kuhn's account, instead of observations determining theory, the theory determines the observations. Since there are no 'theory-neutral' observations, he seems to be going further than simply saying that a new paradigm shows us things we did not notice before. The world is actually different for different paradigms. 'In a sense that I am unable to explicate further,' he writes, 'the proponents of competing paradigms practice their trades in different worlds.'[11] For instance, scientists once believed in a substance called phlogiston (which was emitted during combustion) and now they do not. The concept of 'mass' in Newtonian physics has a very different meaning from the concept of 'mass' in Einsteinian physics. Although the same word continues to be used, their meanings are given by the paradigms within which they occur. Since the world is always seen only through a paradigm, there is a problem as to how those working within different paradigms can discuss their ideas with each other. If scientific theories cannot be measured against anything external to themselves, they cannot be judged correct or mistaken, true or false. In the 'revolutionary' stage of a given scientific discipline, contending paradigms are strictly *incommensurable*. There is no neutral ground that can be used to adjudicate between them.

Why, then, should scientists change their paradigm? It is important to remember that Kuhn is neither a scientist nor a philosopher as much as a historian of science. He recognizes the fact of scientific change but stresses that his interest is mainly in the kind of community that emerges after a time of crisis. He points out that individual scientists embrace a new paradigm 'for all sorts of reasons and usually for several at once', but has left himself without any means for giving a rational account of that change. It cannot be because of an appeal to experience, since experience is governed by the paradigm. Nor can it be through the discovery of a fatal error, since what counts as error is also controlled by the paradigm. He invokes 'idiosyncrasies of autobiography and personality' and even 'the nationality or the prior reputation of the innovator and his teachers'.[12] Those who resist the new paradigm cannot be said to be wrong, and he says of the historian of science: 'At most he may wish to say that the man who continues to resist after his whole profession has been converted has *ipso facto* ceased to be a scientist.'[13] Since 'there is no standard higher than the assent of the relevant community',[14] he argues that we may 'have to relinquish the notion, explicit or implicit, that changes of paradigm carry scientists and those who learn from them closer and closer to the truth'.[15]

Thus philosophy of science, which traditionally sought to give a rational justification for scientific activity and a rational reconstruction of the way theories logically depend on each other, has now dissolved into history and sociology. Science is no longer the awesome offspring of the human reason interacting with an objective reality, but simply what one particular historical community happens to do. By focusing on the scientific community, Kuhn draws out the way in which norms and standards are enforced by the community. His early critics were quick to point out, however, that while he had given a reasonable explanation of disagreement among scientists, he was unable to explain the regular emergence of consensus in science. For, if scientific theories cannot be compared, then how do we account for the speed with which the opposition is won over to a new paradigm? Extra-scientific considerations alone cannot explain the ability of the scientific community to resolve its disagreements so quickly.

In his later papers, Kuhn distanced himself from the free-wheeling relativism that others extracted from his position.[16] He softened his conception of 'incommensurability' and repudiated charges that he had made the practice of science irrational. He clarified his position as being a rejection of *rule-governed inference* when it came to choosing between competing paradigms. 'In a debate over choice of theory, neither party has access to an argument which resembles a proof in logic or formal mathematics.'[17] Consensus is possible because there *are* shared values and criteria of theory-choice, but different scientists will weigh the criteria differently and also differ in the way they interpret the application of a criterion and so reach different conclusions. The appraisal of theories is more like the rationality of value judgements in other areas of life than the rationality of rules. One may accept this wholeheartedly, while still expressing the criticism that Kuhn's tendency to speak of different 'worlds' for different paradigms lapses into incoherence, since it is difficult to talk of there *being* different realities without becoming vulnerable to the charge that one is still in some sense talking about reality.

Remaining for the moment with Kuhn, the rationality he ascribes to science is still strictly limited. He is still reluctant to use the concept of 'truth'. So we cannot talk of one theory as more 'true' than another, nor can we say that the practice and theories of science are more 'true' than, say, those of an astrologer or a witchdoctor. Thus he is unable to explain the success of science, the remarkable predictive and manipulative power of modern science. Any theory of scientific change must surely account for scientific *progress*— why the scientific community holds Einsteinian Special Relativity, for example, to be a *truer* account of reality than Newtonian mechanics. Kuhn somehow subscribes to a firm belief in such progress while remaining within a purely sociological framework of explanation. Whether this is logically tenable is seriously open to question.

Kuhn's anti-empiricism fitted the mood of the times. His anti-realist tendencies find their logical culmination in the work of Paul Feyerabend. For Feyerabend, scientists are 'salesmen of ideas and gadgets, they are not judges of truth and falsehood'.[18] He takes an 'anything goes' approach to all assertions, procedures, inferences and conclusions. Once the foundations of empirical knowledge are set aside, and there is nothing to put in its place, we no longer talk about reality but about people's beliefs about reality, from truth to what is held to be true. For Feyerabend, what counts as 'reality' depends on our choice: 'We concede that our epistemic activities may have a decisive influence even upon the most sordid piece of cosmological furniture—they may make gods disappear and replace them by heaps of atoms in empty space.'[19] Elsewhere he writes, 'There exists . . . a plurality of standards just as there is a plurality of individuals. In a free society, however, a citizen will use the standards to which (s)he belongs: Hopi standards, if he is a Hopi: fundamentalist Protestant standards, if he is a fundamentalist.'[20]

We have seen in the previous chapter how such relativistic assaults on the concept of objective truth tend to be incoherent, if not actually self-contradictory. Feyerabend is asserting *as true* the proposition that there is no such thing as truth. He launched a vituperative assault on Popper and all other defenders of 'objective knowledge', an assault the justification of which was rendered doubtful by Feyerabend's own claims! But this seemed to have escaped his notice, so intoxicated was he with his newly discovered cognitive freedom, a freedom which he apparently withholds from those who criticize him. Similar inconsistencies are found among those literary scholars who argue that 'anything goes' when it comes to reading a text, since meanings are created by readers, but who angrily accuse critical reviewers of 'distortion' where their own texts are concerned!

It is one thing to say that theories/paradigms can govern how we see and experience the world, but quite another to make it impossible any longer for human thought and language to refer to a real world. It is one thing to admit that the analysis of the concept of truth has been problematic, but quite another to regard it as 'illusory' and to give it up altogether as a human goal. It is one thing to question whether experience is the only source of knowledge, but quite another to assert that knowledge and moral values are only a matter of social convention like driving on the right or the left side of the road. It is one thing to argue for opportunity of choice between different traditions and theories as a good *strategy* in the discovery of truth, but quite another to deny that any view is better than any other or some reasons more valid than others.

7.3   Personal Knowledge

The thought of Michael Polanyi (1891–1976) blows like a refreshing breeze over the stagnant swamps of contemporary philosophy of science. Polanyi, unlike all the other philosophers we have mentioned above, was a practising research chemist as well as being a philosopher and historian of science. He sought to understand science from the perspective of the working scientist and not from the finished product of 'scientific knowledge'. His aim was to reform the epistemological basis of science, to resolve the dilemma posed by the rending asunder of the 'objective' and 'subjective' poles of knowledge, which he believed had left their disastrous mark on modern society. He called his approach a 'post-critical philosophy' because it rejects the false understanding of scientific objectivity that has dominated western culture since the Enlightenment. But he does so in a way that rescues science from the quagmire of relativism.

Polanyi is indebted to fellow-scientists such as Einstein who emphasized the logical gap that exists between scientific ideas and empirically given experience. Theories are creations of the human mind, wonderfully imaginative guesses which cannot be captured by some systematically applied procedure. Although empirical data may suggest what a theory should be, the latter cannot be deduced from the former. In this he is reminiscent of Popper. But we must not leap to the conclusion that scientific concepts and theories are purely subjective entities in the human mind. They derive from and disclose the actual rational structure of the real world; they are formed under the impact which the world makes upon our minds as we humbly seek to understand it and reflect its rationality. This is a theme that we discussed in chapter 6. It leads to Polanyi's conception of scientific objectivity as recognizing:

. . . that the discovery of objective truth consists in the apprehension of a rationality which commands our respect and arouses our contemplative admiration; that such discovery, while using the experience of our senses as clues, transcends experience by embracing the vision of a reality beyond the impression of our senses, a vision which speaks for itself in guiding us to an ever deeper understanding of reality . . .[21]

Polanyi expresses in a more sophisticated idiom the Augustinian dictum *credo ut intelligam*: I believe that I may understand. There is no knowing without trusting, and trusting is the way to knowing. The art of scientific discovery is a skill like other skills, whether perception, learning a language, riding a bike or using a tool. Like other skills it can be passed on only by example from generation to generation and learned to a certain extent by imitation. Like other skills its premisses cannot be explicitly articulated. In Polanyi's words, 'We know more than we can tell'. Scientific discovery shares with all other skills the fact that the premisses of the skill are not understood by us before we actually start performing it. We learn the skill first, only then do we reflect on it. A child learns to speak by imitating adults. To do this the child must accept on trust that the words the adults use are meaningful. This is a 'tacit knowledge' which the child then expresses in imitation and practice. There are no explicit rules by which the language is learned. By a whole series of tacit judgements the child achieves a similar 'indwelling' in language as do his parents and so grasps the meaning of words and of language. From childhood to manhood he must trust before he can understand.

So too in scientific work. We accept that science is a meaningful activity and a valid system of thought. We believe in science in order to know through science. And since there are no formal rules to guide us in scientific discovery, we entrust ourselves to a Master from whose examples we pick up the skill. Since we have already explored (in the previous chapter) the first aspect of such 'faith', let us here examine in a little more detail this second aspect which Polanyi highlights: 'He who would learn from a master by watching him must trust his example. He must recognize as authoritative the art which he wishes to learn and those of whom he would learn it.'[22]

Polanyi insists that the authority of science is essentially traditional. The scientific tradition is passed on through personal contact between teachers and learners. This is true from the elementary level through to the highest levels of original research. We rely on the authority of teachers until we are in a position to come to see for ourselves that what is taught is true. In other words, doubt can never be the first step on the road to knowledge. Critical doubt is a secondary intellectual activity. It comes into play only after we have thoroughly assimilated the scientific tradition as embodied in textbooks, scientific journals and the personal authority of a skilled practitioner who is certified by the scientific community to be a competent teacher.

Only after a long period in which the student has submitted herself to the authority of the tradition is she qualified to work alongside a scientist who is doing original research on problems which are not only unsolved, but perhaps not even recognized except by this scientist. It is while watching this scientist at work, seeing how he selects fresh lines of inquiry, reacts to new clues and unforeseen difficulties, evaluates ambiguous evidence, discusses other scientists' work, and keeps speculating about hundreds of possibilities that may never be realized, that the vision of science is passed on and the student learns the skill of research. There are no objective criteria by which the work of the scientist can be judged; he, along with his peers, is the one who sets the standards and determines the criteria, and—in doing so—accepts the risks of failure as well as the possibility of success. The question of success and failure may not be settled for a long time. Einstein's theories were, after much debate, accepted on the basis of their intrinsic beauty and comprehensiveness, but it was only long afterward that there was any experimental demonstration of their truth.

This authority, which is essentially personal and informal in character, and to which the student submits in order to learn, is there to bring her into contact with a reality greater than herself. The whole process of assimilating the art and premises of science is very similar to the actual structure of scientific discovery itself. The theory and the experiments we perform, the scientific tradition embodied in the textbooks which we use and accept on authority, are there as 'clues' which we tacitly integrate into the background map in our minds and thus intuit the rationality in nature to which they point us.

This tacit dimension in human knowledge is an important aspect of Polanyi's epistemology. Consider a surgeon using a probe to explore a cavity which cannot be observed directly.

He doesn't pay attention to the pressure of the probe on his hand because his 'focal awareness' is on the patient's body. His 'subsidiary awareness' of the instrument in his hand is tacit. The probe is an extension of himself, he *indwells* the probe. But when he was a student and first introduced to this instrument, no doubt he did give his central attention to it. But with experience he comes to rely on it. A time may come when he feels it is no longer adequate for the task at hand and needs to be replaced. But as long as he is using it, he must continue to trust it. He uses it a–critically. He cannot both rely on it and doubt it at the same time.

This is why Polanyi uses the term 'personal knowledge': only a person can relate subsidiaries to a focus and sustain such an integration. The error of rationalism and empiricism (and its offshoot positivism) has been that they tried to replace such personal participation in the act of understanding by some explicit, systematic procedure. But this is what we cannot do. Not only because many of the clues and subsidiaries are unspecifiable, but primarily because we are dealing with an act of integration and not deduction. We cannot give an explicit explanation of an act of tacit integration. So there is no foundationalist justification for science, nor any strict proof of any part of science.

Every working scientist indwells the scientific tradition as a whole, as well as the reigning paradigm in his or her field of inquiry. Without such a commitment to the tradition, science would collapse. At any moment in history some part of the tradition may be under critical scrutiny, but this scrutiny is possible only if the tradition as a whole is accepted tacitly. The authority of this tradition is maintained by the scientific community. It is held together by the free assent of its members, and exercised in practice by those who determine which article will be accepted for publication in research journals and which rejected, and by those in charge of appointments to research and teaching posts in universities and other institutions.

In his writings Polanyi has given examples of many theories which were rejected without discussion simply because they fell outside the accepted tradition. Unless the tradition was protected from every maverick idea, science could not develop. At the same time, if the tradition did not make room for questioning and radical innovation, science would stagnate.

Innovation, however, can be responsibly accepted only from those who are already skilled 'indwellers' of the tradition. And one new fact, or even several new facts, do not suffice to displace an established paradigm. This can happen only when a new paradigm is offered in its place, one that conveys an alternative vision of reality that commends itself by its beauty, rationality and comprehensiveness. The acceptance of such a vision is a personal act in which I commit myself in the knowledge that I am in a cognitive minority and could be proved wrong. It involves personal commitment to the new paradigm (or theory) and the willingness to risk one's scientific reputation.

But it is not on that account merely subjective. The scientist who commits himself to the new vision does so—as Polanyi puts it— with 'universal intent'. He believes it to be objectively true, and he therefore causes it to be widely published, invites discussion and criticism, and seeks to persuade his fellow scientist that it is a true account of reality. He may have to wait several years before there is convincing experimental verification of his vision. But at no stage is it merely a subjective opinion. It is held with 'universal intent' as being a true account of reality which all people ought to accept and which will prove itself true both by experimental verification and also by opening the way to fresh discovery.

So the scientific tradition expresses freedom, but not anarchy. The tradition is not infallible but it does provide a firm framework for research. There are universal norms which have to be respected if research is not to become futile. Speculation is limited by what has been established as true. This Republic of Science (Polanyi's phrase for the scientific community) is pluralist in the sense that it is not controlled from any one centre, and scientists are free to differ from one another and to argue with one another. But because it believes that there is an objective reality to be known, differences of opinion are not simply left to coexist as wonderful examples of 'tolerance'. Instead they are fiercely debated, argued over and investigated further until one vision prevails over all the others as being more true or else some fresh way of seeing things opens up and enables the others to be seen as but partial glimpses of the same truth. It is because scientists operate within the same premises and values that agreement between them is at all possible.

In summary, the diffused authority of the Republic of

Science rests on the fact that each member of the community is informed by one and the same tradition, that each acknowledges the same set of past masters and the authority of the ideals and standards tacitly handed down from each generation. The past masters can be criticized and the tradition improved, but only because the authority of the tradition is assumed in all such criticism. In Polanyi's own words: 'We can see here the wider relationship, upholding and transmitting the premisses of science, of which the master-pupil relationship forms one facet. It consists in the whole system of scientific life rooted in a common tradition. Here is the ground on which the premisses of science are established; they are embodied in a tradition, the tradition of science. The continued existence of science is an expression of the fact that the scientists are agreed in accepting one tradition, and that all trust each other to be informed by this tradition.'[23]

7.4   Mission Implications

There are obvious lessons here for Christian education and mission. Polanyi himself saw an analogy between the theological task and scientific research, but it was left to theologians such as Thomas Torrance and Lesslie Newbigin to draw out the full implications of his epistemology for Christian theologizing and missionary endeavour. There are strong similarities between the practice of Christian discipleship and the practice of scientific research. Both are learned through submission to a received tradition. The Christian tradition, embodied in the biblical writings and the history of their interpretation in different ages and places, expresses and carries forward —like the scientific tradition— certain ways of looking at things, certain models for interpreting experience. Unlike science it involves us in questions about the ultimate meaning and purpose of things and human life- questions which modern science excludes as a matter of methodology. As Newbigin puts it, 'The models, concepts, and paradigms through which the Christian tradition seeks to understand the world embrace these larger questions. They have the same presuppositions about the rationality of the cosmos as the natural sciences do, but it is a more comprehensive rationality based on the faith that the author and sustainer of the cosmos has personally revealed his purpose.'[24]

Like the scientist, the Christian believer has to learn to

indwell the tradition. This is what is involved in developing a 'Christian mind'. We do not study the Bible as an end in itself, but rather in order to read the world *through* the Bible. Its models and concepts are things which we do not simply examine from the perspective of another set of models (drawn from, say, the Enlightenment tradition or a Confucian tradition) but have to become the models through which we understand the world. We have to internalize them and to dwell in them. And, as in the case of the pupil learning physics or biology, this has to be in the beginning an exercise of personal faith. But being personal does not mean that it is subjective. Newbigin uses Polanyi's terminology to argue that 'The faith is held with universal intent. It is held not as "my personal opinion" but as the truth which is true for all. It must therefore be publicly affirmed, and opened to public interrogation and debate. Specifically, as the command of Jesus tells us, it is to be made known to all nations, to all human communities of whatever race or creed or culture. It is public truth.'[25]

This parallel, however, is not complete. 'In the case of the scientific community, the tradition is one of human learning, writing, and speaking. In the case of the Christian community the tradition is that of witness to the action of God in history, action which reveals and effects the purpose of the Creator. These actions are themselves the reality which faith seeks to understand. Thus the Christian understanding of the world is not only a matter of "dwelling in" a tradition of understanding; it is a matter of dwelling in a story of God's activity, activity which is still continuing. The knowledge which Christian faith seeks is knowledge of God who has acted and is acting.'[26]

Another difference lies in the distinction between 'discovery' and 'revelation'. The scientist says, 'I have discovered that . . .'; the prophet declares 'God spoke to me'. But does the use of the word 'revelation' mean that reason has been left behind? Obviously not. Both the scientific discovery and the spoken word have God as their ultimate source. In both instances they become the starting point of a fresh tradition of reasoning in which the significance of these disclosures is explored, developed, tested in experience, and extended into further areas. Reason operates in the tradition based on revelation no less rigorously than it does in the tradition based on discovery. So to pit reason against revelation, as is common in some Christian as well as non-Christian circles, is nonsensical. Reason, as we have seen above, is not an independent source of information. It bites on what it receives. It is always embodied in a tradition. The difference between the scientific tradition and the biblical tradition is not that one relies on reason and the other on revelation. 'The difference lies at the point of contrast between the two ways of expressing the original experience: "I have discovered" and "God has spoken".'[27]

7.5   Alienated Minds

Idolatry carries its own backlash. The worship of any idol provokes the emergence of its counter-idol in the course of time. By speaking of human knowledge as being always a *personal* involvement with a reality beyond the self, Polanyi pointed a way beyond the false antitheses (or idolatries) of objectivism and subjectivism, reason and culture, autonomy and tradition, which have bedevilled the modernist project from its beginnings in the European Enlightenment. Knowledge is available to all who are willing to personally commit themselves to its quest, to take personal responsibility for it, and to publicly share that knowledge with others while acknowledging the possibility that one may be wrong. We cannot evade personal responsibility for our assertions of truth.

This vision of knowledge runs counter to the foundationalism of many medieval and modern epistemologies. It is *not* the case that one is warranted in accepting some belief only if it can be inferred from propositions which are self-validating, known impersonally and indisputably. It is not the case that scientific reasoning is *fundamentally* different from reasoning in other realms such as theology or law, for the rational appraisal of scientific theories is also a rationality of human judgement and not a rationality of rules. This does not imply that there is no structured, intelligible reality outside our own conceptions and beliefs, nor that we must give up truth as the aim of theoretical inquiry, nor even that we can never come to know truth. Although many who have been impressed by the difficulties of foundationalism have allowed themselves to be attracted towards one or more of these other positions, Polanyi has shown convincingly that these are invalid conclusions. The rejection of a false certainty does not entail scepticism about truth. Rather, it is to acknowledge a created rationality appropriate to our situation as fallible, fallen human knowers.

Polanyi's description of how science works is a far cry from the mythology of science expressed by many non-scientific philosophers and modern theologians. For instance, Don Cupitt, an outspoken, self-styled 'radical' theologian, contrasts what he labels 'traditional dogmatic thinking' with the supposedly 'critical thinking' of science in the following manner: 'As we see most clearly in the case of scientific method, critical thinking uses methodical doubt as a way to truth . . . Open, sceptical and puritanical, it is (or should be) systematically dedicated to self-criticism. It demythologizes, it detects and discards illusions with almost obsessive zeal. In terms of traditional dogmatic thinking such a temper of mind is subversive, destructive and nihilistic.'[28]

What is disconcerting is to find these errors duplicated in the contemporary Christian church. Not infrequently in writings about inter-faith dialogue we encounter the (unrecognized) assumption that the writer has access to a privileged position, outside of tradition and culture, from which he can survey the whole world of religious beliefs and conclude that they are 'partial and symbolic expressions' of an ineffable, universal Mystery. Or else we are told that, in the light of the collapse of 'the project of modernity', we now have to give up all notions of 'universality' and 'objectivity' and speak of our Christian tradition as being simply 'one conversation among others'. Other related theologies espouse a relativistic twilight where there are no objective controls ('anything goes') on textual interpretation, and the reader's creativity reigns supreme. At the other end of the ecclesiastical spectrum we encounter attempts to 'prove' the truth of Christianity on the basis of 'indubitable evidence' and to capture the 'essence' of the gospel in a context-independent, rationalist framework.

It is apparent that both 'liberals' and 'fundamentalists', each of whom perceives the other as the arch-enemy, are far more deeply united than they think: they are both victims of the mood-swings of post-Enlightenment western culture. If the church is to be obedient to her vocation to confront the multiform idolatries of the modern world, she must begin by repenting of ways of thinking about truth, tradition and authority that derive from an alien mindset.

Finally, we should never forget that, in the biblical perspective, the 'darkening of human minds' is ultimately rooted in the hardening of the human heart towards God and one's fellow human beings (cf. Rom. 1:18ff; Eph. 4:17ff). The fallen human reason, which is restored to its proper functioning by divine revelation and redemption, finds talk of sin distasteful. Postmodernist relativism shares with Enlightenment modernism a naive belief in the human power to overcome evil. In the former case, not by the sustained application of reason to human affairs but by reconstructing our 'world' through the endless free play of language, the creation of 'new vocabularies'. Thus, 'sin' and 'evil' are banished at one stroke. A Christian confrontation with modernity cannot, therefore, remain at the level of epistemology. It must address the mysterious perversity of the human will and its need for reconciliation and liberation.

Notes

[1] R. Descartes, *Discourse On Method, and Other Writings*, trans. F.E. Sutcliffe (Harmondsworth: Penguin, 1968), Discourse 2, p. 37

[2] R. Niebuhr, *The Nature and Destiny of Man*, 2 vols (New York: Scribner, 1941–1943) 1:137–38

[3] Quoted in E. Cassirer, *Kant's Life and Thought* (New Haven and London: Yale University Press, 1981) pp. 227f

[4] Op. cit. Discourse 4, p. 53

[5] Ibid. opening of Meditation 2, p. 102

[6] E. Gellner, *Reason and Culture* (Oxford: Blackwells, 1992) p. 91

[7] A. MacIntyre, *Whose Justice? Which Rationality?* (Notre Dame: University of Notre Dame Press, 1988) p. 6

[8] T.S. Kuhn, *The Structure of Scientific Revolutions* (Chicago: University of Chicago Press, 1962, 2nd edition enlarged, 1970)

[9] E.g., K. Popper, *The Logic of Scientific Discovery* (London: Hutchinson, 1959)

[10] Kuhn, op. cit. p. 111

[11] Ibid. p. 150

[12] Ibid. p. 153

[13] Ibid. p. 159

[14] Ibid. p. 94

[15] Ibid. p. 170

[16] See 'Reflections on my Critics' and 'Logic of Discovery or Psychology of Research?' in *Criticism and the Growth of Knowledge*, eds. I. Lakatos and A. Musgrave (Cambridge: Cambridge University Press, 1970); 'Objectivity, Value Judgement, and Theory Choice' and 'Second Thoughts on Paradigms', in *The Essential Tension* (Chicago: University of Chicago Press, 1977)

[17] T.S. Kuhn, 'Reflections on my Critics' in I. Lakatos and A. Musgrave (eds), *Criticism and the Growth of Knowledge* (Cambridge: Cambridge University Press, 1970) p. 260

[18] P. Feyerabend, *Philosophical Papers, Vol II: Problems of Empiricism* (Cambridge: Cambridge University Press, 1981) p. 31

[19] P. Feyerabend, *Science in a Free Society* (London: New Left Press, 1978) p. 70

[20] P. Feyerabend, *Philosophical Papers*, vol. II, op. cit. p. 27

[21] M. Polanyi, *Scientific Thought and Social Reality* (Oxford University Press, 1977) p. 101. See also *The Tacit Dimension* (New York: Doubleday & Co., 1966); *Science, Faith and Society* (Chicago: University of Chicago Press, 1964)

[22] M. Polanyi, *Science, Faith and Society*, p. 15

[23] Ibid. p. 52

[24] L. Newbigin, *The Gospel in a Pluralist Society* (Grand Rapids: Eerdmans, 1989) p. 49

[25] Ibid. p.50

[26] Ibid. pp. 50–1

[27] Ibid. p. 60

[28] D. Cupitt, *The Sea of Faith* (BBC Publications, 1984) pp. 252–3

8

The Cross and Idols

'Then the chief priests and the Pharisees called a meeting of the
Sanhedrin. "What are we accomplishing?", they asked. "Here is
this man performing many miraculous signs. If we let him go on
like this, everyone will believe in him, and then the Romans will
come and take away both our temple and our nation" '

—John 11:47–48

The reasons for the crucifixion of Jesus are complex. But it is
clear that in announcing the dawn of God's new order (the
'kingdom of God') and in his teaching about the blessings and
demands of that new order, Jesus was, from the very outset of
his ministry, coming into direct conflict with the power
structures of his world. To announce that Israel's God was king
was not a new message in Israel. It was, after all, the heart of
the nation's faith. What *was* new was the announcement that,
in and through the humble ministry of this Jesus of Nazareth,
the king was reclaiming his world from the false gods who
reigned in his place. This was depicted as the fulfilment of the
Abrahamic promise. Indeed Jesus consistently understood
himself to be not simply another prophet in the line of
Abraham and Moses, but rather the fulfilment of all that the
prophets spoke of and longed for (e.g. Lk. 4:16–21; 10:23,24;
24:25–27; Matt. 11:2–14; 16:13–17; Jn. 5:39,40,45–47; 8:56).

8.1 Power Confrontations

The Roman empire, in the period of the New Testament, was
the heir of Babylon, both as a military power and, more
importantly, as the spiritual embodiment of all that biblical
Babylon symbolized. The Greco-Roman culture despised
humility and physical weakness. Her pagan gods were gods of
strength. They offered their devotees power, military conquests, fabulous wealth and immortality. As for the Jews in the
time of Jesus, they had, as so often in their chequered history,

lost sight of their God-given national vocation. While remaining physically separate and culturally distinct from both their pagan overlords and other nations, they were spiritually indistinguishable from them. They had begun to think of Yahweh too in terms of pagan notions of power. The kingdom of Yahweh had become for them synonymous with the universal rule of the nation of Israel and Yahweh's public destruction of their enemies. Even the early disciples of Jesus were captivated by a vision of Jesus as another Judas Maccabeus (or, even better, a Jewish Ceasar), setting up his throne in Jerusalem and calling forth God's wrath on the nations, with them as his honoured assistants (e.g. Mk. 10:32ff). They expected Jesus to inaugurate Yahweh's kingdom among men of influence and wealth, to exclude foreigners and 'sinners' (the term the religious establishment used for the common people who couldn't keep all the obligations of the Mosaic Law), and to execute vengeance on their national foes.

What a shock they were in for! Reading through the gospel narratives we quickly become aware of how disturbing was Jesus' redefinition of the kingdom of God. He overturned all the expectations of his disciples, let alone that of the nation's leaders, concerning the nature of God and the salvation he was inaugurating. Those who had been consigned to the margins of society (e.g. women, lepers, tax-collectors, Samaritans) suddenly found themselves invited to enjoy the in-breaking of God's rule in their midst. Life with Jesus seemed to be one constant round of celebration. He declared that God's kingdom was a gift to be received, not something to be earned. It was open to all who were prepared to become like 'little children' (Mk. 10:15)— in other words, like the 'nobodies' of society, insignificant people, those who had no possessions to boast of, whether political power, social status, economic wealth, religious merit, moral or intellectual achievement. Such people are unlikely to dictate to God what God should do and shouldn't do, whom God should accept and whom he shouldn't. Jesus saw in them the representatives of the true Israel, a new 'people of God' to be reconstituted around himself.

In the name of Israel's king, who was also the king of all creation, Jesus challenged the leaders of Israel by crossing social and political barriers which kept people apart. He often violated social taboos (e.g. the purity laws which operated like a caste-system in the Judaism of his day). Unlike contemporary

Jewish rabbis, he not only associated with women but discussed theology with them (e.g. Jn. 4:19ff), and invited them, along with men, to be his disciples. Even his healing 'signs' had deep political implications. For people such as the lepers and the woman with the haemorrhage (Mk. 5:24ff), their disabilities meant exclusion from membership of Israel. They could not enter the Temple which was the focal point of Jewish national identity (lepers were not allowed even into Jerusalem). By healing and embracing lepers, Jesus not only healed them physically but also restored them socially. And the power that lay at the heart of God's kingdom was not the self-assertive power of pagan rulers, he said, but the power of self-giving service. It was power to love people, even one's enemies, to the point of dying for them.

The Jesus of the gospels, unlike the Jesus of religious sentimentalism, is both gentle and tough, witty and serious, stern and tenderhearted. The one thing the people who met him could not do was to stereotype him. He demolished all their labels and expectations, upset their attempts to pigeonhole him as a prophet, a wonder-worker, or a conventional rabbi. He was vilified as a 'glutton and a drunkard', accused of consorting with prostitutes and other 'low life', resented for his scathing wit as much as for his relentless exposure of religious pretentiousness. As Lord Hailsham, a former Lord High Chancellor of Britain, marvels in his autobiography, 'The tragedy of the Cross was not that they crucified a melancholy figure, full of moral precepts, ascetic and gloomy . . . What they crucified was a young man, vital, full of life and the joy of it, the Lord of life itself . . . someone so utterly attractive that people followed him for the sheer fun of it.'[1]

The novelist Dorothy Sayers, too, has described with her characteristic pungency the impact of Jesus: 'The people who hanged Christ never, to do them justice, accused him of being a bore— on the contrary, they thought him too dynamic to be safe. It has been left for later generations to muffle up that shattering personality and surround him with an atmosphere of tedium. We have very efficiently pared the claws of the Lion of Judah, certified him "meek and mild" and recommended him as a fitting household pet for pale curates and pious old ladies. To those who knew him, however, he in no way suggested a milk-and-water person; they objected to him as a dangerous firebrand.'[2]

One of the most disturbing thing about Jesus, and that which finally sealed his execution, was the radical way he understood himself as being and doing everything that the Temple in Jerusalem stood for. Not only did he heal and restore people to community life, he offered them free and unmerited forgiveness for their sins, thus claiming to reconcile them to God. In doing so he was subverting the entire sacrificial cultus in the Temple. The Temple was the place to which every Jew went to be cleansed from an impurity and to be forgiven for his sins. The daily and annual sacrifices, administered by the Temple priesthood, were a reminder of the holiness of God and the costly nature of his love for sinful Israel. They also expressed the worshipper's response of faith-commitment. The Temple was also the place where the glory of God was believed to dwell: it was the symbol of Yahweh's personal presence among his covenant people. In short, the Temple represented everything that made Israel unique in the world.

But Jesus changed all that. Forgiveness of sin was now found in him, not in the Temple cult. He claimed the authority to cancel the debt of sin and offer new life in the Holy Spirit (one of the gifts that would follow the inauguration of the new order of the kingdom of God— e.g. Ezek. 36:25–27; Ezek. 37; Is. 32:15f; Joel 2:28). In driving out the money-lenders from the Temple courts and 'cursing' a fig tree on the way to the Temple (Mk. 11:12ff) he acted out two dramatic parables against the Temple— and, by implication the whole nation. He wept over the city and its temple, and warned of its impending destruction (Matt. 23:37-24; 25). In other words, Jesus saw that Israel had failed in its calling to be God's agent of healing for the nations. The Temple had become an object of national idolatry and religious power-mania. Far from siding with the Jewish nationalists in their fanatical violence against Rome, Jesus saw the present Roman occupation and the impending destruction of Jerusalem by the Roman armies as God's just punishment on a people who had forsaken the very God whose name was constantly on their lips. It was his human body that would be the new Temple (Jn. 2:19–22), the meeting-place between God and humankind. This was why to honour him was to honour God, to reject him was to reject God, to know him was to know God, and even to see him was to see God (e.g. Jn. 5:19ff; 14:8ff; Lk. 10:16). He would also fulfil the destiny of Israel himself: bear her judgement at the hands of pagan powers, demonstrate perfect filial obedience to her God, reveal the glory of God by making atonement for the sin of the nations and so drawing them into his light.

The death of Jesus, then, was the battle-ground between God and the powers of evil represented by religious and political idolatry. In Jesus we see the one human being who refused to bow at the shrine of any idol. He thus attracted the venom of all who benefit from the worship of idols as well of the demonic powers which idolatry evokes. All our collective human rebellion was poured out on him. So the cross reveals the true nature of idolatry: Jesus was condemned to death, not by the irreligious and the uncivilized, but by the highest representatives of Jewish religion and Roman law, because his claims and his way of life undermined both the idolatry of achievement (whether religious or secular) and the idolatry of power in all human relationships.

8.2   The God of the Cross

However, the cross also reveals God's response to that idolatry. Even in his suffering and death, Jesus resisted the temptation (which he confronted right through his public ministry) to fight evil on its own terms. Indeed he allowed evil to do its worst to him. Paradoxically, the point of apparent defeat became the moment of greatest triumph. It was the victory of divine weakness over human strength, of the word of truth over the machinations of power, of self-surrendering love over self-grasping hate. The bodily resurrection sealed that victory by reversing the human verdict passed on Jesus and showing that idolatry and death would not have the last word in God's creation. But it is important to remember that the New Testament writers saw that victory accomplished, not only through the resurrection, but at the point of Jesus' death. It was the offering of his life in death that proclaimed the glory of God (e.g. Jn. 12:23ff; 13:31, 1 Cor. 1:22–25; Col. 2:15). It is in this context that the all-important question arises: who is this who sets up his rule in the world by dying under the full weight of its evil?

The world, including many Christians, assume that they know already what the word 'God' means and then try to see whether it is appropriate or not to fit Jesus into that meaning.

But the witness of the New Testament writers lies in the other direction. They argue that we don't really know who the Creator of the universe is until we look at Jesus, and especially at Jesus crucified. This is a staggering claim. To worship one who was obviously a human creature like the rest of us would seem to be the very pinnacle of idolatry. But the earliest Christians, all of whom came from the strongest monotheistic tradition in the world, not only found themselves addressing this Jesus in the language they traditionally used of God himself, but made this the launching-pad for their campaign against all idolatry!

The German theologian Eberhard Jungel puts this well:

> The traditional language of Christianity insists on the fact that we must *have said to us* what the word "God" should be thought to mean. The presupposition is that ultimately only the speaking God himself can say what the word "God" should provide us to think about. Theology comprehends this whole subject with the category of revelation . . . Therefore, when we attempt to think of God as the one who communicates and expresses himself in the person Jesus, then we must always remember that this man was *crucified*, that he was killed in the name of God's law. For responsible Christian usage of the word "God", the Crucified One is virtually the real definition of what is meant with the word "God". Christian theology is therefore fundamentally the theology of the Crucified One.[3]

Similarly, in a popular book entitled *Who Was Jesus?*, the British New Testament scholar Tom Wright points out that the Christian doctrine of incarnation 'was never intended to be about the elevation of a human being to divine status. That's what, according to some Romans, happened to the emperors after they died, or even before.' Wright continues, 'The Christian doctrine is all about *a different sort of God*– a God who was so different to normal expectations that he could, completely appropriately, become human in, and as, the man Jesus of Nazareth. To say that Jesus is in some sense God is of course to make a startling statement about Jesus. It is also to make a stupendous claim about God.'[4]

These claims, which lie at the heart of the biblical gospel, are what makes Christ and Christian faith unique. The English poet Edward Shillito, writing after the savage butchery of the First World War (1914–1918) when men slaughtered each

202 Gods That Fail

other in the defence of modern gods they could not even name, pointed to the wounds of Jesus as God's only credentials to a suffering humanity:

> The other gods were strong; but Thou wast weak;
> They rode, but Thou didst stumble to a throne;
> But to our wounds only God's wounds can speak,
> And not a god has wounds, but Thou alone.[5]

The unknown author of the Epistle to the Hebrews expands on the theme of Jesus having fulfilled every aspect of Old Testament Law. He is both the high priest and the sacrificial victim, the altar and the way through the curtain into the Holy of Holies. He is a prophet superior to Moses, a priest superior to Aaron and Melchizedek. He is 'crowned with glory and honour' (2:9) as the Son whom God 'appointed heir over all things' (1:2). He is the pioneer, the one who having 'tasted death for everyone' (2:9) is able to free 'those who all their lives are held in slavery by their fear of death' (2:15) and lead them into the final Jerusalem, the city of the living God. Those who follow him are already 'receiving a kingdom that cannot be shaken' (12:28). They have no need of any further religious performance, for by being in himself the reality that the Law dimly pointed to, Jesus has revealed the latter to be simply 'a shadow of the good things to come' (10:1).

In the light of this reality, it was fitting that those who still sought to preserve temple and nation (Jn. 11:48) should lead Jesus outside the city gate of Jerusalem to be judicially executed in the place where the carcasses of the sacrificial animals were burned (13:11,12). It was not the 'sinners' but the religious who flung him away. So, the author concludes his exposition of Jesus' significance with the logical call to his fellow Christians: 'Let us, then, go to him outside the camp, bearing the disgrace he bore. For here we have no enduring city, but we are looking for the city that is to come' (13:13,14). The disciples of Jesus are called to go out to where Jesus already is: *discarded by religion*. They are to share his 'disgrace', the ridicule and hatred that every ancient religious community directs at those who dare to say that piety and tradition can separate us from God and that the 'ungodly' may be closer to experiencing God's kingdom than the 'righteous' (as in e.g. Rom. 4:5; Lk. 18:9–14). This 'going outside' is a picture of Christian conversion. But the writer does not depict this as a conversion from one religion to another, as if what was being offered in the gospel was a superior religion ('Christianity') to live by. Rather, it is fundamentally a conversion from every form of religious identity to Jesus Christ.

Here the epistle to the Hebrews comes full circle. The whole argument draws us back to the opening verse of the epistle, the foundation from which this new perspective springs: 'In the past God spoke to our forefathers through the prophets at many times and in various ways, but in these last days he has spoken to us by his Son. . . .' (1:1) The apostle John puts it like this, 'For the law was given by Moses; grace and truth came through Jesus Christ. No one has ever seen God, but God the One and Only, who is at the Father's side, has made him known' (Jn. 1:17,18). Jesus does not supplant religion (taking 'law' and 'prophets' above in their broadest sense) by confronting and rejecting it. Rather, he lifts the whole discourse to a different level of reality altogether: knowing God is a matter of 'grace and truth', not of 'law', and he is the one who uniquely brings both to humankind. He embodies both in his own person. Law can only follow grace, and all our views of God, the world and ourselves now have a new criterion of truth: the crucified and risen Jesus. It is here that the Creator of the universe (in the words of Martin Luther) 'pours out not sun or moon, nor heaven and earth, but his own heart and his dearest Son, and even suffers him to shed his blood and die the most shameful of all deaths for us shameful, wicked and ungrateful people'.[6] The death of God's own Son is the only adequate measure of what God thinks of our sin; and the death of God's own Son is the only adequate basis on which we may be forgiven that sin.

The cry of dereliction on the cross, 'My God, my God, why have you forsaken me?' is at the very heart of the gospel. Jesus enters the depths of despair that sin dispenses and humanity suffers in its alienation from God. In the words of the apostle Paul, 'God made him who had no sin to be sin on our behalf, so that in him we might become the righteousness of God' (2 Cor. 5:21) To meditate on what happened at Golgotha is, as Jürgen Moltmann has emphasized in recent times, to be led beyond an abstract monotheism and a secular atheism to a full-blooded trinitarian understanding of ultimate reality. The cross discloses God's true identity as the holy and loving Father and as the loving and obedient Son who offers himself in the Holy Spirit for sinful humanity. We see the Father's grief in the handing over of the Son to death out of holy love for the world, and the Son suffering abandonment by the Father in loving obedience to him. The Fatherlessness of the Son is matched by the Sonlessness of the Father. Father and Son are most deeply separated in their forsakenness, at the same time most deeply united in their mutual surrender.[7] And at the point where (to the world) God seemed to be most totally absent, at that point (to the eye of post-Easter faith) he was most profoundly revealed.

This is how Moltmann expresses God's involvement with us in the death of Jesus: 'In Jesus he does not die the natural death of a finite being, but the violent death of the criminal on the cross, the death of complete abandonment by God . . . God does not become a religion, so that man participates in him by corresponding religious thoughts and feelings. God does not become a law, so that man participates in him through obedience to a law. God does not become an ideal, so that man achieves community with him through constant striving. He humbles himself and takes upon himself the eternal death of the godless and godforsaken, so that all the godless and the godforsaken can experience communion with him.'[8] There is no rejection, degradation or loneliness he has not assumed in the cross of Jesus.

Here we are face to face with the supreme challenge to idolatry: the Crucified God (to use Luther's bold phrase). In renouncing the privileges of an idol, by becoming flesh and embracing our human weakness, vulnerability, suffering and death, he overturns the world. He thus frees us from the quest for powerful idols by becoming himself a victim of idolatry. We have see how idolatry dehumanizes the idolater as well as the victims. The crucified God, in the historical form of a dehumanized victim himself, converts dehumanized men and women into truly human beings.

We noted in an earlier section Martin Luther's stirring protest at the 'Philosophers' God' in the name of the 'crucified God'. Luther spoke out of his personal experience of God's grace, wonderfully illuminating the epistles of Paul which he had begun to study and teach students in the university town of Wittenburg. In the Heidelberg Disputation of 1518 he further contrasted the 'theologians of glory' with the 'theologians of the cross'. Here he was drawing on two biblical passages, Exodus 33:18ff and Romans 1:20ff. In Exodus 33, Moses asks God, 'Show me your glory'. He receives the answer, 'You cannot see my face; for man shall not see me and live.' Instead, God places Moses in the cleft of a rock and covers him with his hand until his glory has passed by. Then God takes away his hand and Moses catches a glimpse of his back, but not of his face full of glory.

For Luther, the 'theologians of glory' seek to know God directly in his obvious divine power, wisdom and majesty. But he includes this within the idolatry described by Paul in Rom. 1:20ff. Men misuse the knowledge of God given in creation. This leads to idolatry and inflated human pride. So God reveals himself in a way that deals with human idolatry and destroys human pride. Such knowledge of God is a saving knowledge which brings sinful men and women into a right relationship with God and harmony with the rest of creation. This is the theology of the cross. It recognizes God precisely where he has 'hidden' himself, in his sufferings and in all that which the theologians of glory consider to be weakness and foolishness.

God cannot meet us when he is clothed in his majesty. 'Do not get mixed up with this God,' said Luther, 'Whoever wishes to be saved should leave the majestic God alone— for he and the human creature are enemies'. In this life God never meets us in that way nor does he want us to try to approach him that way. The brilliance of his glory would be too terrible to bear. The God we need is the 'God who is clothed in his promises-God as he is present in Christ . . . We know no other God than the God clothed with his promises. If he should speak to me in his majesty, I would run away—just as the Jews did. However when he is clothed in the voice of a man and accommodates himself to our capacity to understand, I can approach him.' Elsewhere he wrote, 'Thus you may find God in Christ, but you cannot find God outside of Christ even in heaven.'[9] Religious intellectualism and moralist activism alike belong to the realm of idolatry. They seek to carve out an area of human autonomy, to shake off the creature's dependance on the Creator. They are centred on human achievement, and not on receptivity to the divine gift. They refuse to 'let God be God'. Only the theology of the cross, which learns to think of God and life through the wounds of Christ, anchors us in reality. For God is now free to be God.

In all this Luther was echoing, in sparklingly fresh and vivid language, the central convictions of New Testament preaching. For instance, listen to the apostle Paul himself:

> Where is the wise man? Where is the scholar? Where is the philosopher of this age? Has not God made foolish the wisdom of the world? For since in the wisdom of God the world through its wisdom did not know him, God was pleased through the foolishness of what was preached to save those who believe. Jews demand miraculous signs and Greeks look for wisdom, but we preach Christ crucified: a stumbling block to Jews and foolishness to Greeks, but to those whom God has called, both Jews and Greeks, Christ the power of God and the wisdom of God (1 Cor. 1:21ff).

Although the God of the cross is also the Creator of the human mind, and although all true knowledge is grounded ultimately in his wisdom, God refuses to subject the message of the cross to the judgement of human wisdom. For this would be to dethrone himself as God and to enthrone man. It would be to capitulate before human sin, not to save humanity from its sin. Thus God's strategy for the remaking of humanity— for the saving of the world from its foolish and self-destructive idolatry— is centred in the shame of the cross. The cross, by overturning our notions of power and wisdom, dethrones our self-centredness and humanizes us. It glorifies God, enabling us now to serve him in our humanity.

From the perspective of human wisdom, the cross is a mad aberration, a sick joke. In his masterly survey of crucifixion in the antiquity, Martin Hengel has reminded us of the horror and revulsion which it universally engendered. Only rebellious slaves and the worst kind of criminals were executed by crucifixion in the Roman empire. Little wonder that 'the heart of the Christian message, which Paul described as the "word of the cross" . . . ran counter not only to Roman political thinking, but to the whole ethos of religion in ancient times and in particular to the ideas of God held by educated people'.[10] The early Christian apologists were acutely conscious of the scorn that the message of the cross met with among the sophisticated men and women of the Greco-Roman world. Thus Justin Martyr (c.100–165) observed that the basis for the offence caused by Christian preaching was Christian belief in the divine status of the crucified Jesus and his significance for salvation: 'They say that our *madness* consists in the fact that we put a *crucified man* in second place after the unchangeable and eternal God, the Creator of the world.'[11]

That the early followers of Jesus lived and died for such a foolish message must surely be the biggest evidence in support of its veracity. It is the very absurdity of the 'word of the cross' that is its best *apologia*. For a Jewish audience, the confession 'Christ [the Messiah] died . . .' was an unprecedented scandal, contradicting the prevailing messianic expectations. Hengel also points out that while, among the Stoics for instance, an ethical and symbolic interpretation of the crucifixion was possible, 'to assert that God himself accepted death in the form of a crucified Jewish manual worker from Galilee in order to break the power of death and bring salvation to all men could only seem folly and madness to men of ancient times. Even now, any genuine theology will have to be measured against the test of this scandal.'[12]

The social consequences of this new preaching are also evident:

> Brothers, think of what you were when you were called. Not many of you were wise by human standards, not many were influential; not many were of noble birth. But God chose the foolish things of the world to shame the wise; God chose the weak things of the world to shame the strong. He chose the lowly things of this world and the despised things– and the things that are not— to bring to nothing the things that are, so that no one may boast before him (1 Cor. 1:26ff).

Here is a church *of* the poor and *for* the poor that springs into being as a result of gospel preaching. Such a radical gospel must not be confused with the recently fashionable tendency in Asian theological circles to identify the church with the 'peoples of Asia' and evangelism with political activism, the latter usually paraded in semi-Marxist categories. The Korean theologian Kim Yong-Bock, for example, takes it for granted that 'the most basic theological affirmation is that the peoples of Asia are the children of God . . . The dalits, janata, minjung, the poor, oppressed, women and the ethnically and culturally alienated in Asia are the very people of God.'[13] The work of the Christian church, then, is to identify with those who are already the people of God in order to bring them freedom from *han* (feelings of brokenness, resentment, helpless anger—

all of which can form a potentially revolutionary source of psychic energy). He continues, 'God's work among the suffering people in Asia is the establishment of God's sovereign rule of justice, in which the people become sovereign.'[14] Likewise, a report by a group of ecumenial Asian theologians asserts that 'the very Third World people—the oppressed poor, the minjung, the blacks, and women— who are the victims of dominating capitalist powers also contain within themselves the dynamic of revolution and liberation. Marxism is perhaps the best tool for them to become liberated and to revolutionize toward a new, humane, just world order.'[15]

One is forced to wonder: is this what the wisdom of the cross has been reduced to? The radical vision of sin that the cross gives has now been diluted and domesticated into a purely secular concept of being wronged by others; there is no need anymore for 'grace and truth' to liberate us from the ideological distortions of all forms of power, only the transfer of power from one social group to another. The writer seems to betray a naive view of oppressed peoples. Neither Jesus nor Paul had any illusions about human oppression. Though the message of salvation for the rich and powerful comes through the poor (and depends on their willingness to identify with the poor), the poor themselves are not automatically saved by their poverty. Sin runs deeper than the socio-political structures in which it is often embodied. The crucifixion narratives themselves show us that though Jesus was executed along with two criminals, both of whom suffered the same humiliation and degradation that he suffered, he was greeted with two very different responses. One man demanded freedom as his right, the other threw himself on Jesus' mercy while acknowledging his own guilt. Were they both liberated by the cross? One wonders further: is the reduction of the gospel to a call for the political liberation of the 'oppressed masses' itself another manifestation of modern idolatry— specifically, the replacement of human persons by collective abstractions? And does this not serve to perpetuate the dehumanizing tendencies of such idolatry in our world?

A similar reductionist approach is apparent in the renowned Sri Lankan Jesuit Aloysius Pieris' exhortation to the Asian Church to be 'baptized' in the 'Jordan of Asian religiosity' and to be 'crucified' on the 'Cross of Asian poverty'. We have already seen that the latter calling is indeed a consequence of faith in One who was rejected for challenging the power-structures and idolatry of his society. But the way Pieris develops the former is more dubious. He describes Jesus' voluntary baptism at the hands of John the Baptizer as an identification with 'the stream of an ancient spirituality',[16] and draws from this the implication that 'the first and last word about the local church's mission to the poor in Asia is total identification . . . with monks and peasants who have conserved for us, in their *religious socialism*, the seeds of liberation that *religion* and *poverty* have combined to produce'.[17]

But this is surely reading into the text what Pieris wants to say anyway! Jesus did identify himself with the Jewish renewal movement taking place around John in the Judaean wilderness. But John speaks of Jesus as one 'more powerful than I, whose sandals I am not fit to carry', and who would himself baptize the people not with water but with 'the Holy Spirit and fire', and sought to deter Jesus saying, 'I need to be baptized by you, and do you come to me?' (Matt. 3:11–14). Eventually it is John who submits to Jesus' request! Is Pieris prepared to say that the Hindu and Buddhist traditions of spirituality relate to Jesus in the way that John's 'stream of an ancient spirituality' does? Evidently not. We can share both Pieris' concern for the poor and his call to the church to learn from Asian religious traditions without indulging in such selective biblical exegesis.

Third World Christians, struggling under oppressive regimes and unjust global economic structures, would do well to heed the wisdom of that great Christian pastor, theologian and martyr under the Nazis, Dietrich Bonhoeffer (1906–1944). In the opening chapter (entitled 'Ethics as Formation') of his famous *Ethics*, Bonhoeffer, having reminded his readers that 'only by God's executing judgement upon himself can there be peace between him and the world and between man and man' and that 'what befell Christ befalls every man in him'[18], warns them: 'Neither the triumph of the successful nor the bitter hatred which the successful arouse in the hearts of the unsuccessful can ultimately overcome the world. Jesus is certainly no apologist for the successful men in history, but neither does he head the insurrection of shipwrecked existences against their successful rivals.'[19] Bonhoeffer continues, 'In the cross of Christ God confronts the successful man with the sanctification of pain, sorrow, humility, failure, poverty, loneliness and despair. That does not mean that all this has a value in itself, but it receives its sanctification from the love of God, the love which takes all this upon itself as its just reward. God's acceptance of the cross is is his judgement upon the successful man. But the unsuccessful man must recognize that what enables him to stand before God is not his lack of success as such, not his position as a pariah, but solely the willing acceptance of the sentence passed on him [i.e. in Christ] by the divine love.'[20]

For Bonhoeffer, it is only the 'form of Jesus Christ', which is the form of the cross as opposed to the form of human plans and programmes, that truly confronts the world and defeats it. Only in the cross of Christ, that is, as those upon whom God has executed sentence, do we recognize and realize our true form. We do not fundamentally transform the world with our ideas or our principles or our revolutions, but it is the Risen Christ, who bears the new world within himself, who transforms men and women into conformity with himself.

> To be conformed with the Incarnate— that is to be a real man . . . The quest for the superman, the endeavour to outgrow the man within the man, the pursuit of the heroic, the cult of the demigod, all this is not the proper concern of man, for it is untrue . . . To be conformed with the Incarnate is to have the right to be the man one really is. Now there is no more pretence, no more hypocrisy or self-violence, no more compulsion to be something other, better and more ideal than what one is. God loves the real man. God became a real man.[21]

Surely there is no more liberating message than this, for victim and for victimizer! Human beings can become truly human because God became truly human. This is why we cannot accomplish our own transformation, but it is rather God who takes our human form into his own form so that we may become, *not God*, but, in the eyes of God, *human*. The church is no less than the risen Christ taking form among human lives. The church bears, for the sake of all, the form which is the proper form of all humanity. To quote again Bonhoeffer's own words, 'The Church is the man in Christ, incarnate, sentenced, and awakened to new life. In the first instance, therefore, she has nothing to do with the so-called religious functions of man, but with the whole man in his existence in the world with all its implications. What matters in the Church is not religion but the form of Christ, and its taking form amidst a band of men'.[22]

What unites most ancient Eastern religions and modern Western secular humanisms is the quest for *techniques of power*: techniques that will confer self-mastery and/or the mastery of the natural order. The gods of the Indian and Chinese pantheons are essentially personifications of various forms of power. Devotion and ritual, less demanding than the rigorous contemplative techniques of the mystics, have as their goal freedom from vulnerability, suffering and contingency. The right formula, the correct devotional posture, the appropriate prescribed offering . . . these are the preoccupations of the traditional devotee. In the modern technocratic world, finding the right advertising slogan, the correct management method, or the appropriate political style have come to dominate the lives of many men and women. Manipulation of the 'spiritual' realm is now combined with the manipulation of the human and material realms in the technocratic spirituality of the New Age. The cross of Christ, which directs us to the powerlessness and suffering of God freely embraced, stands as the great antidote to the obsession with technique, religious and secular. The disciples of Christ, secure in the gracious love of God, have nothing to offer the world but their own vulnerability.

8.3   The Cross Among the Nations

Returning to the theme of Jesus crucified outside the gates of Jerusalem, the disciples of Jesus must also be where he is: *rejected by nationalism*. They are to share his 'disgrace' (Heb. 13:13), the isolation and hatred that is incurred when we dare to identify with those of other national communities and to think globally rather than parochially. The cross of Jesus reconciled Jew and Gentile, slave and free, men and women by bringing them all down to the same level as sinners and raising them all to the same level as children of God. United in sin, even more united in grace (e.g. Eph. 2:11–18; Gal. 3:26–29). The reconciliation of the cross thus has horizontal as well as vertical dimensions: it is what makes both individualism and nationalism flat contradictions of the message of the cross. The gospel is universal at its very heart.

However, just as being converted from religion to Jesus does *not* imply the rejection of all that is good, true and beautiful in the world of religion; so, being outside nationalism does not imply the denigration of national cultures. In fact, the very reverse. It is only when we dare to 'step out' of our national cultures (not necessarily physically, but by striving to look at things in the frame-work of the gospel), that we develop a critical appreciation of our own nation's greatness and also of its particular idolatries.

We saw earlier how the Christian movement was viewed by the Romans with perplexity and suspicion, partly because it distanced itself from common religious observances which were often associated with 'good citizenship'. One second-century apologist, pleading for the toleration rather than repression of Christians, described them in this way:

> Christians are not distinguished from the rest of mankind by country or language or customs . . . Their doctrine has not been discovered through any inventive faculty or the careful thought of pretentious men . . . While they live in cities both Greek and oriental, as falls to the lot of each, and follow the customs of the country in dress, food, and general manner of life, they display the remarkable status of their citizenship. They live in countries of their own, but as sojourners. They share all things as citizens; they suffer all things as foreigners. Every foreign land is their native place, every native place is foreign . . .[23]

But this attitude of relativizing political citizenship in the light of higher realities did not mean that Christians failed to take local cultures seriously. In truth, it was the very opposite. From its inception, Christian mission affirmed cultural specificity while remaining universal in its scope. The events of Pentecost were understood as a reversal of Babel. The miraculous gift of 'tongues' was symbolic of the church's vocation, to continue the ministry of Jesus to the nations under his continuing leadership and empowering. Pentecost served to 'sanctify' vernacular languages as adequate channels of access to the truth of God. From the point of view of the gospel, no culture is inherently unclean in the eyes of God, nor is any culture the exclusive norm of truth. This commitment to a *Christian pluralism* (which endorsed social and linguistic diversity) was not mere tolerance. It was to recognize that, in God's plan of salvation, the heritage of all the nations, purged of all their idolatrous accretions, will ultimately serve his kingdom (e.g. Is. 60; Rev. 22:24).

One of the apostle Paul's great contributions to the early church was his vigilance on two theological fronts: against Jewish cultural hegemony, on the one hand, which sought to impose Jewish norms and customs on non-Jewish converts; and against the syncretizing tendencies of the Greco-Roman cults, on the other, which formed the social context in which most Christian converts lived. The church of Jesus Christ was the first fruits of the 'new creation' which incorporated all that is worthy in the Jewish and Gentile worlds, cleansed through the message of the cross of their demonic elements. Ethnicity is thus legitimized, without being absolutized (e.g. see Acts 15:1–2; Gal. 2:11ff; 3:25–28; Eph. 2:14–22; 1 Cor. 10:14–22, 32; Rom. 15:8–16; Col. 2:13–17; Phil. 4:8).

We have seen how the gospel, which originally set itself against the power of religion and radically questioned the religious way of being in the world, was itself turned into another religion under the patronage of the imperial powers. Constantine became the undisputed emperor of Rome in 312 C.E. believing that the Christ of the Christians had given his armies victory in battle. The genuineness of his 'conversion' is still being debated by historians: it seems it was a curious mixture of religious superstition, genuine admiration for Christians, and political perception. The Edict of Milan the following year led to legal toleration of Christians. Finally in 380 C.E. the emperor Theodosius officially transformed Christianity into the sole state religion, with all the potential for idolatry, corruption and demonization that this entailed. That the church realized that potential to no small degree is a tragic fact of history we have to acknowledge. It was not so much a matter of the state taking over the church as the church taking over the state: with the empire in decline, the church found itself stepping into the power vacuum and taking on the prerogatives of the state. In one sense this was inevitable, and it made possible the preservation of the cultural treasures of Greco-Roman civilization from utter extinction. However, the corrupting influence of temporal power was to undermine the church's spiritual authority abroad more effectively than any imperial decree of persecution could ever have done.

Christianity is still identified with its European past, despite the fact that most Christians today are to be found outside of Europe and North America. Christian mission in the Third World is still perceived by other religious communities as the imposition of 'Western religion' and an implicit belief in the superiority of Western cultural values. Often such perceptions are based on ignorance both of the Christian faith and of the complex entity we call loosely 'Western culture'. It is also often motivated by overt prejudice. But, surely, Christians, for whom the recognition of human failure and the reality of forgiveness is at the heart of the message they proclaim, should ever be willing to confess and repent of the perversions of the gospel which have resulted through the colonial experience. We are not called to be defenders of empirical Christianity, but witnesses to the crucified and risen Christ. And Christ stands as judge of the church in its movement through history, as well as of all historical cultures, belief-systems and structures of power.

Bearing witness to Christ begins with self-criticism. We dare not ignore the lessons of history lest we end up repeating the mistakes of the past. A movement that proclaimed grace and practised justice, a faith that had at its centre a crucified man as the hope of human and cosmic transformation, could not have been converted to a religious civilization like any other without serious damage to its very essence. . . .

However, given the corruptions and betrayals of the faith, we need to point out to our critics in Asia that the missionary activity of the church in our part of the world did not begin with the European expeditions of the sixteenth century and the subsequent expansion of European military, economic and cultural power. The Portuguese, on reaching the south-west coast of India, found an indigeneous Indian Christian community of 100,000 strong and claiming a link with the apostle Thomas.[24] They lived in relative isolation, having once had strong connexions with the Syriac-speaking churches of West Asia which had been crippled since the rise of Muslim power in the seventh century. The first official Christian mission to China was from the Persian patriarch in the mid-seventh century: Christians were moving eastwards in evangelism even as the Muslim Arabs from the south were overruning Zoroastrian Persia. There is evidence of Christian communities in China in the eighth century which, along with Buddhists, suffered persecution under the new imperial dynasty in the ninth century and disappeared mysteriously for the next three hundred years.[25] Christians in Central Asia too disappeared under the savage destructiveness of the Mongol conquests under Tamerlaine in the fourteenth century. Only in Egypt and Ethiopia did ancient non-European churches survive well in to the modern period.

It is a salutary challenge to be reminded (by a leading American historian who has himself served as a missionary in Asia) that the Christian church had its beginnings in Asia: 'Its earliest history, its first centres were Asian. Asia produced the first known church building, the first New Testament translation, perhaps the first Christian king, the first Christian poets, and even arguably the first Christian state. Asian Christians endured the greatest persecutions. They mounted global ventures in missionary expansion the West could not match until after the thirteenth century. By then the Nestorian church (as most of the early Asian Christian communities came to be called) exercised ecclesiastical authority over more of the earth than either Rome of Constantinople.'[26]

The full history of indigenous Christian communities which lived outside the centres of global power still waits to be written. But it would be a much-needed corrective to the way that most non-Christians perceive the history of Christian expansion. Such a history should be read, side by side, with the histories of the persecution and martyrdom of Christians within allegedly 'Christian' Europe itself: the costly witness of Christians who renounced power such as the Franciscans, Benedictines, Waldensians, Wycliffe and the Lollards, Anabaptists and Mennonites, Moravians, the early Methodist movement and many more. The Christians who fled to the American wilderness in the seventeenth century were those persecuted by the Church of England. It may well be the case that, in the period 1492–1914 which saw the gradual dominance of European powers throughout the world, more Christians than any other people have been killed or victimized by these same European powers.

The colonial experience was a complex story, varying from period to period and from country to country. The relationship of Christian missionaries and European churches to that experience is even more complex, and is only now beginning to be explored.[27] It is only those who have never read history, who have never explored the intricate interweavings of human motives in all historical communities, who tend to simplify the last four hundred years of Christian missions to a uniformly evil tale of 'guns and Bibles'. There is another side to this popular version which needs to be written in each society. Unresearched generalizations usually have a political purpose. They buttress ideologies which, as we have seen, serve to disguise either a quest for power or the consolidation of power (in this case, over national Christians).

Without attempting to 'whitewash' atrocities which were often committed in the name of Christ, and many instances of arrogance and insensitivity, we can, nevertheless, point to countless acts of heroism, courtesy and self-sacrifice on the part of western missionaries in every continent. Some of them were among the brightest young intellects of Europe and America. Many died young, others were stricken by disease and ill-health while working in torrid conditions. They pressed every human activity into the service of the gospel, from education for women and outcastes to publishing houses and agriculture. Many of the finest medical and educational institutions still standing on the Indian sub-continent (e.g. Vellore, Luddhiana, Serampore University) were founded by Christians on their own initiative, often against the wishes of the European colonists or their home governments. Indeed, the missionary contribution to medical health in Asia and Africa has been nothing less than extraordinary: from the treatment of leprosy and pioneering discoveries in epidemiology to the develop-ment of national health care systems, the training of primary health care workers and the setting up of educational institu-tions for women doctors and nurses.[28]

While the plunder and oppression of Spain and Portugal, aided and abetted by the Catholic hierarchy, is well-known even in elementary school textbooks, few of us know of men like Antonio de Montesinos or Bartholomew de Las Casas, themselves Catholic missionaries to South and Central Amer-ica in the sixteenth century, who championed the rights of native Indian peoples and vigorously denounced the actions of their own Church hierarchy. Or of evangelicals like van der Kemp, Philip and Kibb in Southern Africa who were hated by the European settlers for their defence of black tribes, and of similar efforts by evangelicals against the Arab slave-trade in East Africa in the nineteenth century.

It was also the case that the interests of missionaries and colonialists, far from being hand-in-glove, usually ran counter to each other. Until 1833, for instance, British missionaries were barred from entering India by the East India Company (the British trading company, set up in 1600, which grew into the world's first multinational commercial empire and was the major power in India until circumstances forced the British crown to intervene directly in India in 1858) for they feared the effect of local conversions on commercial trade. Few people are aware that the pioneering work of Christian scholar-missionaries on ancient Hindu and Buddhist texts, and their translation into European languages, was a key factor in the revival of these religions on the Indian subcontinent in the nineteenth and early twentieth centuries. Even when the scholars were not Christian missionaries, Christian publishing houses were often the first to disseminate the results of their work. For instance, Rhys David's book on Buddhism in 1877, which was the first scholarly work in English on that religion, was published by the Society for the Propagation of Christian Knowledge. (Has any scholarly work on Christianity been published by a Buddhist, Hindu or Muslim publishing house?) How many are aware that the great age of Christian missionary activity has been the twentieth century, and especially the post-colonial era? There are more cross-cultural missionaries at work in today's world than in any stage of human history (and probably more than all of the past centuries combined). And it is estimated that by the first decade of the next century there will be more cross-cultural Protestant missionaries sent from or within the Third World countries than from the West.[29]

The major plank in Protestant mission strategy was always Bible translation. This often involved writing down a vernacular for the very first time, and the creation of grammars and local literatures. This was as true for Europe as for Asia or Africa. Translation of the Bible into over 2000 languages has been the chief instrument of indigenous cultural renewal in many parts of the world. By believing that the truth of the Bible could be distinguished from the language in which it was embodied, and that the vernacular was adequate for participation in the Christian movement, the more serious-minded missionaries and translators have preserved a great variety of languages and cultures from extinction, and lifted obscure tribes and ethnic groups into the stream of universal history.

No one has brought this fact out more vividly than the West African scholar Lamin Sanneh, now a professor at Yale University. He writes, 'In many significant cases, these languages received their first breath of life from Christian interest. This is true whether we are speaking of Calvin and the birth of modern French, Luther and German, Tyndale and English, Robert de Nobili or William Carey and the Indian vernaculars, Miles Brunson and Assamese, Johannes Christaller and Akan in Ghana, Moffatt and Sichuana in Botswana, Ajayi Crowther and Yorruba in Nigeria, and Krapf and Swahili in East Africa, to take a random list from many examples . . . vernacular translation excites vernacular self-confidence, which in turn foments the national sentiment.'[30] Sanneh observes that the Christian view that all cultures may serve God's purpose 'stripped culture of idolatrous liability, emancipating it with the force of translation and usage'.[31] It is perhaps another of the many ironies of Church history that such indigenous renewal should turn into anti-missionary stridency and later into nationalism.

Sanneh invites us to contrast this attitude to culture with that of Hinduism or Islam. To the Hindu and Muslim alike, sacred texts are untranslatable. Sanskrit and Arabic are the divine tongues, and the culture of origin becomes the universal paradigm. Until quite late into this century, many high-caste Hindus believed that in venturing beyond India one became ritually contaminated. While Islam has practised social pluralism, it is 'through tolerance rather than the substitution by the vernacular of Arabic'.[32] The missionary success of Islam is in effect the universalization of Arabic as the language of faith. Every Muslim must step into Arabic on entering the mosque to perform his rites, a daily passage that for many reaches its climax in the annual *hajj*, the pilgrimage to Mecca. When one considers that three out of every four Muslims in the world are non-Arabs, it is clear that this implies a down-grading of their mother tongues in the fundamental acts of piety and devotion. Cultural diversity is regarded, at best, irrelevant or, at worst, a hindrance to faith.

The historian Brian Stanley, in commenting on the failure of much British missionary work in the last century, attributed it not to a failure in motivation, but rather a failure in holiness: 'Missionaries who were acutely conscious of their need to be radically distinctive from "pagan" peoples to whom they were sent, were insufficiently aware of the equal need for them to be distinctive from the racial and cultural assumptions of their own social background . . . their error was not that they were indifferent to the cause of justice for the oppressed, but that their perceptions of the demands of justice were too easily moulded to fit the contours of prevailing Western ideologies.'[33]

The lesson for Christian witness today is plain. The very nature of the gospel implies that we take, with equal serious-ness, both cultural particularity and cultural relativity. The church that is the bearer of the gospel to the nations must be critically aware of its own socio-cultural situation. It must be aware of how far its preaching, lifestyle and methodologies express but also challenge that situation. But the capacity to challenge is possible only if the church takes seriously its own culturally pluralistic nature. A partnership that involves thoughtful, mutual listening among Christians from every tradition and culture within the world-wide church is indis-pensable for faithful and united witness to Jesus Christ.

Sadly, possibilities for such partnership look bleak at the present moment of writing. The world ecumenical movement appears to have abandoned its original aim to bring the various confessional churches into visible and organic union with each other. The World Council of Churches' own foundational commitment to 'Jesus Christ as Saviour and God, according to the Scriptures' seems to have fallen into abeyance, no longer expressing the acceptable limits of doctrinal puralism. Although many of its public statements and working documents bear witness to a strong commitment to both biblical authority and world evangelism, its national and international programmes tend to be hi-jacked by the latest political fashion. It tends to breed 'band-wagon Christians' who marginalize all others who may not agree with their particular theological stance or who refuse to identify the gospel with a particular political cause.

Likewise, the evangelical Christian constituency has frag-mented into a number of independent churches and organi-zations, each with its own private agenda and strategy for world evangelism. Plans to orchestrate what is grandly called 'global mission' are usually formulated in some Californian computer-bank or a South Korean megachurch. Anyone who raises fundamental questions regarding the underlying (lack of) the-ology of mission is often simply dismissed as a crypto-liberal. One of the many paradoxes of the evangelical scene is how the glut of communications technology within churches has gone hand-in-hand with an inversely proportional decline in communication between Christians!

It seems to me that many evangelical leaders, especially in the

United States, have been misled by the myth of the Global Village. The fact that I can telephone New York from Colombo more easily than I can, say, Madras, does not mean that the world is getting smaller, let alone that we are coming to understand ourselves across cultural, social and theological barriers. All it reflects is the way technology follows the distorted global networks of economic and political power. As we saw in a previous chapter, those who own the technology of communications set the world's agenda. What counts as 'news', for instance, is what the TV and press moghuls decide is news. As a result of worldwide TV, most people in the Third World have a very one-sided image of westerners and western culture, while it is probably true to say that most westerners today are less informed about other non-western societies (including the way non-Westerners perceive them) than was their parents' generation. Furthermore, as long as American and East Asian Christians are blind to the way their economic and political power distorts their presentation of the gospel, all their well-meaning efforts in 'global mission' will only backfire on the churches of the Third World. Once again the poor are exposed to a Constantinian Christ rather then the Christ of the cross. The alliance of 'big business' expertise with missionary enterprise will prove disastrous, as it always has in the history of the church. Contemporary evangelistic methodologies, with their preoccupation with management techniques and marketing strategies, not only undermine the radical thrust of the gospel but serve to reinforce the identification of the Christian church with the depersonalizing trends in modernity.

8.4   Conclusion

Wherever the cross is preached, it carries the stigma of scorn and shame. We have seen that the cross is intrinsically an object of horror, and the message it embodies is a scandal to the rich, the proud, the powerful and the religious of every age. It is God's answer to the idolatry of the human heart. But this message has been betrayed so often by the Christian church in its own idolatrous associations with wealth and power, that the ridicule it now evokes, among both religious and secular peoples alike, is of a very different kind. Its meaning has been utterly obscured or else trivialized. Today the cross of the risen Jesus can, once again, be a liberating gospel only if it is proclaimed in humility, penitent confession and non-manipulative love. The church must live out the Good News in its proclamation. In other words, the announcement that Jesus is the true and living way to the Father (e.g. Jn. 14:6) can be made only by people who walk the way that Jesus walked.

Lesslie Newbigin, himself a missionary for many years in South India, has summoned Christians, especially those in the West, to challenge the belief-framework within which contemporary culture operates: 'It must call unequivocally for radical conversion, a conversion of the mind so that things are seen differently, and a conversion of the will so that things are done differently. It must decline altogether the futile attempt to commend the biblical vision of how things are by seeking to adjust it to the assumptions of our culture.'[34]

Christians in Asia are exposed to a multitude of cultures, whether religious or secular. We absorb today's dominant culture of modernity through our educational system, the professions and the mass-media, while the assumptions and orientation of our traditional religious cultures still shape our emotional responses, our family life and our 'private' choices. We are in a unique position, straddling cultures ancient and modern and called to bring them into a transforming unity in Jesus Christ.

But we have done what our brethren in the West have often done: turned the focus of the gospel from the public realm of history to that of private 'religious experience', divorced our outer and inner worlds, the spiritual and the material. In the name of Christ, we have blessed brutal regimes of the right and the left; been apathetic towards economic exploitation and social discrimination; celebrated socialism in one generation and capitalism in the next as the manifestation of the kingdom of God; encouraged intolerance and ethnic nationalisms; either denigrated religious traditions or naively hailed them all as 'equally valid pathways to God'. Those among us who are rightly sensitive to the distorting colonial images of Jesus that still flourish in many parts of Asia have, in turn, produced other travesties, equally distorting: e.g. Jesus as Shaman, Mother, Worker, Guerilla . . .

The irony is that those who are most vocal in their contemptuous dismissal of evangelical Christianity as a 'western cultural import' have themselves been seduced by the mindset of the Enlightenment which, as we have seen, was a peculiarly western project, now experiencing its intellectual death-throes. So, for instance, the prominent Indian theologian and ecumenical leader, Stanley Samartha, has argued that claims concerning the Lordship of Jesus over all of life must be confined to the liturgical life and worship of the Christian community, whose sole calling it is to 'contribute to the pool of values' which will undergird and nurture the secular, pluralist character of the Indian state.[35] Here is the old fact-value separation on full display. But, how can values such as 'justice' and 'unity' be affirmed apart from some beliefs about the true nature of things? Isn't the miserable condition of outcastes ('dalits') in India itself an expression of a *just* cosmic order— according to brahmanical Hinduism? Isn't it unjust, given the individualist understanding of human beings in liberal Western states, to interfere with the 'right to unlimited consumption'?

Christian values are grounded in a different vision of things which is given in the historic story of Jesus. The latter calls into question other visions of how things are. To call the church to contribute values prised out of that story, but without proclaiming that story itself, is to call the church to deny its identity and the most important thing it has been entrusted with for the sake of the society to which it belongs. Christians are called to work alongside others in building viable political structures which ensure justice for all peoples, and this is indeed a vitally important aspect of our witness whether in the West or the East. But to separate word and deed, proclamation and service, justice and truth, is to fall victim to the false and dangerous dualisms of modern culture.

If confessing Jesus as the Lord of all life is taken to mean the offer of an other-worldly salvation to abstract 'souls', divorced from their historical existence, and which leaves their relation-ships to the power-structures of their society unchanged, then we are only exchanging one set of idols for another. If, on the other hand, we challenge the power-structures of society on any other foundation than that of the gracious proclamation of the crucified and risen Jesus, and by evading the vulnerabil-ity of the way of the cross, we shall, likewise, be confronting idolatry with idolatry. To affirm clearly and boldly the truth of the gospel, the fact of the sovereignty of Jesus Christ as sole Saviour and Judge of every human enterprise, and to do this in the public domain whether people hear or refuse to hear, that may well be the most profound political action that the church undertakes in any society in any part of the world.

'Dear children, keep yourselves from idols' (1 Jn. 5:21).

Notes

[1] Lord Hailsham, *The Door Wherein I Went* (London: Collins,1975) p. 54

[2] D. Sayers, *Creed or Chaos* (New York: Harcourt Brace & Co, 1949) pp. 5–6

[3] E. Jüngel, *God as the Mystery of the World* (Edinburgh: T & T Clark, 1983) p. 13

[4] N.T. Wright, *Who Was Jesus?* (London: SPCK, 1992) p.5 2 (Italics in text)

[5] Quoted in W. Temple, *Readings in St. John's Gospel* (1939–1940; repr. Macmillan, 1968) p. 366

[6] Quoted in J. Atkinson, *Martin Luther: Prophet to the Church Catholic* (Grand Rapids: Eerdmans/ Exeter: Paternoster, 1983) p. 183

[7] E.g., J. Moltmannn, *The Crucified God* (Eng. trans. London: SCM, 1966) pp. 240ff

[8] Ibid. p. 276

[9] Luther, op. cit., pp. 20,21

[10] M. Hengel, *Crucifixion* (1977) in *The Cross of the Son of God* (London: SCM, 1986) p. 97

[11] Apology I, 13.4, quoted in Ibid. p. 93

[12] Op. cit. p. 181

[13] Kim Yong-Bock, 'The Mission of God in the Context of the Suffering and Struggling Peoples of Asia', in *Peoples of Asia, People of God* (Osaka: Christian Conference of Asia, 1990) p. 12

[14] Ibid. p. 13

[15] *Third World Theologies: Papers and Reflections from the Second General Assembly of the Ecumenical Association of Third World Theologians, December 1986, Oaxtepec, Mexico*, ed. KC Abraham (Maryknoll, NY: Orbis, 1990) p. 20

[16] A. Pieris, *An Asian Theology of Liberation* (Edinburgh: T & T Clark, 1988) p. 48

[17] Ibid. p. 45 (italics in text)

[18] D. Bonhoeffer, *Ethics* (Eng. trans. London: SCM, 1955) p. 13

[19] Ibid. p. 15

[20] Ibid. pp.15,16

[21] Ibid. pp.18,19

[22] Ibid. p. 21

[23] *Epistle to Diognetus*, in H. Bettenson (ed), *The Early Christian Fathers* (Oxford: Oxford University Press, 1956)

[24] S. Neill, *A History of Christian Missions* (London: Penguin, 1964) p. 143. For a recent, balanced survey of the Thomas tradition, see SH Moffett, *A History of Christianity in Asia, vol. 1: Beginnings to 1500* (San Francisco: HarperCollins, 1992) Ch. 2

[25] Moffett, Ibid. Ch. 15

[26] Ibid. p. xiii

[27] See, e.g., B. Stanley, *The Bible and the Flag* (Leicester: Apollos, 1990)

[28] See, e.g., S.G. Browne, F. Davey and W.A.R. Thomson, *Heralds of Health: The Saga of Christian Medical Initiatives* (London: Christian Medical Fellowship, 1985)

[29] B.L. Myers, *The Changing Shape of World Mission* (Monrovia, CA: MARC, 1993) p. 18

[30] L. Sanneh, 'Pluralism and Christian Commitment' in *Theology Today*, vol. 45, April 1988 pp. 21–33

[31] Ibid. p. 27

[32] Ibid. p. 23

[33] Stanley, op. cit. pp. 182–3,184

[34] L. Newbigin, *The Other Side of Nineteen Eighty Four* (Geneva: WCC Publications, 1983) p. 53

[35] S.J. Samartha, *One Christ-Many Religions: Towards a Revised Christology* (Indian ed, Bangalore: SATHRI, 1992)

Index